Arduino Masterclass

Build Electronics Projects from Scratch

Sarful Hassan

Preface

Who This Book Is For This book is designed for beginners, hobbyists, students, and professionals who want to learn Arduino from the ground up. Whether you are an aspiring electronics engineer, a maker looking to build innovative projects, or someone interested in microcontrollers, this book will provide a step-by-step approach to mastering Arduino. Prior programming experience is not required, but familiarity with basic electronics concepts can be helpful.

How This Book Is Organized This book is structured to take you from fundamental concepts to advanced applications, ensuring a smooth learning experience:

- **Chapters 1-8** introduce Arduino, microcontrollers, basic circuit theory, and debugging techniques.

- **Chapters 9-27** cover essential electronic components, power management, coding structures, memory optimization, and communication protocols.

- **Chapters 28-37** dive into sensors and interfacing techniques.

- **Chapters 39-57** focus on practical applications, including motor control, IoT, displays, and smart systems.

- **Chapters 60-64** provide troubleshooting techniques, common mistakes, and sensor calibration guidance.

What Was Left Out To keep this book focused and practical, highly advanced topics such as FPGA integration, deep machine learning applications, and complex PCB design were omitted. However, these subjects can be explored in future editions or complementary resources.

Code Style (About the Code) All code examples in this book are written in a clean, structured, and beginner-friendly manner. Comments are provided to explain key sections, and all examples have been tested on standard Arduino boards. You are encouraged to experiment and modify the code to enhance your learning experience.

Release Notes This is the first edition of *Arduino Masterclass: Build Electronics Projects from Scratch*. Any feedback or suggestions for future editions are welcome. Updates and additional resources may be made available through online platforms.

Notes on the First Edition This edition is the result of extensive research and hands-on experimentation. While every effort has been made to ensure accuracy, errors may still exist. Readers are encouraged to report any issues or suggestions to improve future versions.

MechatronicsLAB Online Learning For additional tutorials, project files, and updates, visit MechatronicsLAB.net. For any queries, you can contact us at mechatronicslab.net@gmail.com.

Acknowledgments for the First Edition I would like to express my gratitude to all those who supported this project, including my mentors, peers, and the Arduino community. Special thanks to my family for their patience and encouragement throughout the writing process.

Table of Contents

Chapter 1: Introduction to Arduino

Arduino is an open-source electronics platform based on easy-to-use hardware and software. It is designed for anyone interested in creating interactive projects. Arduino boards are capable of reading inputs, such as light on a sensor, a finger on a button, or a Twitter message, and turning it into an output, such as activating a motor, turning on an LED, or publishing something online.

History of Arduino

Arduino was created in 2005 by a group of students at the Interaction Design Institute Ivrea in Italy. Their goal was to create a simple, low-cost tool for students and hobbyists to learn and experiment with electronics and programming. Over time, Arduino has grown into a worldwide community with an extensive range of boards, modules, and software support.

History of Arduino Timeline

Year	Event
2005	Arduino project was initiated at Interaction Design Institute Ivrea
2007	First commercial Arduino boards were made available
2008	Arduino community started growing rapidly
2010	Introduction of Arduino Mega for larger projects
2013	Arduino Due released with an ARM-based processor
2015	Arduino split into two entities, Arduino.cc and Arduino.org
2017	Merger of Arduino.cc and Arduino.org, strengthening community support
2020	Introduction of new IoT-enabled Arduino boards

Why Use Arduino?

Arduino is popular for several reasons:

- **Open-source**: Both the hardware and software are freely available for anyone to use and modify.
- **Easy to use**: The Arduino programming language is based on C++ but simplified for beginners.
- **Affordable**: Compared to other microcontroller platforms, Arduino is relatively inexpensive.

- **Versatile**: It can be used for a wide range of applications, from simple LED blinking to complex robotics and IoT solutions.
- **Strong Community Support**: A large community of users provides tutorials, libraries, and troubleshooting help.

Components of an Arduino Board

An Arduino board typically consists of:

- **Microcontroller**: The brain of the board, usually an Atmel AVR or ARM-based chip.
- **Digital and Analog Pins**: Used for connecting input and output devices.
- **Power Supply**: Provides necessary voltage to run the board.
- **USB Interface**: Used for programming the board and power supply.
- **Clock and Reset Button**: Controls timing and resets the board when needed.

Common Arduino Boards

There are various types of Arduino boards, each designed for different applications. Some of the most commonly used include:

- **Arduino Uno**: The most popular board, ideal for beginners.
- **Arduino Mega**: Offers more input/output pins for larger projects.
- **Arduino Nano**: A compact version, great for small projects.
- **Arduino Leonardo**: Includes built-in USB communication capabilities.
- **Arduino Due**: Features a more powerful ARM processor.

Arduino Software (IDE)

Arduino uses an Integrated Development Environment (IDE) for writing and uploading code to the board. The IDE supports:

- **Sketches**: Programs written in the Arduino language.
- **Libraries**: Pre-written code to simplify complex tasks.
- **Serial Monitor**: A tool for debugging and communication with the board.

Getting Started with Arduino

To start using Arduino, follow these steps:

1. **Choose an Arduino Board**: Select the right board based on your project needs.
2. **Install the Arduino IDE**: Download and install the Arduino software from the official website.
3. **Connect the Board**: Use a USB cable to connect the Arduino to your computer.
4. **Write Your First Sketch**: Open the IDE and write a simple program, such as making an LED blink.
5. **Upload the Code**: Click the upload button to transfer the sketch to the Arduino board.
6. **Observe the Output**: Check if the program executes as expected.

Summary

Arduino is an easy-to-use platform that enables beginners and experts alike to create electronics projects. With a vast community, extensive resources, and versatile applications, Arduino has revolutionized DIY electronics, education, and prototyping.

This chapter introduced the basics of Arduino, its history, components, and how to get started. In the next chapter, we will delve deeper into Arduino programming and its core functions.

Chapter 2: Understanding Microcontrollers

A microcontroller is a compact integrated circuit designed to govern a specific operation in an embedded system. It contains a processor, memory, and input/output peripherals on a single chip. Unlike general-purpose computers, microcontrollers are optimized for specific tasks such as controlling home appliances, automobiles, medical devices, and industrial automation systems.

Microcontroller vs. Microprocessor

Feature	Microcontroller	Microprocessor
Components	CPU, RAM, ROM, I/O ports on a single chip	CPU only, requires external RAM, ROM, and peripherals
Power Consumption	Low	High
Cost	Lower	Higher
Application	Embedded systems, IoT devices	Computers, high-performance systems
Complexity	Simple	Complex

Architecture of a Microcontroller

Component	Function
Central Processing Unit (CPU)	Executes instructions and processes data.
Memory (RAM & ROM)	Stores temporary data (RAM) and permanent code (ROM/Flash Memory).
Input/Output Ports (I/O)	Interfaces to connect sensors, actuators, and other devices.
Timers and Counters	Used for time-based operations and event counting.
Analog-to-Digital Converter (ADC)	Converts analog signals to digital data.
Digital-to-Analog Converter (DAC)	Converts digital data to analog signals.
Communication Interfaces	Protocols like UART, SPI, and I2C enable communication with other devices.

Types of Microcontrollers

Type	Example
8-bit Microcontrollers	ATmega328, PIC16F877A
16-bit Microcontrollers	MSP430, dsPIC33
32-bit Microcontrollers	ARM Cortex-M, ESP32
General-purpose Microcontrollers	ATmega328 (used in Arduino)
Industrial Microcontrollers	PIC, ARM-based controllers for automation
IoT Microcontrollers	ESP8266, ESP32 for smart devices
Automotive Microcontrollers	STM32, NXP used in vehicle control systems

Popular Microcontroller Families

Family	Characteristics
AVR (Atmel)	Used in Arduino boards, easy to program, and power-efficient.
PIC (Microchip)	Used in industrial and commercial applications.
ARM (Various Manufacturers)	High-performance microcontrollers used in advanced applications.
ESP (Espressif Systems)	Popular for IoT applications due to built-in Wi-Fi and Bluetooth.

Microcontroller Programming

Language	Use Case
C and C++	Most commonly used for embedded programming.
MicroPython	A Python implementation for microcontrollers.
Assembly Language	Low-level programming for optimized performance.

IDE and Development Tools

Tool	Supported Microcontrollers
Arduino IDE	Arduino-compatible boards
MPLAB	PIC microcontrollers
Keil uVision	ARM-based microcontrollers
PlatformIO	Multiple microcontroller platforms

Applications of Microcontrollers

Field	Example Applications
Consumer Electronics	Televisions, washing machines, remote controls
Automotive Systems	Engine control units, airbag systems, anti-lock braking systems
Medical Devices	Pacemakers, blood glucose monitors, diagnostic equipment
Industrial Automation	Robotics, CNC machines, smart sensors
Internet of Things (IoT)	Smart home devices, wearable technology, remote monitoring systems

Summary

Microcontrollers are an essential component of modern embedded systems, offering low-cost, power-efficient solutions for a wide variety of applications. Understanding their architecture, types, and programming is crucial for designing efficient and innovative electronic systems.

Chapter 3: Arduino Board Overview

Arduino is an open-source electronics platform that consists of both hardware and software. Arduino boards are widely used for prototyping, learning, and IoT applications due to their ease of use and extensive community support.

Types of Arduino Boards

Board Name	Microcontroller	Digital I/O Pins	Analog Input Pins	Communication Interfaces	Special Features
Arduino Uno	ATmega328P	14	6	UART, SPI, I2C	Most commonly used board
Arduino Mega 2560	ATmega2560	54	16	UART, SPI, I2C	More I/O pins for complex projects
Arduino Nano	ATmega328P	14	8	UART, SPI, I2C	Compact size, similar to Uno
Arduino Leonardo	ATmega32U4	20	12	UART, SPI, I2C	Built-in USB communication
Arduino Due	ATSAM3X8E (ARM Cortex-M3)	54	12	UART, SPI, I2C, CAN	32-bit microcontroller, more powerful
Arduino Zero	ATSAMD21G 18 (ARM Cortex-M0)	20	6	UART, SPI, I2C	Ideal for IoT applications
ESP8266 /ESP32	ESP8266/ESP 32	Varies	Varies	Wi-Fi, Bluetooth, UART, SPI, I2C	Built-in wireless communication

Common Features of Arduino Boards

- **Microcontroller**: The main processing unit that executes the program.
- **Digital and Analog Pins**: Used to interface with sensors, actuators,

and other devices.

- **Power Supply**: Can be powered via USB, battery, or external adapter.
- **USB Interface**: Used for programming and serial communication.
- **Clock Speed**: Varies depending on the board; determines processing speed.
- **Flash Memory**: Stores the uploaded code.

Arduino Pinout Overview

Pin Type	Description
Digital Pins (D0 - D13)	Used for digital input/output operations. Some support PWM output.
Analog Pins (A0 - A5/A7)	Used for reading analog values from sensors.
Power Pins	Includes 3.3V, 5V, GND, and Vin for powering external components.
PWM Pins	Specific digital pins (e.g., D3, D5, D6, D9, D10, D11) support Pulse Width Modulation (PWM) for simulating analog output.
Communication Pins	UART (TX/RX), SPI (MISO, MOSI, SCK), and I2C (SDA, SCL) for device communication.
Reset Pin	Used to reset the microcontroller manually.

Choosing the Right Arduino Board

The selection of an Arduino board depends on the project requirements. Here are some guidelines:

- **For Beginners**: Arduino Uno is recommended due to its simplicity and extensive support.
- **For Advanced Projects**: Arduino Mega 2560 offers more I/O pins.
- **For Compact Applications**: Arduino Nano or Pro Mini is ideal.
- **For IoT Applications**: ESP8266 or ESP32 provides built-in Wi-Fi and Bluetooth.
- **For High-Performance Needs**: Arduino Due or Arduino Zero with ARM architecture is suitable.

Chapter 4: Setting Up the Arduino IDE

The Arduino Integrated Development Environment (IDE) is the primary software used to write, compile, and upload code to Arduino boards. It is a user-friendly platform that supports multiple operating systems, including Windows, macOS, and Linux.

Downloading and Installing the Arduino IDE

Follow these steps to download and install the Arduino IDE:

1. **Visit the Arduino Official Website**: Go to www.arduino.cc and navigate to the "Software" section.
2. **Choose Your Operating System**: Select the appropriate version for Windows, macOS, or Linux.
3. **Download the Installer**: Click on the download link and save the file to your computer.
4. **Install the Software**:
    a. **Windows**: Run the installer, accept the license agreement, and follow the on-screen instructions.
    b. **macOS**: Open the downloaded file and drag the Arduino application to the Applications folder.
    c. **Linux**: Extract the archive and run the installation script.

Setting Up the Arduino Board

After installing the IDE, follow these steps to set up your Arduino board:

1. **Connect the Arduino Board**: Use a USB cable to connect your Arduino to the computer.
2. **Select the Board Model**:
    a. Open the Arduino IDE.
    b. Go to "Tools" > "Board" and choose your Arduino model (e.g., Arduino Uno, Mega, Nano).
3. **Select the Port**:
    a. Navigate to "Tools" > "Port" and select the correct COM port.
4. **Install the Necessary Drivers**:
    a. On Windows, the installer usually includes the required drivers.
    b. On macOS and Linux, drivers are typically pre-installed.

Writing and Uploading Code

1. **Open the Arduino IDE** and create a new sketch.
2. **Write a Simple Program**: `void setup() {`

```
    pinMode(LED_BUILTIN, OUTPUT);
}

void loop() {
    digitalWrite(LED_BUILTIN, HIGH);
    delay(1000);
    digitalWrite(LED_BUILTIN, LOW);
    delay(1000);
}
```

3. **Verify the Code**: Click the checkmark button to compile the code.
4. **Upload the Code**: Click the arrow button to upload the sketch to your Arduino board.
5. **Monitor the Output**:
   a. Use the "Serial Monitor" (Tools > Serial Monitor) to view data sent from the Arduino.

Troubleshooting Common Issues

Issue	Solution
Board not detected	Check the USB connection, restart the IDE, or try a different cable.
Compilation error	Ensure the correct board and port are selected. Check for syntax errors.
Upload failed	Press the reset button on the board before uploading.
Serial monitor not working	Verify the correct baud rate is set in the Serial Monitor.

Summary

Setting up the Arduino IDE is an essential step in programming an Arduino board. By installing the software, configuring the board, writing code, and troubleshooting issues, users can successfully develop and deploy their projects. The next chapter will explore fundamental Arduino programming concepts.

Chapter 5: Understanding Digital and Analog Signals

In electronics and microcontroller programming, signals are used to transmit data between components. These signals can be categorized into two types: digital and analog. Understanding the difference between them is crucial for working with sensors, actuators, and communication protocols in Arduino and embedded systems.

Digital Signals

A digital signal consists of discrete values, typically represented as HIGH (1) and LOW (0). These signals are used in binary communication and logic-based operations.

Characteristics of Digital Signals:

- Represented as binary values (0 or 1)
- Used in digital circuits and microcontrollers
- Less susceptible to noise interference
- Suitable for switching applications and logic operations

Examples of Digital Signals in Arduino:

- **Turning an LED on and off**:
```
void setup() {
    pinMode(13, OUTPUT);
}
void loop() {
    digitalWrite(13, HIGH); // Turn LED on
    delay(1000);
    digitalWrite(13, LOW);  // Turn LED off
    delay(1000);
}
```
- **Reading a digital button press**:
```
int buttonState;
void setup() {
    pinMode(2, INPUT);
}
void loop() {
    buttonState = digitalRead(2);
    if (buttonState == HIGH) {
    }
}
```

Analog Signals

An analog signal is a continuous signal that can take an infinite number of values within a given range. These signals are commonly used in sensors and control applications where precise values are needed.

Characteristics of Analog Signals:

- Continuous range of values
- More susceptible to noise interference
- Used for measuring real-world phenomena such as temperature, light, and sound
- Requires Analog-to-Digital Conversion (ADC) for processing by microcontrollers

Examples of Analog Signals in Arduino:

- **Reading a potentiometer value**: int sensorValue;

```
void setup() {
    Serial.begin(9600);
}

void loop() {
    sensorValue = analogRead(A0);
    Serial.println(sensorValue);
    delay(500);
}
```

- **Generating an Analog Output using PWM**: void setup() {
    pinMode(9, OUTPUT);
}

```
void loop() {
    analogWrite(9, 128); // Set PWM duty cycle
    delay(1000);
}
```

Digital vs. Analog Signals: A Comparison

Feature	Digital Signal	Analog Signal
Nature	Discrete (0 or 1)	Continuous range of values
Noise Resistance	High	Low
Processing	Easier, binary logic	Requires ADC for microcontrollers
Examples	Buttons, LEDs, Relays	Sensors, Audio signals, Motor control

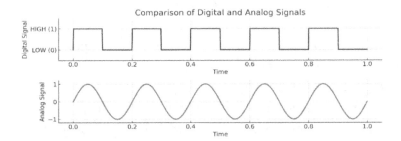

Converting Between Digital and Analog Signals

1. **Analog to Digital Conversion (ADC):**
   a. Converts real-world analog signals into a digital representation.
   b. Example: Reading a temperature sensor value with an Arduino.
2. **Digital to Analog Conversion (DAC):**
   a. Converts digital signals into an analog form.
   b. Example: Generating sound or varying motor speed using Pulse Width Modulation (PWM).

Summary

Understanding the differences between digital and analog signals is essential for working with electronic circuits and microcontrollers. Digital signals are used for logic and switching applications, while analog signals handle continuous values such as sensor readings. Converting between these two types of signals allows for efficient data processing and control in embedded systems.

Chapter 6: Powering Your Arduino

Powering your Arduino board correctly is essential to ensure stable operation and prevent damage. There are multiple ways to supply power to an Arduino, each suitable for different use cases. Understanding these power options will help you choose the best method for your project.

Importance of Proper Power Supply

Ensuring the correct power supply for your Arduino board is crucial for reliable performance. Incorrect power input can lead to various issues, including:

- **Voltage Instability:** Insufficient or excessive voltage can cause erratic behavior or permanent damage.
- **Component Damage:** Applying higher-than-recommended voltage can damage the microcontroller and connected peripherals.
- **Inadequate Current Supply:** If the power source cannot provide enough current, sensors and actuators may not function correctly.
- **Overheating:** Excess voltage, especially when using onboard regulators, can cause overheating and thermal shutdown.
- **System Reliability:** Using a stable power source ensures consistent performance and reduces unexpected resets or failures.

Powering Methods

Arduino boards can be powered using the following methods:

Power Source	Voltage	Common Use
USB Connection	5V	Programming and debugging
Barrel Jack	7-12V	External power supply for standalone operation
VIN Pin	7-12V	Alternative external power source
5V Pin	5V	Direct power input (use with caution)
3.3V Pin	3.3V	For low-power applications
Battery	Varies	Portable applications

1. Powering via USB

- The most common method for powering an Arduino during development.
- Provides a stable 5V supply from a computer or USB adapter.
- Maximum current depends on the USB port (typically 500mA for standard USB 2.0 ports).

2. Powering via Barrel Jack

- Suitable for standalone applications where no computer connection is needed.
- Accepts a voltage range of 7-12V (regulated by onboard voltage regulator).
- Recommended for long-duration projects requiring a reliable power source.

3. Powering via VIN Pin

- Allows an external power source (7-12V) to be connected directly to the board.
- Internally regulated to provide the required voltage.
- Useful when integrating with an external power circuit.

4. Powering via 5V Pin

- Provides direct access to the 5V rail of the board.
- Use caution as bypassing the onboard regulator may lead to damage if incorrect voltage is applied.
- Useful when sharing power between multiple components.

5. Powering via 3.3V Pin

- Provides 3.3V for low-power components.
- Cannot supply high current, typically limited to 50mA.

6. Powering via Battery

- Ideal for portable applications.
- Can be connected via VIN (for 7-12V batteries) or directly to 5V (for 5V batteries like Li-Po or Li-Ion packs).
- Requires careful selection of battery capacity and voltage regulation.

Power Considerations

- **Voltage Regulation:** Ensure the input voltage does not exceed the board's limits.

- **Current Requirements:** Verify that the power source can supply enough current for the board and connected components.
- **Heat Dissipation:** Using higher voltage sources (e.g., 12V) may generate excessive heat in the onboard voltage regulator.
- **Battery Life:** If using a battery, calculate the expected run time based on power consumption.

Note:
- Always check the specifications of your Arduino board before connecting a power source.
- If using external power, ensure it provides stable and regulated voltage to avoid damage.
- For portable applications, consider using a battery with a built-in voltage regulator to maintain stable output.

Warning:
- Supplying voltage beyond the recommended range can permanently damage the microcontroller.
- Avoid connecting power simultaneously through USB and VIN to prevent conflicts.
- Incorrect polarity when connecting an external power source may lead to irreversible damage.

Summary

Properly powering your Arduino ensures stable operation and longevity. The choice of power source depends on your application, with USB being convenient for development and external power options being suitable for standalone projects. Understanding these power methods and the importance of a stable power supply will help in designing efficient and reliable Arduino-based systems.

Chapter 7: Using Serial Monitor

The Serial Monitor is a built-in tool in the Arduino IDE that allows users to communicate with an Arduino board through a computer. It enables real-time debugging, data visualization, and interaction with the microcontroller via the serial interface. Understanding how to effectively use the Serial Monitor is crucial for debugging, monitoring sensor data, and interacting with various peripherals.

What is the Serial Monitor?

The Serial Monitor is a terminal window that displays data sent from the Arduino to the connected computer over a serial connection. It can also send data from the computer to the Arduino, making it a useful tool for testing and debugging.

With the Serial Monitor, you can:

- Display real-time sensor values.
- Send and receive text commands.
- Debug Arduino programs by printing messages and variables.
- Test communication between the Arduino and external devices.

Opening the Serial Monitor

To open the Serial Monitor:

1. Connect the Arduino board to your computer via USB.
2. Open the Arduino IDE.
3. Click on "Tools" > "Serial Monitor" or press **Ctrl + Shift + M**.
4. Set the correct baud rate (e.g., 9600 baud) in the bottom right corner of the Serial Monitor.

If no output is visible, ensure the correct COM port is selected by navigating to "Tools" > "Port" and choosing the appropriate port.

Understanding Baud Rate

Baud rate refers to the speed of data transfer between the Arduino and the computer. Common baud rates include:

Baud Rate	Description
9600	Standard speed for most applications
115200	Faster data transfer, suitable for high-speed applications
4800	Used for slow-speed communication

19200	Medium-speed communication

The baud rate set in `Serial.begin(baudrate);` must match the baud rate selected in the Serial Monitor; otherwise, unreadable characters (garbage values) may appear.

Basic Serial Communication Commands

Command	Description
`Serial.begin(baudrate);`	Initializes serial communication at the specified baud rate.
`Serial.print(value);`	Prints data to the Serial Monitor on the same line.
`Serial.println(value);`	Prints data followed by a new line.
`Serial.read();`	Reads incoming serial data.
`Serial.available();`	Checks if data is available to read.
`Serial.write(value);`	Sends raw binary data over serial communication.

Example: Sending Data to Serial Monitor

```
void setup() {
    Serial.begin(9600); // Start serial communication
at 9600 baud
}

void loop() {
    Serial.println("Hello, Arduino!");
    delay(1000); // Wait for 1 second
}
```

Example: Receiving Data from Serial Monitor

```
void setup() {
    Serial.begin(9600);
    Serial.println("Type something:");
}

void loop() {
    if (Serial.available() > 0) {
```

```
        char input = Serial.read();
        Serial.print("You typed: ");
        Serial.println(input);
    }
}
```

Advanced Example: Interactive LED Control

This example demonstrates how to use the Serial Monitor to control an LED connected to an Arduino.

```
const int ledPin = 13;

void setup() {
    Serial.begin(9600);
    pinMode(ledPin, OUTPUT);
    Serial.println("Type '1' to turn LED ON and '0' to
turn it OFF");
}

void loop() {
    if (Serial.available() > 0) {
        char command = Serial.read();
        if (command == '1') {
            digitalWrite(ledPin, HIGH);
            Serial.println("LED ON");
        } else if (command == '0') {
            digitalWrite(ledPin, LOW);
            Serial.println("LED OFF");
        }
    }
}
```

Using Serial Monitor for Debugging

- **Print variable values**: This helps verify program logic and ensure correct values are used.
- **Monitor sensor readings**: Allows real-time observation of values from temperature, humidity, or motion sensors.

- **Debug communication issues**: If external devices aren't responding, Serial Monitor can help check transmitted and received data.

Troubleshooting Common Issues

Issue	Solution
No output on Serial Monitor	Ensure `Serial.begin(baudrate);` is included in `setup()`.
Garbage values displayed	Match the baud rate in the Serial Monitor with the baud rate in the code.
No data received	Check USB connection and ensure the correct COM port is selected.
Serial Monitor freezes	Close and reopen the Serial Monitor or reset the Arduino board.

Note:

- Always call `Serial.begin(baudrate);` in the `setup()` function to initialize communication.
- The baud rate set in the Serial Monitor must match the value set in the code.
- `Serial.print()` and `Serial.println()` are useful for debugging without additional hardware.

Warning:

- Avoid using excessive `Serial.print()` statements in `loop()`, as it may slow down the execution of other code.
- When reading serial input, ensure to handle multiple characters correctly for commands or numerical inputs.
- Some Arduino boards have a single serial port, so using Serial Monitor and another serial device (e.g., Bluetooth module) may cause conflicts.

Summary

The Serial Monitor is an essential tool for interacting with Arduino boards. It facilitates real-time debugging, data monitoring, and user interaction, making it invaluable for both beginners and advanced users. By understanding its functionality, common commands, and practical applications, users can enhance their ability to troubleshoot and communicate with microcontrollers effectively.

Chapter 8: Debugging Basics

Debugging is an essential skill for working with Arduino and embedded systems. It helps identify and fix errors in code, wiring, and hardware connections. By understanding debugging techniques, users can efficiently resolve issues and improve project stability.

Common Types of Errors

Error Type	Description
Syntax Errors	Mistakes in code structure, such as missing semicolons or incorrect variable names.
Logical Errors	The program runs but does not behave as expected.
Runtime Errors	Errors that occur during execution, such as division by zero.
Hardware Errors	Issues related to incorrect wiring or faulty components.

Using Serial Monitor for Debugging

The Serial Monitor is a powerful tool for debugging Arduino programs. It allows users to print messages and variable values to diagnose issues.

Example: Printing Debug Messages

```
void setup() {
    Serial.begin(9600);
    Serial.println("Debugging started");
}

void loop() {
    int sensorValue = analogRead(A0);
    Serial.print("Sensor Value: ");
    Serial.println(sensorValue);
    delay(1000);
}
```

Identifying Logical Errors

Logical errors can be tricky to spot. By using debug print statements, users can track variable changes and pinpoint unexpected behavior.

Example: Debugging a Conditional Issue

```
int counter = 0;
void setup() {
    Serial.begin(9600);
}
void loop() {
    counter++;
    Serial.print("Counter: ");
    Serial.println(counter);
    if (counter == 5) {
        Serial.println("Counter reached 5,
resetting...");
        counter = 0;
    }
    delay(1000);
}
```

Checking Wiring and Components

- Ensure proper connections by referring to circuit diagrams.
- Use a multimeter to check voltage and continuity.
- Swap suspected faulty components with known working ones.

Using LED Indicators for Debugging

A simple way to debug without Serial Monitor is using LEDs to indicate program state.

Example: Blinking LED as a Debug Indicator

```
const int ledPin = 13;
void setup() {
    pinMode(ledPin, OUTPUT);
}
void loop() {
    digitalWrite(ledPin, HIGH);
    delay(500);
    digitalWrite(ledPin, LOW);
    delay(500);
}
```

Troubleshooting Common Issues

Issue	Possible Solution
No output in Serial Monitor	Ensure `Serial.begin(baudrate);` is called in `setup()`.
Unexpected behavior	Print variable values to check logic flow.
Board not recognized	Check USB connection and COM port.
Components not working	Verify wiring and test with known working components.

Note:

- Always check for loose connections and damaged components.
- Use comments to document debugging steps for future reference.

Warning:

- Avoid infinite loops (`while(1);`) unless intentionally required, as they can cause unresponsive behavior.
- Excessive debugging prints in `loop()` can slow down execution.

Summary

Debugging is a crucial skill for troubleshooting Arduino projects. By using tools like the Serial Monitor, LED indicators, and proper wiring checks, users can efficiently identify and fix issues. Understanding debugging techniques leads to more stable and reliable Arduino applications.

Chapter 9: Ohm's Law and Basic Circuit Theory for Arduino

Understanding the fundamental principles of electricity, including Ohm's Law and basic circuit theory, is essential for working with Arduino. These concepts help in designing circuits, selecting components, and ensuring the safe operation of electronics.

Ohm's Law

Ohm's Law describes the relationship between voltage (V), current (I), and resistance (R) in an electrical circuit:

$V = I \times R$

Where:

- **V** = Voltage (Volts, V)
- **I** = Current (Amperes, A)
- **R** = Resistance (Ohms, Ω)

Example Calculation: If a 5V power source is applied to a 1kΩ resistor, the current flowing through the resistor is: $I = V / R = 5V / 1000Ω = 0.005A = 5mA$

Understanding Circuit Components

Component	Symbol	Function
Resistor	R	Limits current flow and divides voltage.
Capacitor	C	Stores and releases electrical energy.
Inductor	L	Stores energy in a magnetic field.
Diode	D	Allows current to flow in one direction only.
LED	LED	Emits light when current flows through it.
Transistor	Q	Acts as a switch or amplifier.

Basic Circuit Theory

Series Circuits In a series circuit, components are connected end to end, and the same current flows through each component.

- The total resistance: R_total = R1 + R2 + R3 + ...
- Voltage is divided among the components.

Example: Connecting two 1kΩ resistors in series results in a total resistance of: R_total = 1000Ω + 1000Ω = 2000Ω

Parallel Circuits In a parallel circuit, components are connected across the same voltage source, and the total current is divided.

- The total resistance: 1 / R_total = 1 / R1 + 1 / R2 + 1 / R3 + ...
- Voltage remains the same across each branch.

Example: Connecting two 1kΩ resistors in parallel results in a total resistance of: 1 / R_total = 1 / 1000Ω + 1 / 1000Ω = 2 / 1000Ω R_total = 500Ω

Applying Ohm's Law in Arduino Circuits

Choosing the Right Resistor for an LED

- LEDs require a current-limiting resistor to prevent excessive current flow.
- Using Ohm's Law: R = (V_supply - V_LED) / I_LED
- Example: For a 5V supply and a red LED (forward voltage = 2V, desired current = 10mA): R = (5V - 2V) / 0.01A = 300Ω

Measuring Current with a Multimeter

- Set the multimeter to the correct current range.
- Place the probes in series with the circuit to measure current.

Voltage Dividers

- Used to obtain a lower voltage from a higher source.
- Formula: V_out = V_in × (R2 / (R1 + R2))
- Example: Using a 10kΩ and a 5kΩ resistor with a 9V battery: V_out = 9V × (5kΩ / (10kΩ + 5kΩ)) = 3V

Troubleshooting Common Circuit Issues

Issue	Possible Cause	Solution
LED not lighting up	No current-limiting resistor	Add a resistor in series with the LED.
Overheating components	Excessive current flow	Check Ohm's Law calculations and reduce current.
Voltage drop issues	High resistance connections	Use thicker wires or lower resistance paths.
Circuit not working	Loose or incorrect wiring	Double-check connections with a circuit diagram.

Note:

- Always check component ratings before use.
- When using a breadboard, ensure proper connections to avoid open circuits.
- Using a multimeter can help diagnose voltage, current, and resistance values.

Warning:

- Avoid applying excessive voltage to components, as it can damage them.
- Short circuits can cause overheating and damage the Arduino board.
- Always disconnect power before modifying circuits.

Summary

Understanding Ohm's Law and basic circuit principles is essential for designing safe and effective Arduino projects. Knowing how voltage, current, and resistance interact helps in selecting appropriate components and troubleshooting common circuit issues. Applying these concepts ensures successful and stable electronic projects.

Chapter 10: Resistors and Their Uses for Arduino

Resistors are fundamental components in electronic circuits, used to control current flow, divide voltage, and protect sensitive components. In Arduino projects, resistors play a crucial role in ensuring safe operation and proper functioning of sensors, LEDs, and other devices.

Understanding Resistors

A resistor is a passive electrical component that resists the flow of electric current. The resistance value, measured in ohms (Ω), determines how much it restricts the current.

Types of Resistors

Type	Description	Common Use in Arduino
Fixed Resistors	Have a constant resistance value	Current limiting for LEDs, pull-up/down resistors
Variable Resistors (Potentiometers)	Adjustable resistance	Used in sensors and controls
LDR (Light Dependent Resistor)	Resistance changes with light intensity	Light-sensing applications
Thermistors	Resistance changes with temperature	Temperature sensors
Pull-up/Pull-down Resistors	Ensures a defined logic level on inputs	Used in push-button circuits
High-Wattage Resistors	Can handle large power dissipation	Used in power circuits and motor drivers

How to Read a Resistor Value

Most resistors have colored bands representing their resistance value. The color code follows a standard chart:

Color	Digit	Multiplier	Tolerance
Black	0	×1Ω	-
Brown	1	×10Ω	±1%
Red	2	×100Ω	±2%
Orange	3	×1kΩ	-
Yellow	4	×10kΩ	-

Green	5	×100kΩ	±0.5%
Blue	6	×1MΩ	±0.25%
Violet	7	×10MΩ	±0.1%
Gray	8	-	±0.05%
White	9	-	-

Ohm's Law and Resistors in Arduino Circuits

Using Ohm's Law ($V = I \times R$), resistors are selected to regulate current and voltage in circuits. Common applications include:

- **Current Limiting for LEDs:**
  - Example: A 220Ω resistor is used in series with an LED to limit current.
  - Formula: $R = (V\_supply - V\_LED) / I\_LED$
- **Voltage Dividers:**
  - Used to step down voltage levels for sensors or analog inputs.
  - Formula: $V\_out = V\_in \times (R2 / (R1 + R2))$
  - Example: A 10kΩ and 5kΩ resistor combination can step down a 9V signal to 3V.
- **Pull-up and Pull-down Resistors:**
  - Pull-up resistors ensure that a digital input reads HIGH when not actively driven LOW.
  - Pull-down resistors ensure a digital input reads LOW when not actively driven HIGH.
  - Common values used: 4.7kΩ to 10kΩ.

Common Uses of Resistors in Arduino Projects

Application	Resistor Role
LED Protection	Limits current to prevent LED burnout
Button Debouncing	Pull-up/down resistors stabilize button input
Sensor Interfaces	Adjust voltage levels for analog sensors
Current Control	Limits current in transistor circuits
Voltage Dividers	Steps down voltage for components requiring lower input
Motor Driver Circuits	Limits current to protect transistors and ICs
Audio Circuits	Used for tone control and filtering

Example: Using a Resistor with an LED

```
const int ledPin = 9;
void setup() {
    pinMode(ledPin, OUTPUT);
}
void loop() {
    digitalWrite(ledPin, HIGH);
    delay(1000);
    digitalWrite(ledPin, LOW);
    delay(1000);
}
```

In this example, a 220Ω resistor is connected in series with the LED to prevent excessive current.

Advanced Uses of Resistors in Arduino

- **Current Sensing Resistors:**
  - Used in current measurement circuits to monitor power consumption.
  - A low-value precision resistor (e.g., 0.1Ω) is placed in series with a load.
- **Pull-down for MOSFET Switching:**
  - Ensures MOSFET gate turns off properly, preventing unwanted conduction.
- **RC (Resistor-Capacitor) Circuits:**
  - Used for filtering noise and shaping signal waveforms.

Troubleshooting Resistor Issues

Issue	Possible Cause	Solution
LED not lighting up	Resistor value too high	Use a lower resistance (e.g., 220Ω for LEDs)
Overheating components	Incorrect resistor placement	Verify wiring and resistor selection
Fluctuating readings	Missing pull-up/down resistor	Add a pull-up/down resistor to stabilize input
Unexpected voltage drop	Resistor value too high in series circuit	Recalculate based on Ohm's Law

Note:

- Always check resistor values before inserting them into circuits.
- Use a multimeter to verify resistance if unsure.
- Selecting the right resistor value ensures circuit reliability and prevents damage to components.
- Precision resistors are used in circuits requiring accurate voltage control.

Warning:

- Using a resistor with too low a value can cause excessive current flow, potentially damaging the Arduino.
- Exceeding power ratings of resistors can cause overheating and failure.
- Incorrect placement of resistors in voltage divider circuits can result in incorrect voltage levels.
- High-wattage resistors should be used when dealing with power-intensive circuits.

Summary

Resistors are essential components in Arduino circuits, used for current control, voltage division, and signal stabilization. Understanding how to select and use resistors effectively ensures safe and reliable project operation. By applying Ohm's Law and choosing the correct resistor types, Arduino users can build efficient and functional circuits for a variety of applications. Advanced uses, such as current sensing and MOSFET switching, further expand their application in electronics.

Chapter 11: Capacitors and Their Functions for Arduino

Capacitors are essential components in electronic circuits, used for energy storage, filtering, and signal processing. In Arduino projects, capacitors help stabilize power supply fluctuations, filter signals, and store energy for specific applications. Understanding the different types of capacitors and their applications ensures optimal circuit performance.

Understanding Capacitors

A capacitor is a passive electrical component that stores and releases electrical energy. It consists of two conductive plates separated by an insulating material (dielectric). The capacitance value, measured in farads (F), determines how much charge it can store. Larger capacitance values store more charge and release energy more slowly, whereas smaller capacitance values store less charge and respond faster.

Types of Capacitors

Type	Description	Common Use in Arduino
Ceramic Capacitors	Small, non-polarized, fast response	Noise filtering, decoupling
Electrolytic Capacitors	Large capacitance, polarized	Power supply smoothing, energy storage
Tantalum Capacitors	Stable, low leakage current	High-reliability circuits
Film Capacitors	Durable, used for high-voltage applications	Signal processing, power circuits
Supercapacitors	High energy storage, fast charging	Backup power, energy harvesting
Variable Capacitors	Adjustable capacitance	Radio tuning, frequency adjustments

How Capacitors Work in Circuits

Capacitors store electrical charge when voltage is applied and release it when needed. The basic formula for capacitance is:

$Q = C \times V$

Where:

- **Q** = Charge (coulombs, C)
- **C** = Capacitance (farads, F)
- **V** = Voltage (volts, V)

When the voltage across a capacitor changes, the capacitor charges or discharges according to the time constant formula:

$\tau = R \times C$

Where:

- **τ** = Time constant (seconds, s)
- **R** = Resistance (ohms, Ω)
- **C** = Capacitance (farads, F)

A capacitor reaches about 63% of its full charge after one time constant (τ) and is considered fully charged after about five time constants.

Applications of Capacitors in Arduino Projects

Application	Capacitor Role
Power Supply Filtering	Smooths voltage fluctuations and reduces noise
Debouncing Switches	Reduces noise in push buttons, improving stability
PWM Signal Smoothing	Reduces ripple in pulse width modulation (PWM) signals
Energy Storage	Provides temporary power backup in case of voltage drops
Noise Filtering	Removes high-frequency noise from power and signal lines
Coupling and Decoupling	Allows AC signals while blocking DC components
Oscillators and Timers	Used in RC circuits for timing applications
Motor Protection	Reduces voltage spikes from inductive loads

Example: Using a Capacitor for Power Supply Filtering

```
void setup() {
    Serial.begin(9600);
}
void loop() {
    Serial.println("Power stabilized with capacitor");
    delay(1000);
}
```

In this example, a capacitor connected across the power supply reduces noise and stabilizes voltage, improving Arduino performance and preventing resets caused by fluctuations.

Choosing the Right Capacitor for Arduino

- **For Noise Filtering:** Use small ceramic capacitors (0.1µF to 1µF) across power pins of microcontrollers and ICs.
- **For Power Stabilization:** Use electrolytic capacitors (10µF to 1000µF) near voltage regulators to smooth fluctuations.
- **For Energy Storage:** Use supercapacitors (1F or higher) to provide short-term power backups.
- **For High-Frequency Applications:** Use film capacitors for stable operation in RF circuits.

Practical Example: Debouncing a Button Using a Capacitor

When a button is pressed, mechanical contacts may bounce, causing multiple signals instead of one. A capacitor can help debounce the switch.

```
const int buttonPin = 2;
const int ledPin = 13;
bool buttonState = LOW;
void setup() {
    pinMode(buttonPin, INPUT);
    pinMode(ledPin, OUTPUT);
}
void loop() {
    buttonState = digitalRead(buttonPin);
    if (buttonState == HIGH) {
        digitalWrite(ledPin, HIGH);
        delay(50); // Debouncing delay
    } else {
        digitalWrite(ledPin, LOW);
```

```
        }
}
```

A capacitor (typically 10nF to 100nF) placed across the switch terminals helps smooth out bouncing effects and stabilizes button readings.

Troubleshooting Capacitor Issues

Issue	Possible Cause	Solution
Power fluctuations	Insufficient capacitance	Use a larger capacitor near voltage regulators
Incorrect polarity	Reversed electrolytic capacitor	Ensure correct polarity before connecting
Circuit instability	Missing decoupling capacitor	Add a 0.1µF ceramic capacitor near ICs
Signal distortion	Capacitor too large for frequency range	Use appropriate capacitance value based on application
Capacitor overheating	Excessive voltage or current	Verify voltage and current ratings of the capacitor

Note:
- Always check capacitor voltage ratings before use.
- Electrolytic capacitors are polarized; incorrect placement can cause failure.
- Using the correct capacitance ensures stable and efficient circuit operation.
- Decoupling capacitors should be placed as close as possible to IC power pins.

Warning:
- Exceeding voltage ratings can cause capacitor explosion or leakage.
- Connecting polarized capacitors in reverse may lead to failure and short circuits.
- Supercapacitors store large energy; handle with caution to avoid accidental discharge.
- High-frequency circuits require proper capacitor selection to avoid unintended oscillations.

Chapter 12: Diodes and LEDs for Arduino

Diodes and Light Emitting Diodes (LEDs) are essential components in electronics. Diodes control the direction of current flow, while LEDs provide a visual indication of electrical activity. In Arduino projects, both components play a crucial role in circuit protection, signal rectification, and display applications.

Understanding Diodes

A diode is a semiconductor device that allows current to flow in one direction only. It consists of an anode and a cathode. When a positive voltage is applied to the anode, current flows through the diode; otherwise, it blocks the current.

Types of Diodes

Type	Description	Common Use in Arduino
Rectifier Diode	Converts AC to DC	Power supply circuits
Schottky Diode	Low voltage drop, fast switching	Power efficiency applications
Zener Diode	Maintains a fixed voltage	Voltage regulation
Light Emitting Diode (LED)	Emits light when current flows	Visual indicators
Photodiode	Converts light into electrical current	Light sensors, IR receivers

How Diodes Work in Circuits

Diodes function based on their forward and reverse bias characteristics:

- **Forward Bias:** When voltage is applied in the correct direction, the diode conducts electricity.
- **Reverse Bias:** When voltage is applied in the opposite direction, the diode blocks current flow.

The formula governing diode behavior is:

$I = I_s (e^{(Vd / nVt)} - 1)$

Where:

- I = Current through the diode
- I_s = Reverse saturation current

- **Vd** = Voltage across the diode
- **n** = Ideality factor (1-2 depending on the diode type)
- **Vt** = Thermal voltage (~26mV at room temperature)

Understanding LEDs

LEDs are specialized diodes that emit light when current flows through them. They require a current-limiting resistor to prevent excessive current flow.

Choosing the Right Resistor for an LED

Using Ohm's Law (V = IR), we calculate the resistor value for an LED circuit:

- **Example:**
  - Supply Voltage: 5V
  - LED Forward Voltage: 2V
  - Desired Current: 10mA (0.01A)
  - Required Resistor:

R = (5V - 2V) / 0.01A = 300Ω

Common Uses of Diodes and LEDs in Arduino Projects

Application	Component Used	Function
Reverse Polarity Protection	Diode	Prevents damage from incorrect power connections
Power Supply Regulation	Zener Diode	Maintains a stable voltage
Indicator Lights	LED	Provides status indication
Signal Rectification	Rectifier Diode	Converts AC to DC
Infrared Communication	IR LED & Photodiode	Enables wireless data transmission

Example: Controlling an LED with Arduino

```
const int ledPin = 9;
void setup() {
    pinMode(ledPin, OUTPUT);
}
void loop() {
    digitalWrite(ledPin, HIGH);
    delay(1000);
    digitalWrite(ledPin, LOW);
```

```
    delay(1000);
}
```

This example turns an LED on and off every second using an Arduino digital pin.

Troubleshooting Diode and LED Issues

Issue	Possible Cause	Solution
LED not lighting up	Incorrect polarity	Reverse LED connection
Dim LED	Insufficient current	Reduce resistor value
Diode not conducting	Insufficient forward voltage	Check voltage source
Overheating component	Excessive current	Increase resistor value

Note:

- Always check the polarity before connecting a diode or LED.
- Use a current-limiting resistor with LEDs to prevent burnout.
- Zener diodes can regulate voltage, but exceeding their rating can damage them.

Warning:

- Applying reverse voltage to a diode beyond its limit can cause permanent failure.
- Excessive current through an LED can shorten its lifespan.
- Ensure power ratings of diodes match the circuit requirements.

Summary

Diodes and LEDs are crucial components in Arduino circuits. Understanding their properties and correct usage ensures efficient circuit design. Whether used for rectification, protection, or display purposes, these components enhance the functionality and reliability of electronic projects.

Chapter 13: Transistors and MOSFETs for Arduino

Transistors and MOSFETs are essential components in electronic circuits, acting as switches and amplifiers. In Arduino projects, these components are commonly used for controlling high-power devices such as motors, relays, and LEDs. Understanding how transistors and MOSFETs work allows users to design more efficient and powerful circuits.

Understanding Transistors

A transistor is a semiconductor device that can amplify signals or switch electronic loads on and off. It has three terminals:

- **Base (B)**: Controls the transistor operation.
- **Collector (C)**: The main current-carrying terminal.
- **Emitter (E)**: The output terminal.

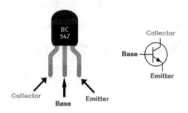

Types of Transistors

Type	Description	Common Use in Arduino
Bipolar Junction Transistor (BJT)	Current-controlled switch	Motor drivers, signal amplification
Field Effect Transistor (FET)	Voltage-controlled switch	High-speed switching applications
Darlington Transistor	Two BJTs combined for high gain	High-power switching

Comparison Table for Different Transistors

Parameter	BJT	MOSFET	Darlington Transistor
Control	Current-controlled	Voltage-controlled	Current-controlled
Efficiency	Less efficient	More efficient	Moderate
Switching Speed	Slower	Faster	Slower
Power Dissipation	High	Low	High
Best for	Small signals	High-power applications	High gain applications
Typical Example	2N2222, BC547	IRF540, IRLZ34N	TIP120, TIP122

How Transistors Work

Transistors operate in three regions:

- **Cutoff Region:** The transistor is OFF, no current flows from collector to emitter.
- **Active Region:** The transistor amplifies the input signal.
- **Saturation Region:** The transistor is fully ON, acting as a closed switch.

Using a Transistor as a Switch

A transistor can control high-power loads using a small signal from an Arduino. The most commonly used transistors in Arduino projects are the **NPN (2N2222)** and **PNP (BC557)** types.

Example: Controlling a Motor Using a BJT

```
const int motorPin = 9;
void setup() {
    pinMode(motorPin, OUTPUT);
}
void loop() {
    digitalWrite(motorPin, HIGH); // Turn on motor
    delay(2000);
    digitalWrite(motorPin, LOW); // Turn off motor
    delay(2000);
}
```

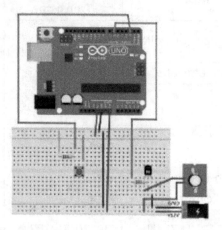

In this circuit, an **NPN transistor (2N2222)** is used to switch the motor ON and OFF based on the Arduino signal. A **1kΩ resistor** should be placed between the Arduino output pin and the transistor base to limit the current.

Understanding MOSFETs

MOSFETs (Metal-Oxide-Semiconductor Field-Effect Transistors) are more efficient than BJTs for switching applications. They have three terminals:

- **Gate (G)**: Controls the MOSFET operation.
- **Drain (D)**: Input for current flow.
- **Source (S)**: Output terminal.

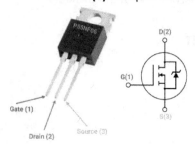

Types of MOSFETs

Type	Description	Common Use in Arduino
N-Channel MOSFET	Switches load on the negative side	Motor control, LED drivers
P-Channel MOSFET	Switches load on the positive side	Power management
Enhancement Mode MOSFET	Normally OFF, turns ON with voltage	General switching
Depletion Mode MOSFET	Normally ON, turns OFF with voltage	Specialty applications

Using a MOSFET to Control High-Power Devices

MOSFETs are preferred for high-power applications due to their low resistance and fast switching.

Example: Controlling an LED Strip with an N-Channel MOSFET

```
const int mosfetPin = 6;
void setup() {
    pinMode(mosfetPin, OUTPUT);
}
void loop() {
    digitalWrite(mosfetPin, HIGH); // Turn on LED strip
    delay(2000);
    digitalWrite(mosfetPin, LOW); // Turn off LED strip
    delay(2000);
}
```

Circuit Diagram

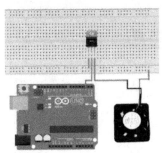

Circuit Diagram Connection Table

Component	Pin Connection
NPN Transistor (2N2222)	Base → Arduino Digital Pin (via 1kΩ resistor), Collector → Motor, Emitter → GND
PNP Transistor (BC557)	Base → Arduino Digital Pin (via 1kΩ resistor), Collector → GND, Emitter → Load
N-Channel MOSFET	Gate → Arduino Digital Pin, Drain → Load Negative, Source → GND
P-Channel MOSFET	Gate → Arduino Digital Pin, Drain → Load Positive, Source → Power Source

Additional Features of Transistors and MOSFETs

- **PWM Control:** Transistors and MOSFETs can be used with Arduino PWM pins to control motor speed and LED brightness smoothly.
- **Current Amplification:** BJTs can amplify weak signals for sensors or microphone circuits.
- **Temperature Sensitivity:** MOSFETs have lower heat dissipation than BJTs, making them more efficient in high-power applications.

Common Applications of Transistors and MOSFETs in Arduino Projects

Application	Component Used	Function
Motor Control	NPN BJT or N-Channel MOSFET	Switching high-power motors
LED Brightness Control	MOSFET	PWM dimming for LED strips
Relay Driver	NPN BJT	Activating high-power relays
Audio Amplification	BJT or MOSFET	Boosting weak signals
Battery Charging Circuit	P-Channel MOSFET	Power management
Inductive Load Switching	MOSFET	Controls solenoids and electromagnets

Note:

- Use a heat sink for high-power transistors and MOSFETs.
- Ensure correct voltage and current ratings for chosen components.
- MOSFETs require a pull-down resistor (10kΩ) at the gate for stable operation.
- BJTs require a base resistor (1kΩ) to limit current and prevent damage.

Warning:

- Overheating transistors can damage circuits.
- Incorrect MOSFET selection can lead to inefficient switching.
- Ensure correct polarity connections to avoid damage.
- Never exceed the voltage or current ratings of transistors and MOSFETs.

Summary

Transistors and MOSFETs are powerful components for switching and amplification in Arduino circuits. Understanding their operation and proper selection ensures efficient circuit performance. Whether controlling motors, LEDs, or other high-power devices, these components are crucial for effective Arduino-based projects. Proper implementation and component selection improve performance, reduce heat dissipation, and enhance reliability.

Chapter: Power Supply for Arduino A to Z

Power is the lifeblood of any electronic circuit, and Arduino projects are no exception. Whether you are designing a small project or working on a larger system, understanding how to properly power your Arduino is crucial to ensure its reliable operation. In this chapter, we will explore various power supply options, how to properly connect them to your Arduino, and how to choose the best power source for your projects.

1. Power Requirements for Arduino

An Arduino board typically requires 5V or 3.3V depending on the model. The **Arduino Uno**, for example, operates at 5V, while some models like the **Arduino Due** operate at 3.3V. Understanding the current and voltage requirements of your Arduino is essential to choose the correct power supply.

- **Voltage**: Most Arduino boards operate at 5V (Uno, Nano) or 3.3V (Due).
- **Current**: The Arduino itself typically draws between 30mA and 50mA, but external peripherals (sensors, motors, LEDs) can increase this significantly.

2. Power Supply Options for Arduino

There are several ways to power your Arduino, depending on the project's requirements. The most common options are:

1. **USB Power**:
    a. The easiest way to power an Arduino is via the USB connection to a computer or a USB power adapter. This provides both power and communication.
    b. **Voltage**: 5V (regulated)
    c. **Current**: Typically 500mA or more
2. **DC Power Jack (Barrel Jack)**:
    a. Most Arduino boards (e.g., Arduino Uno) can be powered through a **DC power jack**. This jack accepts a DC voltage from an external power supply.
    b. **Voltage**: Typically 7V to 12V (Uno) or 6V to 20V (Mega)
    c. **Current**: Depends on the power supply and peripherals connected

3. **Vin Pin:**
    a. The **Vin pin** allows you to supply external voltage directly to the Arduino. This is similar to using the DC barrel jack but bypasses the onboard voltage regulator.
    b. **Voltage:** 7V to 12V recommended
    c. **Current:** Depends on the peripherals
4. **Battery Power:**
    a. **Battery** options include:
        i.   **9V Battery** (Not recommended for heavy-duty projects)
        ii. **AA/AAA Battery Pack** (with a suitable voltage regulator)
        iii. **Li-Po or Li-ion Batteries** (common for mobile and remote projects)
    b. **Voltage:** Depends on battery type (typically 3.7V for Li-ion, 9V for standard packs)
    c. **Current:** Varies depending on battery capacity and load
5. **Power over Ethernet (PoE):**
    a. Some Arduino boards, such as the **Arduino Yun**, support Power over Ethernet (PoE). This allows you to power your Arduino via an Ethernet connection.
    b. **Voltage:** 5V (from Ethernet cable)
    c. **Current:** 500mA or more

3. Voltage Regulation in Arduino

Arduino boards typically have a **voltage regulator** onboard that ensures the correct voltage is supplied to the board, regardless of the voltage supplied to the power input. The onboard regulator converts higher voltages (e.g., 9V from the barrel jack) down to 5V or 3.3V.

- **Linear Regulators:** These are simple and inexpensive but inefficient. They waste excess voltage as heat.
- **Switching Regulators:** More efficient, especially for powering devices requiring higher current or if your power source is battery-operated.

Example: Voltage Regulator Overview

- **5V Regulator (Linear)**: Converts 7-12V input to 5V output, often used in Arduino Uno.
- **Buck Converter (Switching)**: More efficient when powering devices requiring higher currents or when working with battery-powered projects.

4. Choosing the Right Power Supply

When selecting the right power supply for your Arduino project, consider the following factors:

1. **Voltage Requirements**:
   a. Arduino boards require specific voltage levels to operate properly. Always check the **operating voltage** for the board model you are using. For example, the **Arduino Uno** requires 5V, but the **Arduino Due** requires 3.3V.

2. **Current Draw**:
   a. Calculate the **total current** consumption of the entire project, including the Arduino and all connected peripherals (e.g., sensors, motors, LEDs). Make sure the power supply can provide enough current. If not, the Arduino may malfunction or reset.

3. **Powering Motors or High-Current Devices**:
   a. If you plan to control motors, servos, or other high-current devices, you'll need a separate power supply to prevent excessive draw from the Arduino's onboard regulator. For example, use a dedicated 12V power supply for motors while using a separate 5V supply for the Arduino itself.

4. **Portability**:
   a. If you need a portable solution, battery-powered options like **Li-Po** or **Li-ion** batteries are ideal. For larger projects, a **solar panel** combined with a battery might be used.

5. **Efficiency**:
   a. If your project needs to run for extended periods, consider using a **switching regulator** instead of a linear regulator to minimize energy waste and reduce heat generation.

5. Example Connections

1. **Powering via USB**:
   a. Simply connect the **Arduino USB cable** to your computer or USB adapter.
2. **Powering via Barrel Jack**:
   a. Insert a **7V to 12V DC adapter** into the **barrel jack** of the Arduino.
3. **Powering via Vin Pin**:
   a. Connect an external power source (e.g., **9V battery**) to the **Vin** pin and **GND** on the Arduino.
4. **Using a 9V Battery**:
   a. Connect the positive terminal of the battery to the **positive rail** and the negative terminal to the **GND rail** of the Arduino. You can use a **battery clip** to make this connection.

6. Battery Power for Arduino Projects

When working with **battery-powered Arduino projects**, ensure you have the appropriate voltage regulator for stable operation. Below are the types of batteries that can be used:

1. **9V Battery**:
   a. Common but not very efficient for high-current projects.
   b. Can power small projects for a short period of time.
2. **AA or AAA Battery Pack**:
   a. Use multiple batteries in series to achieve the required voltage (e.g., a 6xAA pack for 9V).
   b. Ideal for simple projects that require low current.
3. **Li-ion or Li-Po Battery**:
   a. Provides higher energy density, making them ideal for mobile or wearable projects.
   b. Typically come with a **charging circuit**.

7. Power Management for Arduino Projects

Efficient power management is crucial in ensuring long operation times, especially in remote or battery-powered projects. Consider the following:

1. **Power Saving Techniques**:
   a. Use **sleep modes** in the Arduino to reduce power

consumption during periods of inactivity.
  b. Turn off peripherals when not in use (e.g., motors, sensors).
2. **Charging and Powering with Solar**:
  a. Solar panels combined with **Li-ion batteries** are great for outdoor or autonomous projects. Use a **solar charge controller** to manage the power flow and ensure safe battery charging.

8. Troubleshooting Power Supply Issues
1. **Arduino Not Powering On**:
  a. Check your power supply connections.
  b. Ensure your power supply voltage is within the recommended range for your Arduino model.
2. **Voltage Drops Under Load**:
  a. If you're powering motors or other high-current devices, make sure your power supply is rated for higher current and that you're using a separate supply for high-power devices.
3. **Overheating**:
  a. If your Arduino or voltage regulator gets hot, it could be due to excessive current draw. Consider adding a heatsink or using a more efficient switching regulator.

Summary

Choosing the correct power supply for your Arduino project is vital for both the success and longevity of your work. Understanding your voltage and current requirements, selecting the proper power source, and managing power consumption can ensure your project runs smoothly. Whether you're powering your Arduino through USB, a DC adapter, or batteries, the key is to match the power source to the needs of your project.

Chapter 15: Arduino Environment and Sketch Structure

Arduino is an open-source electronics platform that simplifies hardware and software development. This chapter will provide an in-depth look at the Arduino development environment and explain the structure of an Arduino sketch.

The Arduino IDE

The Arduino Integrated Development Environment (IDE) is the primary tool for writing, compiling, and uploading code to Arduino boards. It consists of several key components:

- **Editor:** A simple interface for writing and modifying code.
- **Message Area:** Displays errors and notifications.
- **Console:** Provides detailed information during compilation and uploading.
- **Toolbar:** Contains buttons for verifying, uploading, opening, and saving sketches.
- **Board and Port Selection:** Allows users to select the appropriate board and communication port.

The Arduino IDE supports multiple platforms, including Windows, macOS, and Linux. Additionally, the newer Arduino Web Editor and Arduino CLI provide alternative ways to work with Arduino sketches.

Sketch Structure

An Arduino sketch is a program written in C/C++ that follows a specific structure:

1. Preprocessor Directives

Preprocessor directives include libraries and define constants that the sketch needs. For example:

```
#include <Wire.h>
#define LED_PIN 13
```

2. Global Variables and Constants

These are declared outside functions to retain their values throughout the program execution:

```
int counter = 0;
const float PI = 3.14159;
```

3. Setup Function

The setup() function runs once when the Arduino board is powered on or reset. It is used to initialize settings such as pin modes and serial communication:

```
void setup() {
    pinMode(LED_PIN, OUTPUT);
    Serial.begin(9600);
}
```

4. Loop Function

The loop() function runs repeatedly, allowing the Arduino to perform continuous tasks:

```
void loop() {
    digitalWrite(LED_PIN, HIGH);
    delay(1000);
    digitalWrite(LED_PIN, LOW);
    delay(1000);
}
```

Additional Functions

Arduino sketches can include user-defined functions to make code modular and reusable:

```
void blinkLED(int duration) {
    digitalWrite(LED_PIN, HIGH);
    delay(duration);
    digitalWrite(LED_PIN, LOW);
    delay(duration);
}
```

Comments and Documentation

Comments improve code readability and help in documentation:

```
// This is a single-line comment
/* This is a
   multi-line comment */
```

Uploading and Running a Sketch

To upload a sketch to an Arduino board:

1. Connect the Arduino to the computer via USB.
2. Select the correct board and port in the Arduino IDE.
3. Click the "Upload" button.
4. Observe the results through the Serial Monitor if needed.

Conclusion

Understanding the Arduino environment and sketch structure is fundamental to developing projects. This chapter provided a detailed overview of the Arduino IDE, sketch structure, and essential functions. Mastering these concepts will enable you to build more complex and efficient Arduino applications.

Chapter 16: Variables and Data Types for Arduino

This chapter explores variables and data types, fundamental concepts in Arduino programming. Variables store values that can change during program execution, while data types define the kind of data a variable can hold. Understanding these concepts is essential for effective programming and memory management in Arduino-based projects.

Key Characteristics of Variables and Data Types

Data Type	Description	Example
int	Stores whole numbers from -32,768 to 32,767.	`int number = 25;`
float	Stores decimal numbers with single precision.	`float temperature = 36.6;`
char	Stores a single character.	`char letter = 'A';`
bool	Stores true or false values.	`bool isReady = true;`
const	Defines constant values that do not change.	`const int maxSpeed = 120;`
long	Stores larger whole numbers from -2,147,483,648 to 2,147,483,647.	`long bigNumber = 100000;`
unsigned int	Stores positive whole numbers up to 65,535.	`unsigned int count = 5000;`
double	Stores double-precision floating-point numbers.	`double precisionValue = 3.14159;`

Basic Rules for Variables and Data Types

Rule	Correct Example	Incorrect Example
Variables must be declared before use.	`int x = 5;`	`x = 5;` (Missing type declaration)
Use appropriate data types for values.	`float pi = 3.14;`	`int pi = 3.14;` (Incorrect type, loses precision)
Constants should be defined using const.	`const int maxVal = 100;`	`int maxVal = 100;` (Allows modification, not a constant)
Boolean values should be true or false.	`bool flag = true;`	`bool flag = 1;` (May work, but not best practice)
Use explicit type conversion when necessary.	`float result = (float)sum / count;`	`float result = sum / count;` (May cause unintended integer division)

Syntax Table

SL	Function	Syntax/Example	Description
1	Declare an Integer	`int num = 10;`	Declares an integer variable.
2	Floating Point	`float pi = 3.14;`	Declares a floating-point variable.
3	Character Variable	`char letter = 'A';`	Declares a character variable.
4	Boolean Variable	`bool flag = true;`	Declares a boolean variable.
5	Constant Variable	`const int maxVal = 100;`	Defines a constant variable.

Syntax Explanation

1. Declare an Integer
What is an Integer? An integer is a whole number without a fractional component. It is commonly used for counting, indexing, and loop control.
```
int num = 10;
```

Example:
```
int count = 5;
Serial.println(count);
```

Example Explanation: This example declares an integer variable count, assigns it a value of 5, and prints it to the serial monitor.

2. Floating Point
What is a Floating-Point Number? A floating-point number stores decimal values, often used in sensor readings and precise calculations.
```
float pi = 3.14;
```

Example:
```
float temperature = 36.6;
Serial.println(temperature);
```

Example Explanation: The variable temperature holds a decimal value and prints it using Serial.println().

3. Character Variable

What is a Character? A character stores a single letter or symbol using the char type, enclosed in single quotes.
```
char letter = 'A';
```

Example:
```
char grade = 'B';
Serial.println(grade);
```

Example Explanation: This example declares a character variable grade and prints it using Serial.println().

4. Boolean Variable

What is a Boolean? A boolean holds either `true` or `false`, used for conditions and logic control.
```
bool flag = true;
```

Example:
```
bool status = false;
Serial.println(status);
```

Example Explanation: The variable `status` is set to `false`, and `Serial.println(status);` prints 0 (false) in Arduino.

5. Constant Variable

What is a Constant? A constant stores a fixed value that cannot change during program execution.
```
const int maxVal = 100;
```

Example:
```
const int maxSpeed = 120;
Serial.println(maxSpeed);
```

Example Explanation: The variable maxSpeed is constant, meaning it remains 120 throughout the program.

Type Conversion and Casting

What is Type Conversion? Type conversion allows changing a variable from one data type to another, either implicitly or explicitly using type casting.
```
int x = 5;
float y = (float)x; // Converts integer to float
Serial.println(y);
```

Example Explanation: This example converts an integer x into a floating-point number y, ensuring it retains a decimal format (5.00).

Chapter 17: Control Structures for Arduino

This chapter covers control structures, which are essential tools in Arduino programming. Control structures allow you to dictate the flow of your program based on conditions and loops. Understanding these structures is crucial for writing efficient and functional Arduino programs that can respond to sensor inputs, user actions, and other dynamic conditions.

Key Characteristics of Control Structures

Control structures allow a program to make decisions (conditional statements) and repeat tasks (loops). These structures enable the program to adapt to different situations, making it more interactive and responsive to various inputs.

Types of Control Structures

Control Structure	Description	Example
if	Executes a block of code if the condition is true.	`if (x > 5) { ... }`
else	Executes a block of code if the condition in `if` is false.	`else { ... }`
else if	Tests multiple conditions sequentially.	`else if (x == 10) { ... }`
switch	Allows multiple conditional branches based on a variable's value.	`switch (x) { ... }`
while	Executes a block of code as long as the condition is true.	`while (x < 10) { ... }`
for	Repeats a block of code a set number of times.	`for (int i = 0; i < 10; i++) { ... }`

Basic Rules for Control Structures

Rule	Correct Example	Incorrect Example
Conditions must be enclosed in parentheses.	`if (x > 10) { ... }`	`if x > 10 { ... }`
Blocks of code in conditional structures should be enclosed in curly braces {}.	`if (x > 5) { ... }`	`if (x > 5) ...`
Ensure the condition in loops will eventually become false to avoid infinite loops.	`while (x < 10) { x++; }`	`while (x > 10) { ... }` (If condition is always true)
Properly define the loop counter for for loops.	`for (int i = 0; i < 10; i++) { ... }`	`for (int i = 0; i < 10) { ... }` (Missing loop counter increment)

Syntax Table

SL	Function	Syntax/Example	Description
1	If Statement	`if (x > 5) { ... }`	Executes the block of code if the condition is true.
2	Else Statement	`else { ... }`	Executes the block of code if the condition in if is false.
3	Else If Statement	`else if (x == 10) { ... }`	Tests a new condition if the previous if or else if conditions are false.
4	Switch Case	`switch (x) { case 1: ... break; default: ... }`	Executes blocks of code based on the value of a variable.
5	While Loop	`while (x < 10) { ... }`	Repeats a block of code while the condition is true.
6	For Loop	`for (int i = 0; i < 10; i++) { ... }`	Repeats a block of code for a set number of times.

Syntax Explanation

1. If Statement

What is an if statement?

An if statement allows you to execute a block of code only when a specified condition is true. It's the foundation for decision-making in Arduino programs.

Syntax:

```
if (condition) {
    // Code to execute if condition is true
}
```

Example:

```
int temperature = 30;
if (temperature > 25) {
    Serial.println("It's hot!");
}
```

Example Explanation:

The program checks if the temperature variable is greater than 25. If this condition evaluates to true, the block of code inside the if statement will execute, printing "It's hot!" to the serial monitor. If the condition is false (i.e., the temperature is 25 or lower), nothing happens. This control structure helps in making decisions based on dynamic inputs.

2. Else Statement

What is an else statement?

The else statement provides an alternative block of code to execute if the condition in the preceding if or else if is false.

Syntax:

```
if (condition) {
    // Code to execute if condition is true
} else {
    // Code to execute if condition is false
}
```

Example:
```
int temperature = 15;
if (temperature > 25) {
  Serial.println("It's hot!");
} else {
  Serial.println("It's not that hot.");
}
```
Example Explanation:
 Here, the program first checks if the temperature is greater than 25. If the condition is true, it prints "It's hot!". If the condition is false (i.e., the temperature is 25 or lower), the program moves to the else block and prints "It's not that hot.". This is a simple way of providing an alternative action when a condition is not met.

3. Else If Statement

What is an else if statement?
 else if provides multiple conditions to test sequentially. Once a true condition is found, the corresponding block of code is executed.
Syntax:
```
if (condition1) {
  // Code to execute if condition1 is true
} else if (condition2) {
  // Code to execute if condition2 is true
} else {
  // Code to execute if all conditions are false
}
```
Example:
```
int temperature = 18;
if (temperature > 25) {
  Serial.println("It's hot!");
} else if (temperature > 15) {
  Serial.println("It's warm.");
} else {
  Serial.println("It's cold.");
}
```

Example Explanation:

In this example, the program first checks if the `temperature` is greater than 25. If `true`, it prints "It's hot!". If the condition is `false`, it checks the next condition with `else if` to see if the temperature is greater than 15. If this second condition is `true`, it prints "It's warm.". If neither of the conditions is `true`, the program will default to the `else` block, printing "It's cold.". The use of `else if` allows for testing multiple conditions in sequence.

4. Switch Case

What is a `switch` statement?

The `switch` statement is a cleaner and more efficient way of handling multiple conditions that check the value of a variable.

Syntax:

```
switch (variable) {
  case value1:
    // Code to execute if variable equals value1
    break;
  case value2:
    // Code to execute if variable equals value2
    break;
  default:
    // Code to execute if no case matches
}
```

Example:

```
int day = 3;
switch (day) {
  case 1:
    Serial.println("Monday");
    break;
  case 2:
    Serial.println("Tuesday");
    break;
  case 3:
```

```
    Serial.println("Wednesday");
    break;
  default:
    Serial.println("Invalid day");
}
```

Example Explanation:
The program checks the value of day using the switch statement. It compares the value of day to each case. When day is 3, it matches case 3 and prints "Wednesday". If none of the cases match, the program executes the default case, printing "Invalid day". This is more efficient than using multiple if-else statements, especially when you have many conditions based on a single variable.

5. While Loop

What is a while loop?
A while loop repeats a block of code as long as the specified condition remains true. It's useful for situations where you don't know the exact number of iterations in advance.

Syntax:
```
while (condition) {
  // Code to execute as long as the condition is true
}
```

Example:
```
int counter = 0;
while (counter < 5) {
  Serial.println(counter);
  counter++;
}
```

Example Explanation:
In this example, the while loop starts with counter set to 0. As long as counter is less than 5, the loop continues. Each time the loop runs, it prints the value of counter and increments it by 1. When counter reaches 5, the condition counter < 5 becomes false, and the loop stops. This loop structure is ideal when the number of iterations is unknown and depends on changing conditions.

6. For Loop

What is a for loop?

A for loop is ideal for repeating code a fixed number of times. It contains an initialization, a condition, and an increment/decrement operation.

Syntax:

```
for (initialization; condition; increment) {
  // Code to execute on each iteration
}
```

Example:

```
for (int i = 0; i < 5; i++) {
  Serial.println(i);
}
```

Example Explanation:

The for loop begins by initializing i to 0. It then checks the condition i < 5. If true, it prints the value of i, then increments i by 1. The loop repeats until i reaches 5, at which point the condition i < 5 becomes false, and the loop stops. This is a great way to execute a block of code a specific number of times, especially when you know the exact number of iterations.

Conclusion

Control structures are powerful tools in Arduino programming, allowing your programs to make decisions and repeat tasks based on changing conditions. Mastery of if, else, else if, switch, while, and for loops will enable you to create more complex and interactive Arduino projects.

Chapter 18: Functions and Their Uses for Arduino

This chapter focuses on functions, a key concept in Arduino programming. Functions allow you to organize and modularize your code, making it easier to write, read, and maintain. Functions help to simplify complex tasks and reduce redundancy by allowing you to reuse blocks of code whenever necessary.

Key Characteristics of Functions

A function is a block of code that performs a specific task and can be called multiple times throughout the program. Functions can take inputs, known as parameters, and can return a value to the calling code.

Types of Functions

Function Type	Description	Example
Built-in Functions	Functions that are predefined in the Arduino library.	`digitalWrite(pin, value);`
User-defined Functions	Functions that the programmer defines for custom behavior.	`int addNumbers(int a, int b) { return a + b; }`
Void Functions	Functions that do not return any value.	`void blinkLED() { digitalWrite(LED_BUILTIN, HIGH); delay(1000); digitalWrite(LED_BUILTIN, LOW); }`
Value-returning Functions	Functions that return a value to the calling code.	`int multiply(int x, int y) { return x * y; }`
Functions with Parameters	Functions that accept inputs to customize behavior.	`void setSpeed(int speed) { analogWrite(motorPin, speed); }`

Basic Rules for Functions

Rule	Correct Example	Incorrect Example
Functions must be defined before they are used in the code.	`int add(int a, int b) { return a + b; }`	`add(a, b);` (Function is used before being defined)
Functions should have a return type specified.	`int multiply(int x, int y) { return x * y; }`	`multiply(int x, int y) { return x * y; }` (Missing return type)
Parameters in functions should be defined with the correct data type.	`void setSpeed(int speed) { analogWrite(motorPin, speed); }`	`void setSpeed(speed) { analogWrite(motorPin, speed); }` (Data type missing)
Use return to send a value from a function back to the caller.	`int getTemperature() { return temperature; }`	`int getTemperature() { temperature; }` (Missing return statement)
Function names should be meaningful and descriptive.	`void turnOnLED() { digitalWrite(LED_PIN, HIGH); }`	`void func() { digitalWrite(LED_PIN, HIGH); }` (Non-descriptive name)

Syntax Table

SL	Function	Syntax/Example	Description
1	Define a Function	`int add(int a, int b) { return a + b; }`	Defines a function that adds two integers and returns the result.
2	Call a Function	`int result = add(3, 4);`	Calls the function with arguments and stores the return value.

| 3 | Void Function | ```
void blinkLED() {
digitalWrite(LED_BUILTI
N, HIGH); delay(1000);
digitalWrite(LED_BUILTI
N, LOW); }
``` | Defines a function that blinks the LED without returning a value. |
|---|---|---|---|
| 4 | Return a Value | ```
int multiply(int x, int
y) { return x * y; }
``` | Defines a function that returns the product of two numbers. |
| 5 | Function with Parameters | ```
void setSpeed(int
speed) {
analogWrite(motorPin,
speed); }
``` | Defines a function that accepts a parameter to set speed. |

Syntax Explanation

1. Define a Function

What is defining a function?
A function is defined using the syntax return_type
function_name(parameters) { ... }. This tells the program what kind of data the function will return (if any), the function's name, and any inputs it will need to perform its task.

Syntax:
```
return_type function_name(parameters) {
   // Code to execute
}
```

Example:
```
int add(int a, int b) {
   return a + b;
}
```

Example Explanation:
This function is called add, and it takes two integer parameters (a and b). It returns the sum of a and b. This function can be called with two integers as arguments, and it will return their sum.

When you call this function, you pass values for a and b, and the function will calculate their sum and send it back as the result.
```

2. Call a Function

What is calling a function?
To use a function, you need to call it, which means you tell the program to execute the function's code by providing any required arguments.
Syntax:
```
function_name(arguments);
```

Example:
```
int result = add(3, 4);
Serial.println(result);
```

Example Explanation:
In this example, the function add is called with the arguments 3 and 4. The function will add these two numbers and return the result (7), which is then stored in the variable result. The program prints result (7) to the serial monitor.
When calling a function, you use the function's name and pass the correct number of arguments in the correct order.

3. Void Function

What is a void function?
A void function does not return a value. It is used when you want to perform an action but don't need to send any result back.
Syntax:
```
void function_name(parameters) {
  // Code to execute
}
```

Example:
```
void blinkLED() {
  digitalWrite(LED_BUILTIN, HIGH);
  delay(1000);
  digitalWrite(LED_BUILTIN, LOW);
  delay(1000);
}
```

Example Explanation:
This function, `blinkLED`, is a void function that blinks the built-in LED. It does not return any value. Instead, it performs an action: turning the LED on for one second, then off for one second, repeatedly. This function could be called in the `loop()` to blink the LED continuously.

4. Return a Value

What does returning a value mean?
Returning a value from a function means sending a result back to the calling code. A function can return only one value at a time.

Syntax:
```
return_type function_name(parameters) {
    return value;
}
```

Example:
```
int multiply(int x, int y) {
    return x * y;
}
```

Example Explanation:
The `multiply` function takes two integers (x and y) and returns their product. The function calculates the product and returns the result. When this function is called, the result can be stored in a variable and used in the program.

5. Function with Parameters

What are parameters?
Parameters are values that you pass to a function when calling it. They allow you to customize the function's behavior each time you use it.

Syntax:
```
void function_name(type parameter1, type parameter2) {
    // Code that uses parameters
}
```

Example:

```
void setSpeed(int speed) {
  analogWrite(motorPin, speed);
}
```

Example Explanation:

This function, setSpeed, takes one parameter, speed, which is an integer. When called, you pass a value for speed, and the function uses it to control the speed of a motor by writing the value to the motorPin. The parameter makes the function reusable with different speeds.

Conclusion

Functions are fundamental building blocks in Arduino programming. They allow you to break down complex tasks into manageable pieces, make your code more readable, and reuse code to reduce redundancy. Mastering the use of functions is key to writing clean and efficient Arduino programs.

Chapter 19: A to Z PWM for Arduino

This chapter focuses on Pulse Width Modulation (PWM), a technique used in Arduino programming to control the power supplied to devices like LEDs, motors, and servos. PWM allows for precise control over the brightness of an LED, the speed of a motor, and many other applications where varying power is required.

Key Characteristics of PWM

PWM is a form of digital signal where the signal is either HIGH (on) or LOW (off) at a fast frequency, with the "duty cycle" determining how long the signal stays HIGH. By adjusting the duty cycle, you can control how much power is delivered to a device. A 100% duty cycle means the signal is always HIGH, while a 0% duty cycle means the signal is always LOW.

PWM Characteristic	Description	Example
Frequency	The number of times the signal repeats per second.	490 Hz (default for most pins on Arduino)
Duty Cycle	The percentage of time the signal is HIGH within one cycle.	50% (signal is HIGH half the time)
Resolution	The number of discrete steps between 0 and 255.	8-bit resolution (0-255)
Output Pin	The pin on the Arduino used for PWM output.	Pin 3, 5, 6, 9, 10, 11 (on most Arduino boards)

Basic Rules for PWM

Rule	Correct Example	Incorrect Example
Use analogWrite() to send a PWM signal.	analogWrite (pin, 128);	analogWrite(pin, 256); (Out of range, should be 0-255)
Only certain pins support PWM output.	analogWrite (9, 128);	analogWrite(12, 128); (Pin 12 does not support PWM)

The value passed to analogWrite() should be between 0 and 255.	analogWrite (3, 255);	analogWrite(3, -10); (Out of range)
PWM can control both analog and digital devices.	analogWrite (3, 127);	analogWrite(4, 100); (Pin 4 does not support PWM)

Syntax Table

SL	Function	Syntax/Example	Description
1	Write PWM signal	analogWrite(pin, value);	Writes a PWM signal to the specified pin with a value from 0 to 255.
2	Pin selection	pinMode(pin, OUTPUT);	Sets the pin to OUTPUT mode, enabling PWM on supported pins.
3	PWM value	analogWrite(9, 128);	Writes a PWM signal with a 50% duty cycle (value of 128).
4	Fade LED (example)	analogWrite(9, brightness);	Example of varying the brightness of an LED using PWM.

Syntax Explanation

1. Write PWM signal

What is writing a PWM signal?
The function analogWrite() is used to send a PWM signal to a pin. The value provided (from 0 to 255) controls the duty cycle of the signal. A value of 0 means the signal is LOW 100% of the time (off), and a value of 255 means the signal is HIGH 100% of the time (on).
Syntax:
analogWrite(pin, value);

Example:
analogWrite(9, 128);

Example Explanation:

In this example, the function `analogWrite(9, 128)` sends a PWM signal to pin 9. The value 128 represents a 50% duty cycle, meaning the signal is HIGH for half of the cycle and LOW for the other half, which results in 50% of the maximum power being delivered to the device connected to pin 9.

This can be used to control devices like LEDs, motors, or any other component that responds to varying power.

2. Pin selection

What is pin selection for PWM?

Before using PWM, the pin must be configured as an output. The `pinMode()` function is used to set the pin to OUTPUT mode so it can send signals.

Syntax:
```
pinMode(pin, OUTPUT);
```

Example:
```
pinMode(9, OUTPUT);
```

Example Explanation:

In this example, `pinMode(9, OUTPUT)` sets pin 9 as an output. This step is essential before using `analogWrite()` to send PWM signals to the pin. You must ensure that the pin supports PWM, as not all pins on the Arduino are capable of generating PWM signals.

3. PWM value

What does the PWM value mean?

The value passed to `analogWrite()` represents the duty cycle of the signal. This value ranges from 0 to 255, where 0 is a 0% duty cycle (always OFF) and 255 is a 100% duty cycle (always ON). Values in between represent different levels of power output.

Syntax:
```
analogWrite(pin, value);
```

Example:

```
analogWrite(9, 128);  // 50% duty cycle
```

Example Explanation:

The value 128 corresponds to a 50% duty cycle, meaning that the signal is ON for 50% of the time and OFF for the other 50%. This is typically used for controlling the brightness of an LED or the speed of a motor.

4. Fade LED (example)

What is fading an LED?

PWM can be used to gradually change the brightness of an LED by varying the duty cycle over time. By using analogWrite() with different values in a loop, you can create a fading effect.

Syntax:

```
analogWrite(pin, brightness);
```

Example:

```
int brightness = 0;
for (brightness = 0; brightness <= 255; brightness++) {
  analogWrite(9, brightness);
  delay(10);
}
for (brightness = 255; brightness >= 0; brightness--) {
  analogWrite(9, brightness);
  delay(10);
}
```

Example Explanation:

This example gradually increases the brightness of an LED connected to pin 9 by increasing the value passed to analogWrite(). It first goes from 0 to 255 and then fades back down from 255 to 0, creating a smooth fade-in and fade-out effect.

The delay(10) creates a small pause between changes to make the fading effect visible to the human eye.

Conclusion

PWM is a powerful technique that allows precise control over devices that require variable power, such as LEDs, motors, and servos. By understanding how to use analogWrite() and adjusting the duty cycle, you can create smooth transitions in brightness, speed, and other variables in your Arduino projects.

Chapter 20: Using Timers and Delays for Arduino

This chapter introduces timers and delays in Arduino programming. Timers are an essential feature of microcontrollers that allow you to manage time-based tasks. Delays, on the other hand, provide a simple way to pause the program execution for a specified duration. Understanding both will enable you to create more responsive and time-controlled Arduino projects.

Key Concepts of Timers and Delays

Timers on the Arduino are hardware-based counters that allow you to measure time intervals and execute actions accordingly. Unlike `delay()`, which halts the entire program for a set period, timers operate in the background, enabling more efficient multitasking. Delays, though simpler, are still useful for basic time control and debugging.

Timer Concept	Description	Example
Timer	A hardware counter that tracks time intervals.	Setting a timer to trigger an interrupt every 1 ms.
Delay()	Pauses program execution for a specified amount of time.	`delay(1000);` causes a 1-second pause.
Millis()	Returns the number of milliseconds since the Arduino started.	Using `millis()` to create non-blocking delays.
Interrupts	Allows the Arduino to react to specific events immediately.	Using interrupts to trigger actions when a button is pressed.

Basic Rules for Timers and Delays

Rule	Correct Example	Incorrect Example
Use `delay()` for simple timing operations.	`delay(1000);` (Wait for 1 second)	`delay(-500);` (Negative value)

Use `millis()` for non-blocking delays.	`if (millis() - lastTime >= interval)`	`millis() < 1000` (Incorrect comparison for timing)
Avoid using `delay()` in time-critical applications.	Use timers or `millis()` to handle time-sensitive tasks.	Relying only on `delay()` for tasks requiring precise timing.

Syntax Table

SL	Function	Syntax/Example	Description
1	Delay execution	`delay(millisec onds);`	Pauses program execution for a set number of milliseconds.
2	Millis timer	`millis();`	Returns the number of milliseconds since the Arduino started.
3	Timer configuration	`` `TCCR0B = TCCR0B & 0b111110000x05;` ``	Configures Timer0 for a 1ms delay.
4	Interrupt handling	`attachInterrup t(digitalPinTo Interrupt(pin) , ISR, mode);`	Sets up an interrupt for a pin change event.

Syntax Explanation

1. Delay Execution

What is a delay?
The `delay()` function is one of the simplest ways to create pauses in your program. When called, it halts program execution for a specified amount of time, allowing other tasks or actions to be executed later.
Syntax:
```
delay(milliseconds);
```

Example:
```
delay(1000);  // Pauses execution for 1 second
```

Example Explanation:

In this example, `delay(1000)` pauses the program for 1000 milliseconds, which is equivalent to 1 second. This is useful when you want to wait before executing the next command.

Limitations of `delay()`:

Using `delay()` in long-running programs can cause issues as it blocks further execution. For example, if you're controlling an LED and need to handle user inputs, the delay will block those inputs from being processed.

2. Millis Timer

What is `millis()`?

`millis()` returns the number of milliseconds that have passed since the Arduino started running the current program. This function is often used to implement non-blocking delays, which allow the program to continue running other tasks while waiting for a certain amount of time to pass.

Syntax:

```
millis();
```

Example:

```
unsigned long previousMillis = 0;
const long interval = 1000;  // 1 second

void loop() {
  unsigned long currentMillis = millis();

  if (currentMillis - previousMillis >= interval) {
    previousMillis = currentMillis;
    // Code to execute after 1 second
  }
}
```

Example Explanation:

In this example, `millis()` is used to create a non-blocking delay. The program checks how much time has passed since the last execution, and if the specified interval (1000 milliseconds) has passed, it executes the code. This approach does not block the execution of other tasks, making it more efficient for time-sensitive applications.

3. Timer Configuration

What is Timer Configuration?
Timers are hardware peripherals within the Arduino that can be configured to generate specific time intervals. These timers can run in the background, enabling more complex scheduling and precise timing without blocking program execution.

Example:
```
TCCR0B = TCCR0B & 0b11111000 | 0x05;  // Configure
Timer0 to overflow every 1ms
```

Example Explanation:
This code configures Timer0 to trigger an interrupt every 1 millisecond. This is a more advanced technique that allows you to use timers for precise time management without relying on `delay()` or `millis()`. Timer interrupts can be used for real-time applications, such as controlling motors or reading sensors at precise intervals.

4. Interrupt Handling

What is an interrupt?
An interrupt is a signal that tells the microcontroller to stop executing the current program and immediately run a special function (known as an interrupt service routine or ISR). Interrupts are commonly used for handling time-sensitive events, such as button presses, sensor readings, or other asynchronous events.

Syntax:
```
attachInterrupt(digitalPinToInterrupt(pin), ISR, mode);
```

Example:
```
void setup() {
  attachInterrupt(digitalPinToInterrupt(2),
buttonPress, FALLING);
}
void buttonPress() {
  // Code to execute when the button is pressed
}
```

Example Explanation:
In this example, the `attachInterrupt()` function is used to call the
`buttonPress()` function every time the button on pin 2 is pressed
(falling edge). Interrupts provide an efficient way to respond to events
without continuously checking for them in the main loop.

Conclusion

Timers and delays are fundamental concepts in Arduino programming.
While `delay()` provides a simple way to pause execution, it can be
inefficient for tasks that require multitasking. Using `millis()` and timers
allows for non-blocking time management, giving your Arduino projects
more flexibility. Interrupts add a further layer of responsiveness by
allowing the program to react immediately to specific events.

Chapter 21: Interrupts and Their Applications for Arduino

Interrupts are a crucial feature in embedded programming, allowing microcontrollers to respond immediately to external events. Instead of waiting for the main program to check for events, interrupts let the system "interrupt" its normal execution to handle more time-sensitive tasks. In Arduino, interrupts are commonly used for tasks like handling button presses, time-sensitive sensor readings, or other real-time operations.

Key Concepts of Interrupts

An interrupt is a signal that tells the microcontroller to temporarily stop executing the main program and run a special function known as an Interrupt Service Routine (ISR). Interrupts can be triggered by various events such as pin state changes, timer overflows, or external signals.

Interrupt Concept	Description	Example
Interrupt Service Routine (ISR)	A special function that executes when an interrupt occurs.	A function that triggers when a button is pressed.
Pin Change Interrupt	Interrupt triggered by changes in pin state (HIGH/LOW).	Interrupt when a button connected to a pin is pressed.
External Interrupt	Interrupt triggered by external devices or signals.	Triggering an interrupt from a sensor or external device.
Edge Triggering	Determines which transition of the signal triggers the interrupt.	Trigger on a rising or falling edge of a signal.

Basic Rules for Interrupts

Rule	Correct Example	Incorrect Example
Interrupt service routines (ISRs) should be kept short and fast.	`ISR(INT0_vect) { digitalWrite( LED_PIN, HIGH); }`	`ISR(INT0_vect) { delay(1000); }` (Delays inside ISRs are not allowed)
Use `attachInterrupt()` to set up pin interrupts.	`attachInterrupt(digitalPinToInterrupt(2), ISR, FALLING);`	`attachInterrupt(2, ISR, FALLING);` (Incorrect pin reference)
Only certain pins support external interrupts.	`attachInterrupt(2, ISR, RISING);`	`attachInterrupt(13, ISR, RISING);` (Pin 13 does not support interrupts on all Arduino boards)
Use the appropriate trigger type for your application (RISING, FALLING, CHANGE).	`attachInterrupt(2, ISR, RISING);`	`attachInterrupt(2, ISR, HIGH);` (Incorrect trigger type)

Syntax Table

SL	Function	Syntax/Example	Description
1	Attach an interrupt	`attachInterrupt(digitalPinToInterrupt(pin), ISR, mode);`	Configures a pin to trigger an interrupt when a specific event occurs.
2	Detach an interrupt	`detachInterrupt(digitalPinToInterrupt(pin));`	Disables the interrupt on a specific pin.
3	Interrupt service routine	`ISR(INT0_vect) { // ISR code }`	The function that gets executed when the interrupt is triggered.

Syntax Explanation

1. Attach an Interrupt

What is attaching an interrupt?

The `attachInterrupt()` function is used to specify which pin should trigger an interrupt, which function should run when the interrupt occurs, and the type of trigger (e.g., rising or falling edge). The interrupt will call the specified function as soon as the event occurs, regardless of what the main program is doing.

Syntax:

`attachInterrupt(digitalPinToInterrupt(pin), ISR, mode);`

Example:

`attachInterrupt(digitalPinToInterrupt(2), buttonPress, FALLING);`

Example Explanation:

In this example, `attachInterrupt(digitalPinToInterrupt(2), buttonPress, FALLING)` tells the Arduino to monitor pin 2 for a falling edge (when the voltage drops from HIGH to LOW). When this happens, the function `buttonPress()` will be called immediately. This setup allows the program to respond to the button press without needing to constantly check the button's state in the main loop.

2. Detach an Interrupt

What is detaching an interrupt?

The `detachInterrupt()` function disables an interrupt on a given pin, meaning that no ISR will be triggered for that pin anymore.

Syntax:

`detachInterrupt(digitalPinToInterrupt(pin));`

Example:

`detachInterrupt(digitalPinToInterrupt(2));`

Example Explanation:

This line of code will remove the interrupt from pin 2. After calling `detachInterrupt()`, no ISR will be triggered for that pin until the interrupt is attached again with `attachInterrupt()`.

3. Interrupt Service Routine (ISR)

What is an ISR?
An Interrupt Service Routine (ISR) is a special function that runs when an interrupt occurs. The ISR should be kept as short and fast as possible because during its execution, other interrupts cannot be processed (known as interrupt nesting). Avoid using functions like delay() or millis() in an ISR, as they rely on timers, and timers cannot be used while an ISR is executing.

Syntax:
```
ISR(INT0_vect) {
    // Code to execute when the interrupt occurs
}
```

Example:
```
ISR(INT0_vect) {
    digitalWrite(LED_PIN, HIGH);   // Turn on LED when
interrupt occurs
}
```

Example Explanation:
This code defines an ISR for interrupt 0 (INT0_vect), which is typically triggered by an external event, such as a pin change. When the interrupt occurs, the LED connected to LED_PIN is turned on. ISRs should be quick and avoid blocking operations like delay() to prevent system performance issues.

Applications of Interrupts
1. **Button Press Handling**
2. Interrupts are commonly used to handle button presses in a way that allows other parts of the program to run without waiting for the button to be pressed.

Example Code:
```
const int buttonPin = 2;   // Pin for button input
const int ledPin = 13;     // Pin for LED output

void setup() {
  pinMode(buttonPin, INPUT);
```

```
  pinMode(ledPin, OUTPUT);
  attachInterrupt(digitalPinToInterrupt(buttonPin),
toggleLED, FALLING);
}

void toggleLED() {
  digitalWrite(ledPin, !digitalRead(ledPin));  //
Toggle LED state
}
void loop() {
  // Main program loop is free to do other tasks
}
```

Explanation:

In this code, when the button connected to pin 2 is pressed (falling edge), the `toggleLED()` ISR is triggered to toggle the LED state. The main program can run independently without checking the button state in every loop iteration.

3. Real-Time Sensor Readings

You can use interrupts to read sensors at precise intervals, making sure that sensor readings are accurate and timely, without having to continuously poll the sensor in the main loop.

Example Code:

```
const int sensorPin = A0;     // Pin for sensor input
volatile int sensorValue = 0;
void setup() {
  pinMode(sensorPin, INPUT);
  attachInterrupt(digitalPinToInterrupt(sensorPin),
readSensor, CHANGE);
}
void readSensor() {
  sensorValue = analogRead(sensorPin);  // Read sensor
value when interrupt triggers
}

void loop() {
  // Main program can handle other tasks
}
```

Explanation:

In this example, the interrupt is triggered by a change in the sensor pin (CHANGE). The ISR reads the sensor value, which can then be used in the main loop for other processing.

Conclusion

Interrupts are a powerful tool in Arduino programming, enabling the microcontroller to respond to real-time events without interrupting the execution of the main program. By using `attachInterrupt()` to configure pin change interrupts and defining ISRs, you can create highly responsive systems that react to buttons, sensors, and other external signals. Remember, keep ISRs short and avoid using blocking functions like `delay()` within them to ensure your system remains responsive.

Chapter 22: Serial Communication Protocols for Arduino

Serial communication is a method used by microcontrollers to exchange data with other devices, such as computers, sensors, and other microcontrollers. In Arduino, serial communication can be performed using several protocols, including UART (Universal Asynchronous Receiver/Transmitter), I2C (Inter-Integrated Circuit), and SPI (Serial Peripheral Interface). Each of these protocols has its strengths and is suitable for different types of applications.

Key Concepts of Serial Communication Protocols

Serial communication protocols enable data exchange between devices using a sequence of bits. UART is commonly used for basic communication over a single line, I2C is ideal for connecting multiple devices over two wires, and SPI is used for faster communication between devices.

Communication Protocol	Description	Example
UART (Universal Asynchronous Receiver/Transmitter)	A protocol that uses two wires for transmitting and receiving data.	Communicating between Arduino and a computer via USB.
I2C (Inter-Integrated Circuit)	A multi-master, multi-slave communication protocol that uses two wires.	Connecting multiple sensors to the same data bus.
SPI (Serial Peripheral Interface)	A synchronous protocol used for high-speed data exchange.	Communicating with SD cards, displays, and sensors.

Basic Rules for Serial Communication

Rule	Correct Example	Incorrect Example
Use `Serial.begin()` to initialize serial communication.	`Serial.begin(9600);`	`Serial.begin(96000);` (Incorrect baud rate)
Always match the baud rate on both devices in UART communication.	`Serial.begin(9600);`	`Serial.begin(115200);` (Mismatch baud rates)
I2C devices must have unique addresses on the same bus.	`Wire.begin(8);`	`Wire.begin(0);` (Address 0 is reserved in I2C)
Use `SPI.begin()` to initialize SPI communication.	`SPI.begin();`	`SPI.begin(0);` (Incorrect syntax for initialization)

Syntax Table

SL	Function	Syntax/Example	Description
1	Initialize Serial Communication	`Serial.begin(baud_rate);`	Sets up serial communication at a specified baud rate.
2	Send Data via Serial	`Serial.print(data);` or `Serial.println(data);`	Sends data over the serial connection (print or print with newline).
3	Initialize I2C Communication	`Wire.begin();`	Initializes the I2C bus for communication.
4	Send Data via I2C	`Wire.write(data);`	Sends data to a device on the I2C bus.
5	Initialize SPI Communication	`SPI.begin();`	Initializes the SPI bus for communication.
6	Send Data via SPI	`SPI.transfer(data);`	Transfers data over the SPI bus.

Syntax Explanation

1. Initialize Serial Communication

What is initializing serial communication?
`Serial.begin()` is used to set up the serial port with a specific baud rate, allowing for communication with external devices such as a computer or another Arduino.
Syntax:
`Serial.begin(baud_rate);`

Example:
`Serial.begin(9600);`
Example Explanation:
This initializes serial communication with a baud rate of 9600 bits per second. The baud rate must match between the Arduino and the device it is communicating with (e.g., a computer). A mismatch in baud rates can cause communication errors.

2. Send Data via Serial

What is sending data via serial?
Once serial communication is initialized with `Serial.begin()`, you can send data using `Serial.print()` or `Serial.println()`. The difference is that `Serial.print()` sends data without a newline character, while `Serial.println()` sends data followed by a newline.
Syntax:
`Serial.print(data);`
`Serial.println(data);`
Example:
```
Serial.print("Temperature: ");
Serial.println(23.5);  // Sends "Temperature: 23.5"
followed by a newline
```
Example Explanation:
This example sends the string "Temperature: " followed by the value 23.5 over the serial connection, and the value is followed by a newline. The data can be received by a serial monitor or another device.

3. Initialize I2C Communication

What is I2C communication?
I2C is a multi-master, multi-slave protocol that allows multiple devices to communicate over just two wires: SDA (Serial Data) and SCL (Serial Clock). `Wire.begin()` initializes the I2C bus.

Syntax:
```
Wire.begin();
```

Example:
```
Wire.begin();
```

Example Explanation:
This initializes the I2C communication. You can specify a device address (optional) when using `Wire.begin(address)` if the device needs a specific address.

4. Send Data via I2C

What is sending data via I2C?
Once the I2C communication is initialized with `Wire.begin()`, you can send data to an I2C device using `Wire.write()`.

Syntax:
```
Wire.write(data);
```

Example:
```
Wire.beginTransmission(8);   // Start communication with
device at address 8
Wire.write(0x01);            // Send a byte of data
(0x01)
Wire.endTransmission();      // End the transmission
```

Example Explanation:
In this example, the Arduino communicates with a device with the address 8. The command `Wire.write(0x01)` sends the byte 0x01 to the device. The `Wire.endTransmission()` function ends the communication.

5. Initialize SPI Communication

What is SPI communication?
SPI is a synchronous communication protocol used for fast data transfer between devices. `SPI.begin()` initializes the SPI bus.

Syntax:
```
SPI.begin();
```

Example:
```
SPI.begin();
```

Example Explanation:
This initializes the SPI communication. SPI uses three pins for communication: MOSI (Master Out Slave In), MISO (Master In Slave Out), and SCK (Clock).

6. Send Data via SPI

What is sending data via SPI?
After initializing the SPI bus with `SPI.begin()`, you can send data using `SPI.transfer()`. This sends one byte of data and simultaneously receives one byte.

Syntax:
```
SPI.transfer(data);
```

Example:
```
byte receivedData = SPI.transfer(0xFF);
```

Example Explanation:
In this example, `SPI.transfer(0xFF)` sends the byte `0xFF` and simultaneously receives a byte from the SPI slave device. The received data is stored in the variable `receivedData`.

Applications of Serial Communication Protocols
1. **UART Communication with a Computer**
2. Serial communication is commonly used to communicate between an Arduino and a computer. It's used for debugging, data logging, and controlling devices through the serial monitor.

Example Code:

```
void setup() {
  Serial.begin(9600);
  Serial.println("Hello, Arduino!");
}

void loop() {
  // Main program logic
}
```

Explanation:

This program initializes serial communication at a baud rate of 9600 and sends "Hello, Arduino!" to the serial monitor.

3. I2C Communication with Sensors

I2C is often used to communicate with sensors like temperature sensors, accelerometers, and other peripherals.

Example Code:

```
void setup() {
  Wire.begin();
  Wire.beginTransmission(8);   // Address of the I2C
device
  Wire.write(0x01);                // Command byte
  Wire.endTransmission();
}

void loop() {
  // Main program logic
}
```

Explanation:

This code demonstrates how to communicate with an I2C device by sending a command byte to the device at address 8.

4. SPI Communication with External Modules

SPI is often used for high-speed communication with devices like SD cards, displays, or sensors.

Example Code:

```
void setup() {
  SPI.begin();
  byte data = SPI.transfer(0xAA);  // Send and receive data
}

void loop() {
  // Main program logic
}
```

Explanation:

This example sends the byte 0xAA over the SPI bus and receives a byte simultaneously from an SPI device.

Conclusion

Serial communication is a fundamental aspect of Arduino programming, allowing the Arduino to interact with other devices. Whether you're using UART for basic communication, I2C for multi-device setups, or SPI for high-speed data transfer, understanding these protocols is key to building complex and efficient projects. Each protocol has its strengths, so it's important to choose the right one based on your project's requirements.

Chapter 23: Arduino Digital and Analog I/O

Input and Output (I/O) are fundamental aspects of any embedded system. Arduino provides a range of digital and analog I/O pins that allow you to read data from external sensors (input) or control devices like LEDs, motors, and relays (output). Digital I/O can either be HIGH or LOW, while analog I/O allows for continuous values within a defined range, which is particularly useful for tasks like reading sensor values or controlling the brightness of an LED.

Key Concepts of Digital and Analog I/O

Arduino boards come equipped with several digital and analog I/O pins, each with different characteristics and capabilities. Digital pins can either be HIGH (on) or LOW (off), while analog pins can read values between 0 and 1023, corresponding to a range of 0 to 5V on most Arduino boards.

I/O Type	Description	Example
Digital Input	Reads either HIGH or LOW values (0 or 1).	Reading a button press or a digital sensor.
Digital Output	Sends HIGH or LOW values (0 or 1) to control devices.	Controlling LEDs, relays, or turning on/off motors.
Analog Input	Reads values in the range of 0-1023 (corresponding to 0V to 5V).	Reading analog sensors, like temperature sensors or light sensors.
Analog Output	Uses PWM (Pulse Width Modulation) to simulate analog output.	Controlling the brightness of LEDs or the speed of motors.

Basic Rules for Digital and Analog I/O

Rule	Correct Example	Incorrect Example
Use pinMode() to set a pin as INPUT or OUTPUT.	pinMode(13, OUTPUT);	pinMode(13, ANALOG); (Invalid mode for digital pin)

Digital input pins return only HIGH (1) or LOW (0).	int buttonState = digitalRead(2);	int buttonState = analogRead(2); (Incorrect function for digital pin)
Analog input pins return a value between 0 and 1023.	int sensorValue = analogRead(A0);	int sensorValue = digitalRead(A0); (Incorrect function for analog pin)
Use analogWrite() to simulate an analog output using PWM.	analogWrite(9, 128);	analogWrite(9, 300); (PWM values should be between 0-255)

Syntax Table

SL	Function	Syntax/Example	Description
1	Set Pin Mode	pinMode(pin, mode);	Configures the specified pin as INPUT or OUTPUT.
2	Read Digital Input	digitalRead(pin);	Reads the state of a digital pin (HIGH or LOW).
3	Write Digital Output	digitalWrite(pin, value);	Sets a digital pin to either HIGH or LOW.
4	Read Analog Input	analogRead(pin);	Reads the analog value from a pin (0-1023).
5	Write Analog Output (PWM)	analogWrite(pin, value);	Writes a simulated analog value (PWM) to a pin (0-255).

Syntax Explanation

1. Set Pin Mode

What is setting the pin mode?

The `pinMode()` function is used to configure a pin to either INPUT or OUTPUT mode. In INPUT mode, the pin is used for reading values (such as from a sensor or switch), while in OUTPUT mode, the pin is used to control devices (such as LEDs or motors).

Syntax:

```
pinMode(pin, mode);
```

Example:

```
pinMode(13, OUTPUT);
```

Example Explanation:

In this example, `pinMode(13, OUTPUT)` sets pin 13 to OUTPUT mode, which allows you to control a device (like an LED) connected to that pin. If you were using a sensor, you would set the pin to INPUT mode.

2. Read Digital Input

What is reading digital input?

The `digitalRead()` function reads the state of a digital pin, either HIGH (1) or LOW (0). Digital input pins are used for things like button presses, switches, or digital sensors.

Syntax:

```
digitalRead(pin);
```

Example:

```
int buttonState = digitalRead(2);
```

Example Explanation:

This code reads the state of pin 2. If the button connected to pin 2 is pressed (HIGH), the value of `buttonState` will be 1. If the button is not pressed (LOW), the value will be 0.

3. Write Digital Output

What is writing digital output?
The `digitalWrite()` function sets a digital pin to either HIGH (on) or LOW (off), allowing you to control devices like LEDs, motors, or relays.
Syntax:
```
digitalWrite(pin, value);
```

Example:
```
digitalWrite(13, HIGH);
```

Example Explanation:
This line of code turns on an LED connected to pin 13 by setting the pin HIGH. To turn it off, you would use `digitalWrite(13, LOW);`.

4. Read Analog Input

What is reading analog input?
The `analogRead()` function reads the value from an analog pin. The value returned is between 0 and 1023, corresponding to an input voltage range of 0 to 5V.
Syntax:
```
analogRead(pin);
```

Example:
```
int sensorValue = analogRead(A0);
```

Example Explanation:
This line of code reads the analog value from pin A0. The value will be between 0 and 1023, representing a voltage range from 0V to 5V (assuming the default reference voltage is 5V).

5. Write Analog Output (PWM)

What is writing analog output?
The analogWrite() function simulates analog output using Pulse Width Modulation (PWM). It takes a value between 0 and 255, where 0 corresponds to OFF and 255 corresponds to fully ON.

Syntax:
```
analogWrite(pin, value);
```

Example:
```
analogWrite(9, 128);
```

Example Explanation:
This line of code writes a PWM signal to pin 9, where 128 represents a 50% duty cycle. This would make an LED connected to pin 9 appear dimmer than if it were running at full brightness (255).

Applications of Digital and Analog I/O
1. **Digital I/O - Button and LED Example**
2. You can use digital input to read the state of a button and use digital output to control an LED.

Example Code:
```
const int buttonPin = 2;
const int ledPin = 13;
int buttonState = 0;

void setup() {
  pinMode(buttonPin, INPUT);
  pinMode(ledPin, OUTPUT);
}
void loop() {
  buttonState = digitalRead(buttonPin);
  if (buttonState == HIGH) {
    digitalWrite(ledPin, HIGH);   // Turn LED on
  } else {
    digitalWrite(ledPin, LOW);    // Turn LED off
  }
}
```

Explanation:

In this example, when the button connected to pin 2 is pressed, the LED connected to pin 13 turns on. If the button is not pressed, the LED turns off.

3. Analog I/O - Reading a Sensor Value

Analog input is typically used for reading sensors like temperature sensors or light sensors.

Example Code:

```
const int sensorPin = A0;
int sensorValue = 0;

void setup() {
  Serial.begin(9600);
}

void loop() {
  sensorValue = analogRead(sensorPin);
  Serial.println(sensorValue);   // Send the sensor
value to the serial monitor
  delay(1000);                   // Delay 1 second
between readings
}
```

Explanation:

This code reads the analog value from a sensor connected to pin A0 and sends the value to the serial monitor. The value will range from 0 to 1023, corresponding to the input voltage.

Conclusion

Digital and analog I/O are essential in making your Arduino projects interact with the real world. Digital I/O is great for simple on/off signals, while analog I/O allows for more nuanced data input and output. Whether you're reading sensor data or controlling devices like LEDs and motors, understanding how to use the I/O pins effectively is key to building responsive and functional Arduino projects.

Chapter 24: Arrays, Strings, and Data Structures for Arduino

Arrays, strings, and data structures are fundamental concepts for organizing and storing data in your Arduino programs. Arrays allow you to store multiple values of the same type, strings are arrays of characters used to represent text, and data structures like structs enable you to group different types of data together. These concepts are critical for efficiently managing data in your Arduino projects, especially when dealing with multiple sensor readings, devices, or configurations.

Key Concepts of Arrays, Strings, and Data Structures

Arduino provides support for arrays and strings, both of which are useful in various applications. Arrays help store collections of data, strings represent text, and structs allow you to create custom data types.

Concept	Description	Example
Arrays	Stores multiple values of the same type.	`int sensorValues[5] = {100, 200, 300, 400, 500};`
Strings	An array of characters used to represent text.	`String greeting = "Hello, Arduino!";`
Data Structures	Custom data types that combine different types of data.	`struct Device { int id; String name; };`

Basic Rules for Arrays, Strings, and Data Structures

Rule	Correct Example	Incorrect Example
Arrays are zero-indexed, meaning the first element is at index 0.	`int values[3] = {1, 2, 3};`	`int values[3] = {1, 2, 3, 4};` (Out of bounds)
Strings are objects that can be manipulated using String functions.	`String name = "Arduino";`	`String name = 123;` (Incorrect data type)
Structs allow you to define a custom type with multiple data	`struct Device { int id;`	`struct Device { int id; String name; id = 1; };` (Invalid

fields.	String name; };	initialization)

Syntax Table

SL	Function	Syntax/Example	Description
1	Define an Array	`int values[5] = {1, 2, 3, 4, 5};`	Initializes an array with five integer values.
2	Access Array Element	`int value = values[2];`	Accesses the third element of an array (index 2).
3	Define a String	`String greeting = "Hello";`	Creates a string variable to store text.
4	Modify a String	`greeting = "World";`	Changes the value of the string variable.
5	Define a Struct	`struct Device { int id; String name; };`	Defines a custom data structure with two fields.
6	Access Struct Field	`device.id = 1; device.name = "Sensor";`	Accesses fields within a struct and assigns values.

Syntax Explanation

1. Define an Array

What is defining an array?
An array allows you to store multiple values of the same data type, making it easier to manage and access data in a compact form. The size of the array is defined when the array is declared.
Syntax:
`type arrayName[size] = {value1, value2, ..., valueN};`

Example:
`int values[5] = {1, 2, 3, 4, 5};`
Example Explanation:
This declares an array named `values` that can hold five integers. The values 1, 2, 3, 4, and 5 are initialized into the array. Arrays in Arduino are zero-indexed, meaning `values[0]` is 1, `values[1]` is 2, and so on.

2. Access Array Element

What is accessing an array element?
You can access a specific element of an array by specifying the index (position) of the element. Remember that the index starts from 0.
Syntax:
```
arrayName[index];
```

Example:
```
int value = values[2];
```

Example Explanation:

This code accesses the third element of the `values` array, which is 3 (since arrays are zero-indexed). The value of `value` will be 3.

3. Define a String

What is defining a string?
A string is an object in Arduino that represents a sequence of characters (text). Strings are often used to manipulate and display textual data.
Syntax:
```
String stringName = "text";
```

Example:
```
String greeting = "Hello, Arduino!";
```
Example Explanation:
This line of code creates a string variable `greeting` and assigns it the value "Hello, Arduino!". The `String` class in Arduino provides various functions to manipulate and work with text.

4. Modify a String

What is modifying a string?
You can change the value of a string using the assignment operator (=). The `String` object provides functions to manipulate text, such as concatenating, appending, or replacing characters.

Syntax:
```
stringName = "newText";
```

Example:
```
greeting = "World";
```

Example Explanation:
This changes the value of the `greeting` string to "World". After this statement, the `greeting` variable will store "World" instead of "Hello, Arduino!".

5. Define a Struct

What is defining a struct?
A struct (short for structure) allows you to group variables of different data types under one custom data type. This is useful when you want to represent complex data that has multiple attributes.

Syntax:
```
struct StructName {
    type1 field1;
    type2 field2;
    ...
};
```

Example:
```
struct Device {
    int id;
    String name;
};
```

Example Explanation:
This defines a struct named `Device` with two fields: `id` (an integer) and name (a string). You can create variables of type `Device` to store data related to devices, such as their ID and name.

6. Access Struct Field

What is accessing a struct field?
You access the fields of a struct by using the dot operator (.). This allows you to retrieve or modify the data stored within the struct.

Syntax:
```
structVariable.fieldName;
```

Example:
```
Device device1;
device1.id = 1;
device1.name = "Sensor";
```

Example Explanation:
In this example, we create a variable device1 of type Device and assign values to its fields. The id is set to 1, and the name is set to "Sensor".

Applications of Arrays, Strings, and Data Structures
1. **Arrays - Storing Multiple Sensor Readings**
2. Arrays are often used to store multiple readings from sensors over time. For example, you could store the temperature readings from a sensor and process them later.

Example Code:
```
int temperatureReadings[10];

void loop() {
  for (int i = 0; i < 10; i++) {
    temperatureReadings[i] = analogRead(A0);   // Read
sensor
    delay(1000);
  }
}
```

Explanation:
This code reads 10 temperature values from an analog sensor connected to pin A0 and stores them in the temperatureReadings array.

3. **Strings - Displaying Messages**
Strings are commonly used to display text on an LCD or the serial monitor. You can easily manipulate and format text using string functions.

Example Code:

```
String name = "Arduino";
String message = "Hello, " + name;
Serial.println(message);
```

Explanation:

This example creates a string name and concatenates it with the string "Hello, ". The final message "Hello, Arduino" is then displayed on the serial monitor.

4. Data Structures - Organizing Complex Data

Structs are useful when you need to represent complex data, such as sensor information or device configurations.

Example Code:

```
struct Sensor {
    int id;
    String type;
    float value;
};
Sensor temperatureSensor = {1, "Temperature", 22.5};

void setup() {
    Serial.begin(9600);
    Serial.print("Sensor ID: ");
    Serial.println(temperatureSensor.id);
    Serial.print("Sensor Type: ");
    Serial.println(temperatureSensor.type);
    Serial.print("Sensor Value: ");
    Serial.println(temperatureSensor.value);
}
```

Explanation:

This code defines a struct Sensor and creates an instance temperatureSensor. It then prints the ID, type, and value of the sensor to the serial monitor.

Chapter 25: Memory Management and Optimization (Including PROGMEM and EEPROM) for Arduino

Memory management is a crucial part of embedded systems programming, particularly when working with resource-constrained devices like Arduino. Understanding how to optimize memory usage and make efficient use of available storage is vital for ensuring your programs run efficiently and without errors. This chapter will explore the different types of memory available in Arduino, how to use PROGMEM for storing data in flash memory, and how to utilize EEPROM for non-volatile storage.

Key Concepts of Memory Management and Optimization

Arduino provides different types of memory, each with specific use cases. These include SRAM (Static RAM), flash memory, and EEPROM (Electrically Erasable Programmable Read-Only Memory). Optimizing your memory usage can help you avoid running out of space or encountering performance issues in your programs.

Memory Type	Description	Example
SRAM	Volatile memory used for storing variables during runtime.	`int counter = 0;`
Flash Memory	Non-volatile memory used to store the program code.	Program code is stored in flash memory by default.
EEPROM	Non-volatile memory used for storing data that persists after resets or power-offs.	`EEPROM.write(address, value);`
PROGMEM	Macro used to store constant data in flash memory instead of SRAM.	`const char message[] PROGMEM = "Hello, World!";`

Basic Rules for Memory Management

Rule	Correct Example	Incorrect Example
Use PROGMEM to store constant data in flash memory.	`const char message[] PROGMEM = "Hello";`	`const char message[] = "Hello";` (Uses SRAM instead of flash)
EEPROM is for non-volatile storage, but has limited write cycles.	`EEPROM.write(0, 123);`	`EEPROM.write(1024, 100);` (Address exceeds EEPROM capacity)
Avoid using EEPROM for large data storage to preserve EEPROM's lifespan.	`EEPROM.write(0, data);`	`EEPROM.write(1023, largeData);` (Large data could wear EEPROM)
SRAM is used for variables during runtime and should be used judiciously.	`int sensorValue = analogRead(A0);`	`int sensorArray[1000];` (Too much SRAM usage)

Syntax Table

SL	Function	Syntax/Example	Description
1	Store Data in PROGMEM	`const type arrayName[] PROGMEM = {value1, value2, ..., valueN};`	Stores constant data in flash memory instead of SRAM.
2	Access Data in PROGMEM	`pgm_read_byte_near( arrayName + index);`	Accesses data stored in flash memory.
3	Write to EEPROM	`EEPROM.write(address, value);`	Writes a byte to a specific address in EEPROM.
4	Read from EEPROM	`EEPROM.read(address);`	Reads a byte from a specific address in EEPROM.
5	Store Data in SRAM	`type variable = value;`	Stores variables in volatile SRAM.

Syntax Explanation

1. Store Data in PROGMEM

What is storing data in PROGMEM?
The PROGMEM macro is used to store data in the flash memory of the Arduino rather than in SRAM. This is especially useful for storing large arrays, strings, or constant data that you don't need to modify during runtime.

Syntax:
```
const type arrayName[] PROGMEM = {value1, value2, ...,
valueN};
```

Example:
```
const char message[] PROGMEM = "Hello, Arduino!";
```

Example Explanation:
This code stores the string "Hello, Arduino!" in flash memory instead of SRAM. Storing data in flash memory reduces the amount of SRAM used, which is often limited on Arduino boards.

2. Access Data in PROGMEM

What is accessing data in PROGMEM?
Since data in flash memory is not directly accessible like SRAM, you must use functions like pgm_read_byte_near() to read the values stored in PROGMEM.

Syntax:
```
pgm_read_byte_near(arrayName + index);
```

Example:
```
char value = pgm_read_byte_near(message + 0);
```

Example Explanation:
This code accesses the first character of the string stored in message (which is in flash memory) using pgm_read_byte_near(). It retrieves the byte at the given index and stores it in value.

3. Write to EEPROM

What is writing to EEPROM?
EEPROM is non-volatile memory, meaning it retains data even after the Arduino is powered off or reset. You can use the EEPROM.write() function to store data in a specific address in EEPROM. However, EEPROM has a limited number of write cycles (typically around 100,000 writes per address), so it should be used sparingly.

Syntax:
```
EEPROM.write(address, value);
```

Example:
```
EEPROM.write(0, 123);
```

Example Explanation:
This writes the byte value 123 to EEPROM at address 0. When you power down and restart the Arduino, this data will persist.

4. Read from EEPROM

What is reading from EEPROM?
You can use EEPROM.read() to retrieve data from EEPROM. Unlike EEPROM.write(), EEPROM.read() doesn't modify the data—it simply retrieves it.

Syntax:
```
EEPROM.read(address);
```

Example:
```
int storedValue = EEPROM.read(0);
```

Example Explanation:
This code reads the byte value stored at address 0 in EEPROM and stores it in storedValue. This value will persist even after the Arduino is powered off and on.

5. Store Data in SRAM

What is storing data in SRAM?
SRAM is used for storing variables that are only needed during the runtime of the program. It is volatile, meaning it loses its data when the Arduino is powered off or reset.

Syntax:
```
type variable = value;
```

Example:
```
int sensorValue = analogRead(A0);
```

Example Explanation:
This code stores the value read from an analog sensor into the sensorValue variable in SRAM. The data will only be available during the program's execution.

Applications of Memory Management and Optimization
1. **Storing Large Constant Data in Flash Memory Using PROGMEM**
2. You can save valuable SRAM by storing large arrays or strings in flash memory with the PROGMEM keyword.

Example Code:
```
const char largeText[] PROGMEM = "This is a large
constant string.";

void setup() {
  Serial.begin(9600);
  char firstChar = pgm_read_byte_near(largeText + 0);
  Serial.println(firstChar);
}
```

Explanation:
This stores the string in flash memory and reads the first character into firstChar during runtime.

3. **Using EEPROM for Non-Volatile Data Storage**
EEPROM can be used to store configuration settings or user preferences that need to persist even after power is lost.

Example Code:

```
int configValue = 42;
EEPROM.write(0, configValue);

void setup() {
  Serial.begin(9600);
  int storedValue = EEPROM.read(0);
  Serial.println(storedValue);  // Outputs 42
}
```

Explanation:

The value 42 is stored in EEPROM and persists even after the Arduino is powered off. It is read back during the next execution.

Conclusion

Efficient memory management is essential for developing reliable and optimized Arduino applications. By using techniques such as PROGMEM to store constant data in flash memory and EEPROM for non-volatile storage, you can maximize the available resources on your Arduino board. Understanding the differences between SRAM, flash memory, and EEPROM, and using them appropriately, ensures that your programs run smoothly and efficiently.

Chapter 26: Debugging and Error Handling for Arduino

Debugging is an essential part of programming that involves identifying and fixing errors in your code. Proper error handling can make your Arduino projects more robust by helping you detect problems and ensure your program behaves as expected. This chapter will cover common debugging techniques, tools, and methods for handling errors in Arduino sketches.

Key Concepts of Debugging and Error Handling

Arduino development can sometimes be tricky, as you might encounter problems related to logic, hardware connections, or communication. Debugging helps you pinpoint issues, while error handling techniques allow you to deal with unexpected situations and prevent your program from crashing.

Concept	Description	Example
Serial Monitor Debugging	Using the Serial Monitor to print out debug information.	`Serial.print("Variable value: "); Serial.println(value);`
Logic Errors	Errors in the program's logic that lead to unexpected behavior.	Incorrect variable assignments or conditions.
Runtime Errors	Errors that occur during the execution of the program.	Infinite loops, division by zero, etc.
**Error Handling with **if	Using conditional checks to manage error situations.	`if (sensorValue < 0) { Serial.println("Error!"); }`
Use of Assertions	Ensuring that certain conditions hold true during execution.	`assert(sensorValue > 0);`

Basic Rules for Debugging and Error Handling

Rule	Correct Example	Incorrect Example
Use `Serial.print()` and `Serial.println()` to debug values.	`Serial.print("Value: ");` `Serial.println(value);`	`Serial.println(value);` (Missing print statement)
Avoid infinite loops without exit conditions.	`while (x < 10) { x++; }`	`while (1) {}` (Infinite loop, will freeze Arduino)
Handle potential errors by checking conditions before acting.	`if (sensorValue > 0) { processData(sensorValue); }`	`processData(sensorValue);` (No check for valid value)
Use `assert()` to ensure assumptions are correct.	`assert(pinMode(pin, OUTPUT) == 0);`	`assert(false);` (Fails without proper conditions)

Syntax Table

SL	Function	Syntax/Example	Description
1	Print Debug Information	`Serial.print("message");`	Prints information to the Serial Monitor for debugging.
2	Conditional Check for Errors	`if (condition) { action(); }`	Performs an action if the condition is met.
3	Use of `assert()`	`assert(condition);`	Ensures that a condition is true; halts program if false.
4	Print Value with Line Break	`Serial.println("message");`	Prints information followed by a newline.
5	Handle Runtime Error	`try { action(); } catch (Exception e) { handleError(); }`	Catch runtime errors (not natively supported in Arduino).

Syntax Explanation

1. Print Debug Information

What is printing debug information?
The `Serial.print()` and `Serial.println()` functions are used to send information to the Serial Monitor. These are essential for tracking variable values and program flow during execution, helping to identify issues in your code.

Syntax:
```
Serial.print("message");    // Prints message without
newline
Serial.println("message"); // Prints message with
newline
```

Example:
```
int sensorValue = analogRead(A0);
Serial.print("Sensor Value: ");
Serial.println(sensorValue);
```

Example Explanation:

This code prints the sensor value to the Serial Monitor for debugging purposes. It helps verify that the sensor is providing the expected output and helps troubleshoot any issues related to sensor reading.

2. Conditional Check for Errors

What is a conditional check for errors?
Conditional checks allow you to verify that certain conditions are met before performing actions. This prevents errors like dividing by zero, performing invalid operations, or acting on unexpected inputs.

Syntax:
```
if (condition) {
   // action to perform
}
```

Example:

```
if (sensorValue >= 0) {
  processData(sensorValue);
} else {
  Serial.println("Error: Invalid sensor value.");
}
```

Example Explanation:

This code checks if the sensor value is valid (non-negative) before processing it. If the value is invalid, an error message is printed to the Serial Monitor.

**3. Use of **assert()

What is the use of assert()?
The assert() function ensures that a condition is true during execution. If the condition is false, the program halts immediately and prints an error message. This is a helpful debugging tool to verify assumptions at runtime.
Syntax:
```
assert(condition);
```

Example:
```
assert(sensorValue >= 0); // Ensures sensor value is
valid
```

Example Explanation:
This code checks whether the sensorValue is greater than or equal to 0. If not, the program halts, making it easier to identify when something goes wrong.

4. Print Value with Line Break

What is printing with a line break?
Using Serial.println() prints a message followed by a new line, which helps in organizing outputs in the Serial Monitor and makes it easier to read multiple debug messages.

Syntax:
```
Serial.println("message");
```

Example:
```
Serial.println("Program started successfully!");
```

Example Explanation:
This prints the message "Program started successfully!" followed by a newline, making it clear when the program has started executing. It's useful for logging the status of the program at different stages.

5. Handle Runtime Errors (Error Handling)

What is error handling?
While Arduino doesn't have native support for try-catch blocks like other programming languages, you can still handle errors by checking conditions and using functions like `Serial.println()` to display error messages. This allows you to prevent crashes and maintain control over the program flow.

Syntax:
```
try {
   // attempt to perform an action
} catch (Exception e) {
   // handle error
}
```

Example:
```
try {
   int value = analogRead(A0);
   if (value < 0) throw "Sensor error";
} catch (const char* msg) {
   Serial.println(msg);
}
```

Example Explanation:
This code attempts to read the sensor value. If the value is invalid (less than 0), it throws an error message, which is then caught and displayed in the Serial Monitor.

Applications of Debugging and Error Handling

1. **Using Serial Monitor for Debugging** You can print variable values or program states to the Serial Monitor to track how your code is progressing and identify where issues arise.

Example Code:
```
int sensorValue = analogRead(A0);
Serial.print("Sensor Value: ");
Serial.println(sensorValue);
```

2. **Conditionally Handle Errors** You can check if a value meets a specific condition before proceeding with a task, ensuring that invalid data or states are handled gracefully.

Example Code:
```
if (sensorValue >= 0) {
  // Process valid sensor data
} else {
  Serial.println("Error: Sensor value is invalid.");
}
```

3. **Using Assertions for Critical Conditions** You can use assert() to ensure that critical conditions in your code are met before proceeding. This is particularly useful during development.

Example Code:
```
assert(sensorValue >= 0); // Ensure that sensor value
is valid
```

Conclusion

Debugging and error handling are essential skills for developing reliable Arduino projects. By using tools like the Serial Monitor to print debug messages, employing conditional checks to avoid errors, and utilizing assert() to enforce valid assumptions, you can ensure your programs run smoothly and are easier to troubleshoot. Proper error handling allows you to detect problems early and maintain control over your system even when unexpected issues occur.

Chapter 27: Power Management Techniques for Arduino

Power management is a key consideration in Arduino-based projects, especially when working with battery-powered devices or remote systems. Efficient power usage can extend battery life, reduce heat generation, and ensure that your system operates reliably over extended periods. This chapter will cover strategies to optimize power consumption in your Arduino projects, including using sleep modes, efficient power sources, and minimizing unnecessary power drains.

Key Concepts of Power Management

Arduino boards, like the Uno or Nano, are designed to operate with a 5V supply, but they can also be powered by a variety of sources including USB, battery, or external power supplies. Managing how your system uses power is crucial to ensure longevity in portable applications. This chapter will focus on reducing power consumption by using sleep modes, reducing clock speeds, and optimizing power-hungry peripherals.

Concept	Description	Example
Sleep Modes	Using sleep modes to reduce power consumption during inactivity.	`LowPower.sleep();`
Low Power Consumption	Minimizing unnecessary power draw from sensors, LEDs, and other peripherals.	Using `digitalWrite()` to turn off unused components.
Power Supply Optimization	Selecting and managing power sources efficiently.	Using a battery with low self-discharge rate.
Efficient Coding Practices	Writing code that reduces the number of active operations and utilizes interrupts.	Using interrupts for sensor readings rather than polling.
Voltage Regulation	Ensuring stable voltage output for the Arduino and connected components.	Using a low-dropout regulator (LDO).

Basic Rules for Power Management

Rule	Correct Example	Incorrect Example
Use sleep modes to reduce power consumption when idle.	`LowPower.sleep();`	Leaving the microcontroller running unnecessarily.
Turn off unused peripherals (e.g., LEDs, sensors) to save power.	`digitalWrite(LED_BUILTIN, LOW);`	Keeping unnecessary peripherals powered on.
Use low-power microcontrollers or chips designed for efficiency.	Using a low-power board like the Arduino Pro Mini.	Using a high-power board like Arduino Mega when not needed.
Minimize sensor polling frequency or use interrupts instead.	`attachInterrupt(digitalPinToInterrupt(pin), ISR, CHANGE);`	Using `digitalRead()` in a loop without delays or interrupts.

Syntax Table

SL	Function	Syntax/Example	Description
1	Use of Sleep Mode	`LowPower.sleep();`	Puts the Arduino into a low-power state to save battery.
2	Turn Off Peripheral	`digitalWrite(LED_BUILTIN, LOW);`	Turns off an LED or any other component to save power.
3	Use Interrupts for Low Power	`attachInterrupt(digitalPinToInterrupt(pin), ISR, CHANGE);`	Uses interrupts to reduce the need for constant polling.
4	Efficient Power Supply	`analogWrite(VCC, LOW);`	Ensures efficient power regulation to connected components.

5	Reduce Microcontroller Speed	`set_sleep_mode(SLEEP_MODE_IDLE);`	Reduces the speed of the microcontroller for lower power.

Syntax Explanation

1. Use of Sleep Mode

What is sleep mode?
Arduino provides sleep modes that can reduce power consumption significantly when the board is idle. By using the LowPower library, you can put the Arduino into a sleep mode where it consumes minimal power until an interrupt or event wakes it up.

Syntax:
```
LowPower.sleep();
```

Example:
```
#include <LowPower.h>

void setup() {
  // Setup code here
}

void loop() {
  // Put the Arduino to sleep for 8 seconds to save power
  LowPower.sleep(8000);
}
```

Example Explanation:
In this example, the LowPower.sleep(8000) function puts the Arduino into a low-power state for 8 seconds, consuming much less power than if the microcontroller were running continuously. This is ideal for applications where the Arduino doesn't need to be active all the time, such as monitoring sensors periodically.

2. Turn Off Peripheral

What is turning off peripherals?
When working with battery-powered systems, it's important to turn off peripherals that are not in use, such as LEDs, sensors, or motors. This can be done by setting their corresponding pins to LOW, which reduces their power consumption.

Syntax:
```
digitalWrite(pin, LOW);
```

Example:
```
digitalWrite(LED_BUILTIN, LOW);   // Turns off the
onboard LED
```

Example Explanation:
In this code, `digitalWrite(LED_BUILTIN, LOW)` turns off the onboard LED to save power. Turning off unused components is a simple but effective way to reduce power consumption.

3. Use Interrupts for Low Power

What are interrupts?
Interrupts allow you to react to specific events or changes in input without constantly polling the sensor or pin in a loop. This allows the Arduino to sleep and only wake up when an event occurs, such as a change in a sensor value or a button press.

Syntax:
```
attachInterrupt(digitalPinToInterrupt(pin), ISR, mode);
```

Example:
```
attachInterrupt(digitalPinToInterrupt(2), wakeUp,
FALLING);

void wakeUp() {
    // Code to execute when the interrupt is triggered
}
```

Example Explanation:
This code attaches an interrupt to pin 2. The Arduino will sleep until a falling edge (LOW to HIGH or HIGH to LOW transition) is detected on pin 2. When this happens, the wakeUp function is called, allowing the Arduino to perform an action without constantly polling for the event.

4. Efficient Power Supply

What is efficient power supply?
Using efficient power regulation and appropriate voltage levels can reduce the power consumption of the Arduino and its connected components. For example, using a low-dropout regulator (LDO) instead of a linear voltage regulator can reduce wasted power.
Syntax:
```
analogWrite(VCC, LOW); // Example of ensuring power
supply regulation
```

Example Explanation:
Using efficient voltage regulators and low-power supply components ensures that the Arduino operates within its optimal power range. This reduces unnecessary heat generation and conserves energy.

5. Reduce Microcontroller Speed

What is reducing microcontroller speed?
The Arduino's processor speed can often be reduced to save power, especially in applications that do not require high processing power. By reducing the clock speed, you reduce the energy used by the processor.
Syntax:
```
set_sleep_mode(SLEEP_MODE_IDLE);  // Example of
reducing power by entering idle mode
```

Example:
```
#include <avr/sleep.h>

void setup() {
  set_sleep_mode(SLEEP_MODE_IDLE);  // Set Arduino to
```

```
idle mode
  sleep_enable();                    // Enable sleep
mode
}

void loop() {
  sleep_mode();                      // Put Arduino
into sleep mode
}
```

Example Explanation:
In this example, the Arduino is set to SLEEP_MODE_IDLE, which reduces its clock speed and allows it to conserve energy when not doing critical work.

Applications of Power Management

1. **Battery-Powered Projects**
2. Power optimization is especially important when working with battery-powered Arduino projects. Using sleep modes, turning off unused peripherals, and minimizing processing time can significantly extend the battery life of your project.

Example Code:
```
LowPower.sleep(10000);   // Sleep for 10 seconds to save
battery
```

3. **Remote Sensing Applications**

In remote sensing applications, where an Arduino is used to monitor environmental data and report it periodically, the Arduino can be put into sleep mode between sensor readings to save power.

Example Code:
```
attachInterrupt(digitalPinToInterrupt(3), readSensor,
FALLING);
```

4. **Wearable Electronics**

For wearable Arduino projects, where minimizing power usage is critical, efficient power management techniques, including low-power sleep modes and efficient power supply regulation, can help prolong the device's operational time.

Example Code:

```
digitalWrite(LED_BUILTIN, LOW);   // Turn off LED when
not needed
```

Conclusion

Effective power management is crucial for ensuring that your Arduino-based projects are energy-efficient, particularly when working with battery-powered systems. By utilizing sleep modes, turning off unnecessary peripherals, using interrupts, and ensuring efficient power regulation, you can greatly extend the operational lifetime of your Arduino projects. Proper power management is essential for developing sustainable, reliable systems, especially for remote sensing, wearable devices, and other portable applications.

Chapter 28: Understanding Sensors

Sensors are essential components in many Arduino projects. They allow your Arduino to interact with the physical world by detecting changes in environmental conditions, such as temperature, humidity, motion, or light. This chapter will introduce the various types of sensors, how to use them with Arduino, and the key considerations for selecting the right sensor for your project.

Key Concepts of Sensors

A sensor is a device that detects changes in physical quantities (e.g., temperature, light, motion) and converts them into electrical signals. Sensors are commonly used in a wide range of applications such as automation, robotics, weather monitoring, and home security.

Concept	Description	Example
Analog Sensors	Sensors that output a continuous voltage signal proportional to the physical quantity being measured.	Temperature sensors like LM35 or light sensors like LDR.
Digital Sensors	Sensors that output discrete signals, usually HIGH or LOW (binary state).	Motion sensors like PIR, proximity sensors, or push buttons.
Sensor Calibration	Adjusting a sensor's output to match known reference values for accurate readings.	Calibrating a temperature sensor to match a known thermometer.
Sensor Sensitivity	The ability of a sensor to detect small changes in the physical quantity.	A highly sensitive microphone picking up faint sounds.
Sensor Resolution	The smallest detectable change in a sensor's output.	An analog temperature sensor that can detect changes of 0.1°C.

Basic Rules for Using Sensors

Rule	Correct Example	Incorrect Example
Check the sensor's voltage requirements before connecting.	`VCC of sensor connected to 5V on Arduino.`	`Connecting sensor's VCC to the wrong voltage level.`
Use `analogRead()` for sensors that output an analog signal.	`sensorValue = analogRead(A0);`	`sensorValue = digitalRead(A0);` (Incorrect for analog sensor)
Use `digitalRead()` for sensors that output digital signals.	`motionDetected = digitalRead(pin);`	`motionDetected = analogRead(pin);` (Incorrect for digital sensor)
Properly calibrate sensors for accurate readings.	`calibrateSensor(sensor);`	`Using uncalibrated sensor directly without adjustments.`
Implement filtering to smooth noisy sensor data.	`sensorValue = (sensorValue + lastValue) / 2;`	`Using raw sensor data without filtering noise.`

Syntax Table

SL	Function	Syntax/Example	Description
1	Read Analog Sensor	`sensorValue = analogRead(pin);`	Reads the value from an analog sensor.
2	Read Digital Sensor	`sensorState = digitalRead(pin);`	Reads the state (HIGH or LOW) of a digital sensor.
3	Map Sensor Value	`mappedValue = map(sensorValue, 0, 1023, 0, 100);`	Maps a sensor's raw output value to a specific range.

4	Sensor Calibration	calibrateSensor (sensor);	Function to calibrate the sensor for accurate readings.
5	Smooth Sensor Data	filteredValue = (lastValue + sensorValue) / 2;	Applies a basic filter to smooth sensor data.

Syntax Explanation

1. Read Analog Sensor

What is reading an analog sensor?
Sensors like temperature sensors (e.g., LM35) or light-dependent resistors (LDR) provide an analog signal, which means their output varies continuously. The Arduino can read this using the analogRead() function, which converts the analog voltage to a digital value.
Syntax:
```
sensorValue = analogRead(pin);
```

Example:
```
int sensorValue = analogRead(A0);  // Read value from
analog pin A0
```

Example Explanation:
This code reads the value from an analog sensor connected to pin A0. The analogRead() function returns a value between 0 and 1023, representing the voltage between 0V and 5V. This value can then be processed or mapped to specific units like temperature or light intensity.

2. Read Digital Sensor

What is reading a digital sensor?
Digital sensors, such as motion sensors or push buttons, have two possible output states: HIGH or LOW. The digitalRead() function is used to read these states.

Syntax:
```
sensorState = digitalRead(pin);
```

Example:
```
int motionDetected = digitalRead(2);  // Read state of
motion sensor on pin 2
```

Example Explanation:
In this example, the motion sensor is connected to digital pin 2. The `digitalRead()` function returns either HIGH (motion detected) or LOW (no motion detected). This is useful for simple binary sensors, such as switches or motion detectors.

3. Map Sensor Value

What is mapping a sensor value?
Sometimes, sensor values need to be converted to a different range for easier interpretation or use. For example, an analog temperature sensor might output values between 0 and 1023, but you want to map these values to a more usable range (like 0 to 100°C).

Syntax:
```
mappedValue = map(sensorValue, 0, 1023, 0, 100);
```

Example:
```
int sensorValue = analogRead(A0);
int temperature = map(sensorValue, 0, 1023, 0, 100);
// Map to temperature range
```

Example Explanation:
This code reads an analog sensor and maps the raw value (0-1023) to a temperature range of 0 to 100°C. The `map()` function is useful for converting sensor outputs to meaningful units.

4. Sensor Calibration

What is sensor calibration?
Sensor calibration involves adjusting a sensor's raw output to match known reference values. For instance, a temperature sensor might need to be calibrated to ensure its readings match a real thermometer.

Syntax:
```
calibrateSensor(sensor);
```

Example:
```
void calibrateSensor(int sensorPin) {
    int rawValue = analogRead(sensorPin);
    float calibratedValue = (rawValue / 1023.0) * 5.0;
// Example calibration formula
}
```

Example Explanation:
This function reads the sensor's raw value and applies a formula to calibrate it. Calibration is crucial to ensure accurate readings, especially for sensors with known offsets or variations in their output.

5. Smooth Sensor Data

What is smoothing sensor data?
Many sensors (such as temperature sensors) can produce noisy data due to fluctuations in environmental conditions or the sensor itself. Smoothing data helps provide a more accurate and stable reading by averaging multiple values.

Syntax:
```
filteredValue = (lastValue + sensorValue) / 2;
```

Example:
```
int sensorValue = analogRead(A0);
filteredValue = (lastValue + sensorValue) / 2;  //
Smooth out sensor noise
lastValue = filteredValue;  // Store the smoothed value
for next iteration
```

Example Explanation:

In this example, the code averages the previous sensor value and the current one to smooth out any noise or rapid fluctuations. This is particularly useful in sensors like analog temperature sensors, where small, random variations in readings are common.

Applications of Sensors

1. **Temperature Measurement**
2. Sensors like the LM35 or DHT11 are often used for temperature measurement in weather stations or HVAC systems. By using analogRead(), you can read the temperature data and control heating or cooling systems.

Example Code:

```
int temperature = analogRead(A0);
temperature = map(temperature, 0, 1023, -40, 125);  //
Map to temperature range
```

3. **Motion Detection**

PIR sensors are commonly used for detecting motion in security systems. By using digitalRead(), you can easily detect motion and trigger alarms or lights.

Example Code:

```
int motionDetected = digitalRead(2);
if (motionDetected == HIGH) {
  Serial.println("Motion detected!");
}
```

4. **Light Sensing**

LDRs (Light Dependent Resistors) are used to detect light intensity and are often used in projects like automatic lighting systems. Using analogRead(), you can control the brightness of lights based on ambient light levels.

Example Code:

```
int lightLevel = analogRead(A1);
lightLevel = map(lightLevel, 0, 1023, 0, 100);  // Map
to percentage
```

5. Distance Measurement

Ultrasonic sensors, such as the HC-SR04, are used for measuring distance. They provide accurate distance readings that can be used in robotic applications.

Example Code:

```
long duration, distance;
digitalWrite(triggerPin, LOW);
delayMicroseconds(2);
digitalWrite(triggerPin, HIGH);
delayMicroseconds(10);
digitalWrite(triggerPin, LOW);
duration = pulseIn(echoPin, HIGH);
distance = (duration * 0.034) / 2;  // Calculate
distance in cm
```

Conclusion

Sensors are integral to most Arduino projects, allowing the system to interact with the environment. Whether you're measuring temperature, detecting motion, or sensing light levels, understanding how to properly interface with sensors is key to creating responsive, intelligent systems. By learning to read sensor values, calibrate sensors, and apply appropriate filtering techniques, you can ensure that your Arduino projects function reliably and accurately in a wide variety of applications.

Chapter 29: Using Temperature Sensors with Arduino

Temperature sensors are one of the most commonly used sensors in Arduino projects. They allow you to measure environmental temperatures and integrate this data into your systems for various applications, such as climate control, weather stations, or temperature monitoring in industrial settings. In this chapter, we'll explore different types of temperature sensors, how to interface them with Arduino, and how to process and use the temperature data.

Key Concepts of Temperature Sensors

Temperature sensors detect temperature changes and convert them into electrical signals that can be interpreted by an Arduino. There are two main types of temperature sensors: **analog** and **digital**.

Concept	Description	Example
Analog Temperature Sensors	Sensors that provide a continuous output voltage that changes with temperature.	LM35, TMP36
Digital Temperature Sensors	Sensors that output a digital signal representing the temperature value.	DS18B20, DHT11
Thermistor	A type of temperature sensor where the resistance varies with temperature.	NTC thermistor (resistance decreases with temperature)
Accuracy	The degree to which a sensor's reading matches the actual temperature.	DS18B20 with ±0.5°C accuracy
Response Time	The time taken for a sensor to respond to temperature changes.	LM35 typically responds within seconds.

Basic Rules for Using Temperature Sensors

Rule	Correct Example	Incorrect Example
Always check the sensor's datasheet for wiring and pinout info.	`LM35 VCC pin to 5V, GND pin to GND, and output to A0.`	Incorrectly wiring the sensor's power or output pin.
For analog sensors, use analogRead() to get the temperature.	`temperature = analogRead(A0);`	`temperature = digitalRead(A0);` (Incorrect for analog sensor)
For digital sensors, use appropriate libraries to read values.	`temperature = ds18b20.getTemp erature();`	`temperature = analogRead(5);` (Incorrect for digital sensor)
Use calibration or formulas to convert raw values to temperature.	`temperature = (sensorValue * 5.0 / 1023.0) * 100;`	Using raw sensor readings directly without conversion.
Apply appropriate filtering to smooth temperature data.	`temperature = (lastTemp + currentTemp) / 2;`	Ignoring noise in the sensor's data without smoothing.

Syntax Table

SL	Function	Syntax/Example	Description
1	Read Analog Temperature Sensor	`temperature = analogRead(pin);`	Reads the value from an analog temperature sensor.
2	Read Digital Temperature Sensor	`temperature = ds18b20.getTemp erature();`	Reads the temperature value from a digital sensor like DS18B20.
3	Convert Analog Sensor to Celsius	`temperature = (sensorValue * 5.0 / 1023.0) * 100;`	Converts raw sensor data from LM35 to temperature in Celsius.

4	Initialize DS18B20 Sensor	`ds18b20.begin();`	Initializes the DS18B20 sensor for temperature readings.
5	Read Temperature from DS18B20	`float temperature = ds18b20.getTemperature();`	Reads the temperature from DS18B20 and returns it as a float.

Syntax Explanation

1. Read Analog Temperature Sensor

What is reading an analog temperature sensor?
Analog temperature sensors, like the LM35, provide a voltage that corresponds to the temperature. The Arduino uses the `analogRead()` function to get the voltage, which is then converted to a temperature using a formula or conversion factor.
Syntax:
```
temperature = analogRead(pin);
```

Example:
```
int sensorValue = analogRead(A0);
float temperature = (sensorValue * 5.0 / 1023.0) * 100;
// LM35
```

Example Explanation:
This code reads the value from an LM35 connected to analog pin A0. The sensor provides a voltage that is proportional to the temperature. The formula (`sensorValue * 5.0 / 1023.0) * 100` converts the analog reading to a temperature in Celsius, where each unit of sensor reading corresponds to 0.01°C.

2. Read Digital Temperature Sensor

What is reading a digital temperature sensor?
Digital temperature sensors like the DS18B20 or DHT11 send temperature readings as digital data. These sensors require specific libraries to interface with them, as they communicate via protocols like OneWire or I2C.

Syntax:
```
temperature = ds18b20.getTemperature();
```

Example:
```
#include <OneWire.h>
#include <DallasTemperature.h>

OneWire oneWire(2);  // Pin connected to the DS18B20
DallasTemperature sensors(&oneWire);

void setup() {
   sensors.begin();
}

void loop() {
   sensors.requestTemperatures();
   float temperature = sensors.getTempCByIndex(0);
   Serial.println(temperature);
   delay(1000);
}
```

Example Explanation:
In this example, the DallasTemperature library is used to interface with the DS18B20 digital temperature sensor. The sensors.getTempCByIndex(0) function retrieves the temperature in Celsius from the first (and only) DS18B20 sensor connected to pin 2.

3. Convert Analog Sensor to Celsius

What is converting an analog sensor reading to Celsius?
Many temperature sensors like the LM35 provide an analog signal whose value needs to be converted to a temperature. For the LM35, the voltage is linearly proportional to the temperature in Celsius, with 10mV per degree.

Syntax:
```
temperature = (sensorValue * 5.0 / 1023.0) * 100;
```

Example:
```
int sensorValue = analogRead(A0);
float temperature = (sensorValue * 5.0 / 1023.0) * 100;
// LM35
```

Example Explanation:
In this example, the analogRead() function reads the raw value from the LM35 sensor. The formula converts this raw data into Celsius by scaling it according to the LM35's voltage-to-temperature conversion factor.

4. Initialize DS18B20 Sensor

What is initializing the DS18B20 sensor?
Before reading data from a DS18B20 temperature sensor, you must initialize the sensor using the begin() function from the DallasTemperature library. This prepares the sensor to take measurements.

Syntax:
```
ds18b20.begin();
```

Example:
```
#include <OneWire.h>
#include <DallasTemperature.h>
OneWire oneWire(2);  // Pin connected to DS18B20
DallasTemperature sensors(&oneWire);
void setup() {
   sensors.begin();  // Initialize sensor
}
```

Example Explanation:

This code initializes the DS18B20 sensor by calling `sensors.begin()`. The `OneWire` library handles communication, and the `DallasTemperature` library simplifies reading temperature values.

5. Read Temperature from DS18B20

What is reading the temperature from a DS18B20 sensor?

After initializing the DS18B20, you can use the `getTemperature()` function to read the temperature in Celsius. The sensor communicates the temperature over the OneWire protocol, and the library handles the conversion.

Syntax:

```
temperature = ds18b20.getTemperature();
```

Example:

```
float temperature = ds18b20.getTemperature();  // Get
temperature from DS18B20
```

Example Explanation:

This function retrieves the current temperature reading from the DS18B20 sensor in Celsius. It's a straightforward way to access temperature data once the sensor is initialized.

Real-life Applications Project: Temperature Monitoring System

In this project, you will create a simple temperature monitoring system using the **LM35** analog temperature sensor. The system will display the current temperature in Celsius on the Serial Monitor.

Required Components

Component	Description
LM35 Temperature Sensor	Analog temperature sensor that outputs a voltage proportional to the temperature.
Arduino Uno	Microcontroller board used to process the sensor data.
Breadboard	Platform for connecting components.
Jumper Wires	Wires used for making connections between components.
USB Cable	Used to connect Arduino to a computer.

Circuit Connection Table

Component	Pin Connection
LM35 Temperature Sensor	VCC to 5V, GND to GND, Output to Analog Pin A0
Arduino Uno	Pin A0 connected to the output of the LM35 sensor.	

Project Code

```
int sensorPin = A0;  // Pin where LM35 is connected
int sensorValue = 0;  // Variable to store the raw
sensor data
float temperature = 0; // Variable to store the
temperature in Celsius

void setup() {
  Serial.begin(9600); // Start the serial communication
}

void loop() {
  sensorValue = analogRead(sensorPin); // Read the
value from LM35
  temperature = (sensorValue * 5.0 / 1023.0) * 100; //
Convert the value to Celsius
```

```
  Serial.print("Temperature: ");
  Serial.print(temperature);  // Display the
temperature in Celsius
  Serial.println(" C");

  delay(1000);  // Wait for a second before taking
another reading
}
```

Code Explanation:

- **sensorPin**: Specifies the analog pin where the LM35 sensor is connected.
- **analogRead(sensorPin)**: Reads the analog voltage output by the LM35 sensor.
- **(sensorValue * 5.0 / 1023.0) * 100**: Converts the raw analog value into a temperature in Celsius.
- The temperature is then displayed on the Serial Monitor every second.

Expected Results

- **Serial Monitor Output:**

Every second, the Serial Monitor will display the current temperature in Celsius, such as:

```
Temperature: 23.50 C
Temperature: 23.52 C
Temperature: 23.53 C
```

- **Physical Result:**

As the temperature in the room changes, the values displayed on the Serial Monitor will change accordingly. For example, if you place the LM35 sensor near a heat source, the temperature should increase.

Chapter 30: Light and IR Sensors with Arduino

Light and infrared (IR) sensors are essential components in many Arduino-based projects. These sensors detect light intensity or infrared radiation, enabling the Arduino to interact with its environment in a wide range of applications, from motion detection to remote control systems.

Key Concepts of Light and IR Sensors

Light sensors are devices that measure the amount of light falling on them. They can be used for a variety of applications, including controlling lighting systems, measuring ambient light, or detecting light in security systems. IR sensors, on the other hand, detect infrared radiation emitted by objects, typically used in motion sensing, obstacle detection, and remote control systems.

Concept	Description	Example
LDR (Light Dependent Resistor)	A type of resistor whose resistance decreases as light intensity increases.	LDR sensor used in light level detection.
Photodiodes	Semiconductor devices that generate current when exposed to light.	Used in optical communication or light detection.
IR LED (Infrared LED)	An LED that emits infrared light used in IR sensors and communication.	Used in remote controls, security systems, and robots.
IR Receiver	A sensor that detects infrared light from an IR LED.	Commonly used in remote control systems.
Analog and Digital Output	Sensors can provide either analog or digital outputs.	Analog: LDR, Digital: IR Receiver
Range of Detection	The distance at which a sensor can detect light or infrared radiation.	LDR: Short range, IR: Can vary based on sensor model.

Basic Rules for Using Light and IR Sensors

Rule	Correct Example	Incorrect Example
Always check the sensor's output type (analog or digital).	`int lightLevel = analogRead(A0);` (For LDR)	`digitalRead(A0);` (Incorrect for analog sensors like LDR)
Use a resistor with an LDR to create a voltage divider.	`int sensorValue = analogRead(A0);`	Directly connecting LDR without resistor.
For IR sensors, ensure correct alignment with the IR LED.	`IRReceiver.receiveSignal();`	Aligning the IR sensor away from the signal source.
Calibrate the sensors for specific lighting conditions if necessary.	`int threshold = 500;` `if(sensorValue < threshold) { // Action }`	Using raw sensor values without considering the environment.
For IR communication, use libraries to handle signal encoding.	`IRremote.begin();`	Using IR without necessary decoding libraries.

Syntax Table

SL	Function	Syntax/Example	Description
1	Read LDR (Analog)	`lightLevel = analogRead(A0);`	Reads the analog value from the LDR and converts it into a light level.
2	Read IR Receiver (Digital)	`irValue = digitalRead(2);`	Reads the digital value from the IR receiver.
3	Send IR Signal	`irsend.sendNEC(address, 32);`	Sends an IR signal using the IR LED.

4	IR Remote Control Setup	`IRrecv.enable IRIn();`	Initializes the IR receiver to start receiving signals.
5	LDR Calibration	`if(lightLevel < threshold) { // Action }`	Compares the light level with a threshold value.

Syntax Explanation

1. Read LDR (Analog)

What is reading an LDR (Light Dependent Resistor)?
An LDR is a light-sensitive resistor, whose resistance decreases with increasing light intensity. By creating a voltage divider circuit with a fixed resistor, you can measure the voltage across the LDR with analogRead(), which gives a value corresponding to the light intensity.
Syntax:
```
lightLevel = analogRead(A0);
```

Example:
```
int lightLevel = analogRead(A0);
```

Example Explanation:
This code reads the voltage across an LDR connected to analog pin A0 and stores the resulting value (ranging from 0 to 1023) in the variable lightLevel. The value represents the intensity of light, where 0 means no light and 1023 means maximum light.

2. Read IR Receiver (Digital)

What is reading an IR receiver?
An IR receiver detects infrared signals from an IR LED (like those used in remote controls). It outputs a digital signal, either HIGH or LOW, depending on whether it detects a signal or not.
Syntax:
```
irValue = digitalRead(2);
```

Example:
```
int irValue = digitalRead(2); // Pin connected to IR
receiver
```

Example Explanation:
This code reads the digital value from the IR receiver connected to pin 2. If the receiver detects an infrared signal, it will return a HIGH value; otherwise, it will return LOW.

3. Send IR Signal

What is sending an IR signal?
Sending an IR signal involves transmitting data using an IR LED. The Arduino can be programmed to send specific signals, such as those used in remote control systems, by using an IR library and an IR LED.
Syntax:
```
irsend.sendNEC(address, 32);
```

Example:
```
#include <IRremote.h>

IRsend irsend;

void setup() {
  irsend.sendNEC(0xF7C03F, 32); // Send a predefined IR
signal
}

void loop() {
  // No continuous action required
}
```

Example Explanation:
This code uses the IRremote library to send a specific IR signal (0xF7C03F) via an IR LED. The sendNEC() function sends a signal using the NEC protocol. You can replace 0xF7C03F with the desired signal address.

4. IR Remote Control Setup

What is setting up an IR remote control receiver?
Setting up an IR receiver allows the Arduino to receive infrared signals from an external remote control. You must initialize the receiver before reading incoming data.

Syntax:
```
IRrecv enableIRIn();
```

Example:
```
#include <IRremote.h>

IRrecv irrecv(2); // Pin connected to IR receiver

void setup() {
  irrecv.enableIRIn(); // Start the IR receiver
}

void loop() {
  if (irrecv.decode(&results)) {
    long int decCode = results.value; // Decode the
received signal
    irrecv.resume(); // Receive the next value
  }
}
```

Example Explanation:
The enableIRIn() function initializes the IR receiver. Once enabled, the receiver listens for infrared signals. If a signal is detected, it is decoded and stored in the results object.

5. LDR Calibration

What is LDR calibration?
In many cases, you may want to use the LDR for controlling actions based on light intensity. For example, you can turn on a light when the light intensity drops below a certain threshold.

Syntax:

```
if(lightLevel < threshold) {
    // Action (turn on light, activate system, etc.)
}
```

Example:

```
int lightLevel = analogRead(A0);
int threshold = 512; // Mid-range light level

if (lightLevel < threshold) {
    digitalWrite(13, HIGH);   // Turn on LED or system
}
```

Example Explanation:

This code reads the light level and compares it with a defined threshold. If the light level is below the threshold (indicating low light conditions), it triggers an action, such as turning on an LED or another system.

Real-life Applications Project: Light-Activated Night Light System

In this project, you will use an **LDR** to automatically turn on an LED when the light intensity falls below a certain threshold (e.g., at night).

Required Components

Component	Description
LDR (Light Dependent Resistor)	Light sensor to measure ambient light levels.
Arduino Uno	Microcontroller board used to control the system.
LED	Light-emitting diode used to indicate the system's state.
10k Ohm Resistor	Used to create a voltage divider circuit with the LDR.
Breadboard	Platform for connecting components.
Jumper Wires	Wires for making connections.

Circuit Connection Table

Component	Pin Connection
LDR	One end to 5V, the other end to Analog Pin A0 and 10kΩ resistor connected to GND.
LED	Long leg to Pin 13, short leg to GND.

Project Code

```
int ldrPin = A0;            //


 Pin where LDR is connected
int ledPin = 13;            // Pin where LED is
connected
int lightLevel = 0;         // Variable to store the LDR
value
int threshold = 512;        // Light level threshold

void setup() {
  pinMode(ledPin, OUTPUT);  // Set LED pin as OUTPUT
  Serial.begin(9600);       // Start serial
communication
}

void loop() {
  lightLevel = analogRead(ldrPin); // Read LDR value
  if (lightLevel < threshold) {    // If light is below
threshold
    digitalWrite(ledPin, HIGH);    // Turn on the LED
  } else {
    digitalWrite(ledPin, LOW);     // Otherwise, turn
off the LED
  }

  delay(500);  // Delay for half a second
}
```

Expected Results

- **Serial Monitor Output**: The Arduino will continually read the LDR value, and the LED will be turned on when the light intensity falls below the threshold (i.e., when it gets dark).
- **Physical Result**: When the light in the room dims (e.g., at night), the LDR detects the change and activates the LED, simulating a night light system. During the day, the LED will remain off.

Chapter 31: Motion Sensors with Arduino

Motion sensors are vital in projects where the detection of movement is required. These sensors are widely used in applications such as security systems, automation, and robotics. They can detect the presence of motion, whether it's human activity or the movement of objects, and relay this information to an Arduino for further processing.

Key Concepts of Motion Sensors

Motion sensors detect changes in the environment, often using technologies like infrared (IR), ultrasonic sound, or passive infrared (PIR). These sensors can trigger events based on movement detection, which makes them perfect for systems such as alarms, lighting control, or even robotics.

Concept	Description	Example
PIR (Passive Infrared) Sensor	Detects infrared radiation (heat) emitted by objects.	Used in motion detection for security systems.
Ultrasonic Motion Sensor	Uses sound waves to detect distance and presence of objects.	Used in robotic applications for obstacle detection.
Microwave Motion Sensors	Uses microwave radiation to detect motion.	Used in industrial automation and security.
Detection Range	The maximum distance at which a sensor can detect motion.	5 meters for PIR sensors, up to 10 meters for ultrasonic sensors.
Analog vs Digital Output	Sensors can output either analog or digital data.	PIR: Digital; Ultrasonic: Analog or Digital
Trigger Mode	Mode in which the sensor outputs data when motion is detected.	Triggered when movement occurs or continuously updated.

Basic Rules for Using Motion Sensors

Rule	Correct Example	Incorrect Example
Always choose a sensor based on the project's motion detection needs.	PIR motion sensor for detecting human presence.	Ultrasonic sensor for motion detection in the dark.
Calibrate sensors for the expected environment (e.g., distance, temperature).	Set PIR sensitivity to suit room size.	Ignoring environmental factors (temperature, size).
Ensure correct sensor orientation for proper detection.	PIR sensor facing towards entry door.	Placing ultrasonic sensor on the ceiling.
Use appropriate wiring and check sensor compatibility with Arduino.	PIR sensor to digital pin.	Using analog pins for digital sensors like PIR.
Always power sensors with the recommended voltage and current.	PIR sensor works on 5V power supply.	Providing too much or too little voltage.

Syntax Table

SL	Function	Syntax/Example	Description
1	Read PIR sensor (Digital)	motionDetected = digitalRead(PIN);	Reads the digital output from a PIR sensor.
2	Measure distance with ultrasonic	distance = sonar.ping_cm();	Measures distance using ultrasonic sensor (in centimeters).
3	Trigger event on motion detection	if (motionDetected == HIGH)	Executes an action when motion is detected.
4	Setup PIR sensor	pinMode(PIRPin, INPUT);	Initializes the PIR sensor to read its output.

5	Display motion detection message	`Serial.println("Motion detected!");`	Prints a message when motion is detected.

Syntax Explanation

1. Read PIR sensor (Digital)

What is reading a PIR sensor?
A PIR sensor outputs a digital signal: HIGH when motion is detected, and LOW when there is no motion. This digital signal can be read using `digitalRead()` in Arduino.
Syntax:
```
motionDetected = digitalRead(PIRPin);
```

Example:
```
int motionDetected = digitalRead(2);   // Read PIR sensor on pin 2
```

Example Explanation:
This code reads the digital value from a PIR sensor connected to pin 2. If motion is detected, the sensor outputs HIGH, and if no motion is detected, it outputs LOW. The `motionDetected` variable will store this value for further actions.

2. Measure distance with ultrasonic sensor

What is measuring distance with an ultrasonic sensor?
Ultrasonic sensors work by emitting high-frequency sound waves and measuring the time it takes for them to bounce back. This allows the sensor to calculate the distance to an object, which can be used for motion detection or obstacle avoidance.
Syntax:
```
distance = sonar.ping_cm();
```

Example:

```
#include <NewPing.h>

#define TRIGGER_PIN 12
#define ECHO_PIN 11
#define MAX_DISTANCE 200
NewPing sonar(TRIGGER_PIN, ECHO_PIN, MAX_DISTANCE);
void loop() {
  int distance = sonar.ping_cm(); // Measure distance
in cm
  Serial.println(distance);
  delay(500);
}
```

Example Explanation:

This example uses the NewPing library to measure distance using an ultrasonic sensor connected to trigger pin 12 and echo pin 11. The function ping_cm() returns the distance in centimeters. The result is printed on the Serial Monitor.

3. Trigger event on motion detection

What is triggering an event on motion detection?

Once motion is detected by a sensor, you can trigger an event (e.g., turning on a light, activating an alarm, or sending a message). The event is executed if the PIR sensor returns a HIGH signal.

Syntax:

```
if (motionDetected == HIGH) {
  // Action to perform when motion is detected
}
```

Example:

```
if (motionDetected == HIGH) {
  digitalWrite(13, HIGH);  // Turn on LED when motion
is detected
} else {
  digitalWrite(13, LOW);   // Turn off LED when no
motion
}
```

Example Explanation:
In this example, if motion is detected (i.e., the PIR sensor returns HIGH), it turns on an LED connected to pin 13. If no motion is detected, it turns off the LED.

4. Setup PIR sensor

What is setting up a PIR sensor?
Before reading data from the PIR sensor, it must be set up correctly. This involves setting the sensor pin as an input and optionally configuring its sensitivity if the sensor supports it.

Syntax:
```
pinMode(PIRPin, INPUT);
```

Example:
```
void setup() {
  pinMode(2, INPUT);  // Set pin 2 as input for PIR sensor
  Serial.begin(9600);  // Start serial communication
}
```

Example Explanation:
This code sets pin 2 as an input to read data from the PIR sensor. The serial communication is also initialized to display the sensor's status on the Serial Monitor.

5. Display motion detection message

What is displaying a motion detection message?
Once motion is detected, you might want to output a message to inform the user. This can be done using `Serial.println()` to display a message on the Serial Monitor.

Syntax:
```
Serial.println("Motion detected!");
```

Example:

```
if (motionDetected == HIGH) {
  Serial.println("Motion detected!");
} else {
  Serial.println("No motion detected.");
}
```

Example Explanation:

This code prints a message on the Serial Monitor when motion is detected. It provides feedback to the user about the current state of the sensor.

Real-life Applications Project: Motion-Activated Alarm System

In this project, a **PIR motion sensor** will be used to detect movement. If movement is detected, the system will trigger an alarm or turn on a light.

Required Components

Component	Description
PIR Motion Sensor	Detects motion using passive infrared technology.
Arduino Uno	Microcontroller to process sensor data.
Buzzer	Produces a sound when motion is detected.
LED	Visual indicator for motion detection.
Resistor	For proper sensor calibration.
Breadboard and Wires	For connecting components.

Circuit Connection Table

Component	Pin Connection
PIR Motion Sensor	VCC to 5V, GND to GND, OUT to Pin 2
Buzzer	Positive leg to Pin 9, Negative leg to GND
LED	Long leg to Pin 13, short leg to GND

Project Code

```
int pirPin = 2;        // Pin where PIR sensor is
connected
int ledPin = 13;       // Pin where LED is connected
```

```
int buzzerPin = 9;          // Pin where Buzzer is
connected
int motionDetected = 0;     // Variable to store PIR
sensor value

void setup() {
  pinMode(pirPin, INPUT);     // Set PIR pin as INPUT
  pinMode(ledPin, OUTPUT);    // Set LED pin as OUTPUT
  pinMode(buzzerPin, OUTPUT); // Set Buzzer pin as
OUTPUT
  Serial.begin(9600);         // Start

 serial communication
}

void loop() {
  motionDetected = digitalRead(pirPin);   // Read PIR
sensor
  if (motionDetected == HIGH) {
    digitalWrite(ledPin, HIGH);   // Turn on LED
    digitalWrite(buzzerPin, HIGH); // Turn on Buzzer
    Serial.println("Motion detected!");
  } else {
    digitalWrite(ledPin, LOW);    // Turn off LED
    digitalWrite(buzzerPin, LOW); // Turn off Buzzer
    Serial.println("No motion detected.");
  }
  delay(500); // Delay for half a second
}
```

Expected Results

- **Serial Monitor Output**: You will see "Motion detected!" or "No motion detected" displayed in the Serial Monitor.
- **Physical Result**: When motion is detected by the PIR sensor, the LED will turn on, and the buzzer will emit a sound. When no motion is detected, both the LED and the buzzer will remain off.

Chapter 32: Ultrasonic Sensors with Arduino

Ultrasonic sensors are used to measure the distance between the sensor and an object by emitting sound waves and measuring the time it takes for them to bounce back. These sensors are widely used in robotics, distance measurement systems, and obstacle detection applications.

Key Concepts of Ultrasonic Sensors

Ultrasonic sensors work based on the principle of sound waves. The sensor emits a high-frequency sound pulse and waits for it to bounce back from an object. The time it takes for the sound pulse to return is used to calculate the distance between the sensor and the object.

Concept	Description	Example
Trigger Pin	The pin used to send a pulse to the ultrasonic sensor.	Pin 12 is typically used for the trigger.
Echo Pin	The pin used to receive the reflected sound pulse.	Pin 13 is typically used for the echo.
Distance Measurement	The time taken for the sound pulse to return is used to calculate the distance.	Used to avoid obstacles in robotics.
Working Principle	The sensor emits sound pulses at a high frequency and measures the time taken for the sound to return.	Used in applications like parking sensors or distance meters.
Ultrasonic Range	The typical range is between 2 cm and 400 cm.	The HC-SR04 can measure from 2 cm to 400 cm accurately.
Analog vs Digital Output	Ultrasonic sensors typically output digital signals.	Outputs a pulse width that corresponds to the distance.

Basic Rules for Using Ultrasonic Sensors

Rule	Correct Example	Incorrect Example
Always ensure the sensor is properly oriented for accurate detection.	Ultrasonic sensor facing directly towards the target.	Sensor placed at an angle that reduces accuracy.
Use the correct pins for trigger and echo connections.	Trigger pin to pin 12, Echo pin to pin 13.	Confusing trigger and echo pins.
Consider the minimum and maximum range for your application.	HC-SR04 sensor with a range of 2-400 cm for obstacle avoidance.	Using a sensor with too narrow or wide a range.
Power the sensor using the recommended voltage.	HC-SR04 works with 5V power supply.	Powering the sensor with more than the recommended voltage.
Account for the sensor's refresh rate.	Ensure the sensor has enough time between measurements.	Reading the sensor too frequently and causing inaccurate results.

Syntax Table

SL	Function	Syntax/Example	Description
1	Initialize sensor	Ultrasonic ultrasonic(trigger Pin, echoPin);	Initialize the ultrasonic sensor with trigger and echo pins.
2	Measure distance	distance = ultrasonic.read();	Read the distance from the ultrasonic sensor.
3	Set trigger and echo pins	pinMode(triggerPin , OUTPUT); pinMode(echoPin, INPUT);	Configure the sensor pins as OUTPUT and INPUT.

4	Trigger ultrasonic sensor	`digitalWrite(trigg erPin, HIGH);`	Send a pulse to trigger the sensor.
5	Calculate distance	`distance = (pulseDuration / 2) / 29.1;`	Calculate the distance using the pulse duration.

Syntax Explanation

1. Initialize sensor

What is initializing the sensor?

To use the ultrasonic sensor, you must initialize it by specifying the trigger and echo pins. These pins will be used to send and receive the sound pulse.

Syntax:

```
Ultrasonic ultrasonic(triggerPin, echoPin);
```

Example:

```
Ultrasonic ultrasonic(12, 13);  // Trigger pin 12, Echo pin 13
```

Example Explanation:

In this example, we initialize the ultrasonic sensor on pins 12 and 13 for the trigger and echo. These pins will be used for distance measurement.

2. Measure distance

What is measuring the distance?

The ultrasonic sensor measures the distance to an object by calculating the time taken for the sound pulse to return. This is read using the read() function.

Syntax:

```
distance = ultrasonic.read();
```

Example:

```
int distance = ultrasonic.read();
```

Example Explanation:
The read() function returns the distance in centimeters from the ultrasonic sensor. The result is stored in the distance variable, which can be used for further actions like obstacle detection.

3. Set trigger and echo pins

What is setting the trigger and echo pins?
Before you use the sensor, you need to configure the trigger pin as an OUTPUT and the echo pin as an INPUT. The trigger pin sends the pulse, and the echo pin receives it.
Syntax:
```
pinMode(triggerPin, OUTPUT);
pinMode(echoPin, INPUT);
```

Example:
```
pinMode(12, OUTPUT);    // Set trigger pin as output
pinMode(13, INPUT);     // Set echo pin as input
```

Example Explanation:
In this example, pin 12 is set as the OUTPUT pin for sending the trigger pulse, and pin 13 is set as the INPUT pin to receive the echo. This configuration is necessary for the sensor to function properly.

4. Trigger ultrasonic sensor

What is triggering the ultrasonic sensor?
To initiate the measurement, you send a HIGH signal to the trigger pin. This causes the sensor to emit a sound pulse.
Syntax:
```
digitalWrite(triggerPin, HIGH);
```

Example:
```
digitalWrite(12, HIGH);    // Send trigger pulse
```
Example Explanation:
The digitalWrite(12, HIGH) command sends a HIGH signal to the trigger pin (pin 12). This causes the ultrasonic sensor to emit a pulse.

5. Calculate distance
What is calculating the distance?
Once the pulse is sent, the sensor waits for the pulse to return. The time it takes for the pulse to return is used to calculate the distance using the formula:

```
distance = (pulseDuration / 2) / 29.1;
```

Syntax:
```
distance = (pulseDuration / 2) / 29.1;
```

Example:
```
long pulseDuration = pulseIn(echoPin, HIGH);  // Measure pulse duration
int distance = (pulseDuration / 2) / 29.1;    // Calculate distance
```

Example Explanation:
The pulseIn() function measures the time the pulse takes to return, and this time is used to calculate the distance in centimeters.

Real-life Applications Project: Ultrasonic Obstacle Avoidance System

In this project, an ultrasonic sensor will be used to measure the distance between the sensor and obstacles in its path. If the object is too close, the system will take appropriate action, like stopping a motor or triggering an alarm.

Required Components

Component	Description
Ultrasonic Sensor (HC-SR04)	Measures distance to objects using ultrasonic sound waves.
Arduino Uno	Microcontroller to process sensor data.
Servo Motor	To demonstrate obstacle avoidance by moving an object.
Jumper Wires	For connecting components on the breadboard.
Breadboard	Used to hold and organize components.

Circuit Connection Table

Component	Pin Connection
Ultrasonic Sensor	VCC to 5V, GND to GND, Trigger to pin 12, Echo to pin 13
Servo Motor	Signal pin to pin 9, VCC to 5V, GND to GND
Arduino Uno	5V to VCC, GND to GND

Project Code

```
#include <Servo.h>
int triggerPin = 12;
int echoPin = 13;
Servo myServo;
void setup() {
  pinMode(triggerPin, OUTPUT);
  pinMode(echoPin, INPUT);
  myServo.attach(9);  // Servo motor connected to pin 9
  Serial.begin(9600); // Start serial communication
}
void loop() {
  long pulseDuration = pulseIn(echoPin, HIGH); // Read
the echo pin
  int distance = (pulseDuration / 2) / 29.1;    //
Calculate distance
  Serial.print("Distance: ");
  Serial.println(distance);
  if (distance < 10) {  // If the object is less than
10 cm away
    myServo.write(90);    // Move the servo motor to 90
degrees (avoid obstacle)
  } else {
    myServo.write(0);     // Keep the servo motor in the
initial position
  }
  delay(500); // Delay between readings
}
```

Expected Results

- **Serial Monitor Output**: The Serial Monitor will display the distance measured by the ultrasonic sensor in centimeters.

Chapter 33: Humidity Sensors with Arduino

Humidity sensors measure the amount of water vapor in the air. These sensors are essential in many applications such as weather stations, greenhouses, and climate control systems. By understanding how to use humidity sensors with Arduino, you can build projects that monitor and regulate humidity levels.

Key Concepts of Humidity Sensors

Humidity sensors work by detecting the amount of moisture in the air. There are different types of humidity sensors, including capacitive, resistive, and thermal types. The most commonly used sensor in Arduino projects is the DHT11 or DHT22, which provides both temperature and humidity readings.

Concept	Description	Example
Sensor Type	Humidity sensors come in resistive, capacitive, and thermal types.	DHT11 is a resistive humidity sensor.
Output Type	Most humidity sensors provide a digital or analog output.	DHT11 provides a digital signal for both temperature and humidity.
Accuracy	The accuracy of humidity sensors varies based on the model.	DHT11 has an accuracy range of ±5% RH.
Temperature and Humidity	Many humidity sensors also measure temperature.	DHT11 and DHT22 can measure both temperature and humidity.
Response Time	The time it takes for the sensor to detect changes in humidity.	DHT11 has a response time of about 1-2 seconds.

Basic Rules for Using Humidity Sensors

Rule	Correct Example	Incorrect Example
Always initialize the sensor before reading data.	dht.begin();	Reading data before calling dht.begin();`

Use proper delays between readings to avoid inaccurate results.	delay(2000); (for 2 seconds delay)	delay(100); (too short of a delay for accurate readings)
Ensure the sensor is within the operating temperature and humidity range.	Operating range: DHT11 (20%-90% RH)	Using sensor in extreme humidity or temperature conditions.
Handle sensor errors gracefully in case of connection failure.	if (!dht.read()) { Serial.println(" Error reading sensor"); }	Ignoring error messages or failing to handle errors.

Syntax Table

SL	Function	Syntax/Example	Description
1	Initialize sensor	dht.begin();	Initializes the DHT sensor for reading.
2	Read humidity	humidity = dht.readHumidity();	Reads the humidity value from the sensor.
3	Read temperature	temperature = dht.readTemperature();	Reads the temperature value from the sensor.
4	Error checking	if (isnan(humidity)) { Serial.println("Failed to read humidity!"); }	Checks if the sensor reading is valid.

Syntax Explanation

1. Initialize sensor

What is initializing the sensor?

Before reading data from the sensor, you need to initialize it using the begin() function. This ensures that the sensor is ready for communication and data collection.

Syntax:

dht.begin();

Example:
```
DHT dht(2, DHT11);   // Create DHT object with pin 2 and
DHT11 sensor type
dht.begin();         // Initialize the sensor
```

Example Explanation:
Here, we create a DHT sensor object on pin 2 and specify that it is a DHT11 sensor. The dht.begin() function prepares the sensor to be used for reading humidity and temperature data.

2. Read humidity

What is reading humidity?
The readHumidity() function is used to obtain the humidity value from the sensor. The value is typically returned in percentage relative humidity (RH).
Syntax:
```
humidity = dht.readHumidity();
```

Example:
```
float humidity = dht.readHumidity();
```

Example Explanation:
This line reads the humidity value from the DHT11 sensor and stores it in the humidity variable. If the sensor fails to return a valid value, the result will be NaN (Not a Number).

3. Read temperature

What is reading temperature?
The readTemperature() function is used to get the temperature value from the sensor. The temperature can be read in Celsius or Fahrenheit.
Syntax:
```
temperature = dht.readTemperature();
```

Example:
```
float temperature = dht.readTemperature();
```

Example Explanation:
This line reads the temperature in Celsius from the DHT11 sensor and stores it in the `temperature` variable. Similarly to humidity, the function returns NaN if the sensor cannot read the data.

4. Error checking

What is error checking?
It's important to check for errors after attempting to read data from the sensor. If the sensor fails to provide a valid reading, handling errors appropriately can ensure the system remains robust.

Syntax:
```
if (isnan(humidity)) {
  Serial.println("Failed to read humidity!");
}
```

Example:
```
if (isnan(temperature)) {
  Serial.println("Failed to read temperature!");
}
```

Example Explanation:
This code checks whether the `humidity` or `temperature` value is NaN (which indicates a failed sensor reading) and prints an error message to the Serial Monitor.

Real-life Applications Project: Humidity and Temperature Monitoring System

In this project, we will build a simple humidity and temperature monitoring system using the DHT11 sensor. This system can be used in applications such as greenhouse monitoring, weather stations, and HVAC systems.

Required Components

Component	Description
DHT11 Sensor	Measures both temperature and humidity.
Arduino Uno	Microcontroller to read sensor data and control outputs.
Breadboard	For organizing the components.
Jumper Wires	For connecting components.
LCD Display	Display the humidity and temperature readings.

Circuit Connection Table

Component	Pin Connection
DHT11 Sensor	VCC to 5V, GND to GND, Data to pin 2
Arduino Uno	5V to VCC, GND to GND
LCD Display	Connect according to LCD wiring instructions (e.g., pin 12, 11, 5, 4, 3, 2 for 16x2 LCD)

Project Code

```
#include <DHT.h>
#include <LiquidCrystal_I2C.h>

#define DHTPIN 2
#define DHTTYPE DHT11

DHT dht(DHTPIN, DHTTYPE);
LiquidCrystal_I2C lcd(0x27, 16, 2);

void setup() {
  lcd.begin(16, 2);
  dht.begin();
  lcd.print("Humidity & Temp");
  delay(2000);
}

void loop() {
  float humidity = dht.readHumidity();
  float temperature = dht.readTemperature();

  if (isnan(humidity) || isnan(temperature)) {
```

```
    lcd.print("Sensor error!");
  } else {
    lcd.clear();
    lcd.setCursor(0, 0);
    lcd.print("Humidity: ");
    lcd.print(humidity);
    lcd.print("%");
    lcd.setCursor(0, 1);
    lcd.print("Temp: ");
    lcd.print(temperature);
    lcd.print("C");
  }
  delay(2000);  // Wait for 2 seconds before updating
again
}
```

Expected Results

- **Serial Monitor Output**: Displays the current temperature and humidity values every 2 seconds.
- **Physical Result**: On the LCD, you will see the current humidity and temperature displayed. If there's a sensor error, it will show "Sensor error!" instead.

Chapter 34: Pressure Sensors with Arduino

Pressure sensors are devices that measure the pressure of gases or liquids. These sensors are widely used in applications ranging from weather monitoring, altitude measurement, and fluid level detection to industrial automation systems. Understanding how to interface pressure sensors with Arduino can help you develop projects that require pressure monitoring.

Key Concepts of Pressure Sensors

Pressure sensors work by detecting the force applied by a gas or liquid on a membrane inside the sensor. This force is converted into an electrical signal, which can then be read by the Arduino. Common pressure sensors for Arduino include the BMP180, BMP280, and the MPL3115A2, which also measure temperature and altitude.

Concept	Description	Example
Pressure Type	Sensors may measure absolute, relative, or differential pressure.	BMP180 measures absolute pressure, MPL3115A2 measures relative pressure.
Output Type	Pressure sensors typically output analog or digital signals.	BMP280 provides digital output via I2C or SPI.
Accuracy	The accuracy depends on the sensor's quality and the measurement range.	BMP180 has an accuracy of ±1 hPa (hectopascal) for pressure.
Sensor Range	The sensor's pressure range defines the minimum and maximum measurable pressures.	BMP280 ranges from 300 to 1100 hPa (hPa stands for hectopascal).
Temperature and Altitude	Some pressure sensors also measure temperature and altitude.	BMP180 measures both pressure and temperature.

Basic Rules for Using Pressure Sensors

Rule	Correct Example	Incorrect Example
Initialize the sensor before reading pressure data.	`bmp.begin();`	Attempting to read before bmp.begin();`
Make sure the sensor is calibrated if necessary.	`bmp.setCalibra ted();`	Skipping calibration on new sensor models.
Use proper delay times to allow the sensor to stabilize.	`delay(500);`	Reading data without delay (can result in incorrect readings).
Handle errors and sensor failure gracefully.	`if (!bmp.begin()) { Serial.println ("Sensor error!"); return; }`	Not handling errors or failing to check sensor readiness.

Syntax Table

SL	Function	Syntax/Example	Description
1	Initialize the sensor	`bmp.begin();`	Initializes the BMP sensor for reading pressure and temperature.
2	Read pressure data	`pressure = bmp.readPressure() ;`	Reads the pressure value from the sensor (in Pa).
3	Read temperature	`temperature = bmp.readTemperatur e();`	Reads the temperature value from the sensor (in °C).
4	Error handling	`if (!bmp.begin()) { Serial.println("Er`	Checks if the sensor is connected and working correctly.

		ror initializing sensor"); }	

Syntax Explanation

1. Initialize the sensor

What is initializing the sensor?
Before using the sensor, it must be initialized. The begin() function ensures that the sensor is properly connected and ready for data readings.
Syntax:
```
bmp.begin();
```

Example:
```
Adafruit_BMP280 bmp;
if (!bmp.begin()) {
    Serial.println("Error initializing sensor.");
    while (1);
}
```

Example Explanation:
This line of code checks if the BMP280 sensor is properly connected. If the sensor cannot be initialized, an error message is printed to the Serial Monitor, and the program halts.

2. Read pressure data
What is reading pressure data?
The readPressure() function retrieves the current pressure reading from the sensor. The value returned is typically in pascals (Pa), which can be converted to other units like hPa or mmHg.
Syntax:
```
pressure = bmp.readPressure();
```
Example:
```
float pressure = bmp.readPressure(); // Pressure in pascals
Serial.print("Pressure: ");
Serial.print(pressure / 100.0F); // Convert to hPa
Serial.println(" hPa");
```

Example Explanation:
The readPressure() function returns the pressure in pascals (Pa). In this example, the reading is converted to hectopascals (hPa) for easier interpretation.

3. Read temperature

What is reading temperature?
The readTemperature() function retrieves the temperature in Celsius from the sensor. This value is helpful when using the pressure data to calculate altitude or monitor environmental conditions.

Syntax:
```
temperature = bmp.readTemperature();
```

Example:
```
float temperature = bmp.readTemperature();
Serial.print("Temperature: ");
Serial.print(temperature);
Serial.println(" C");
```

Example Explanation:
The readTemperature() function returns the temperature in Celsius. In this example, the temperature is printed to the Serial Monitor.

4. Error handling

What is error handling?
It is important to handle potential errors when working with sensors. The code should check if the sensor is properly initialized and whether the data received is valid.

Syntax:
```
if (!bmp.begin()) {
  Serial.println("Error initializing sensor.");
  return;
}
```

Example:

```
if (!bmp.begin()) {
  Serial.println("Failed to initialize the BMP280
sensor.");
  while (1); // Stop program execution
}
```

Example Explanation:

In this code, the if (!bmp.begin()) checks whether the sensor was initialized successfully. If not, the error message is printed, and the program execution is halted to avoid further complications.

Real-life Applications Project: Atmospheric Pressure and Altitude Monitoring System

In this project, we will use the BMP280 sensor to monitor atmospheric pressure and calculate the altitude of the sensor based on the pressure reading. This system can be used for weather stations, drones, and environmental monitoring.

Required Components

Component	Description
BMP280 Pressure Sensor	Measures atmospheric pressure and temperature.
Arduino Uno	Microcontroller to read sensor data and control outputs.
Breadboard	For organizing the components.
Jumper Wires	For connecting components.
LCD Display	Displays the pressure and altitude data.

Circuit Connection Table

Component	Pin Connection
BMP280 Sensor	VCC to 5V, GND to GND, SDA to A4, SCL to A5 (for I2C communication)
Arduino Uno	5V to VCC, GND to GND
LCD Display	Connect according to LCD wiring instructions (e.g., pin 12, 11, 5, 4, 3, 2 for 16x2 LCD)

Project Code

```cpp
#include <Wire.h>
#include <Adafruit_Sensor.h>
#include <Adafruit_BMP280.h>
#include <LiquidCrystal_I2C.h>

Adafruit_BMP280 bmp;      // I2C
LiquidCrystal_I2C lcd(0x27, 16, 2);

void setup() {
  lcd.begin(16, 2);
  if (!bmp.begin()) {
    lcd.print("Sensor Error!");
    while (1);
  }
  lcd.print("Pressure & Altitude");
  delay(2000);
}

void loop() {
  float pressure = bmp.readPressure() / 100.0F; // in
hPa
  float altitude = bmp.readAltitude(1013.25); //
Assuming sea level pressure is 1013.25 hPa

  lcd.clear();
  lcd.setCursor(0, 0);
  lcd.print("Pressure: ");
  lcd.print(pressure);
  lcd.print(" hPa");

  lcd.setCursor(0, 1);
  lcd.print("Altitude: ");
  lcd.print(altitude);
  lcd.print(" m");
  delay(2000); // Update every 2 seconds
}
```

Expected Results

- **Serial Monitor Output**: Displays the pressure and altitude readings every 2 seconds.
- **Physical Result**: On the LCD, the current pressure and altitude will be displayed. The pressure value will change based on the environment, and altitude will adjust according to the atmospheric pressure.

Chapter 35: Sound Sensors and Microphones with Arduino

Sound sensors are devices used to detect sound levels in the environment, and when interfaced with Arduino, they can be used for a variety of applications such as noise detection, sound-activated switches, and audio signal analysis. These sensors typically work by converting sound waves into electrical signals, which are then processed by the Arduino to take actions like triggering events or reading sound levels.

Key Concepts of Sound Sensors

Sound sensors are designed to detect the intensity of sound waves. Some microphones output analog signals that correspond to sound levels, while others provide digital signals that indicate whether the sound exceeds a certain threshold. Understanding how to connect and read these signals with Arduino is essential for building sound-responsive systems.

Concept	Description	Example
Sound Detection	Sound sensors detect changes in sound pressure levels.	A sound sensor may trigger a response when a sound exceeds a threshold.
Output Type	Some sensors provide analog output (variable sound levels), while others provide digital output (sound/no sound).	Analog output (e.g., LM393) or digital output (e.g., KY-037).
Sensitivity	Sensitivity refers to the sensor's ability to detect soft sounds or loud sounds.	A microphone with higher sensitivity can detect quieter sounds.
Frequency Response	The frequency range determines what types of sounds the sensor can detect.	Most sound sensors detect audible sound frequencies (20 Hz to 20 kHz).
Application	Sound sensors can be used in noise detection, security systems, sound-activated devices, and more.	Detecting claps to trigger a light or alarm system.

Basic Rules for Using Sound Sensors

Rule	Correct Example	Incorrect Example
Ensure that the sound sensor's output pin is correctly connected to an Arduino pin.	`analogRead(A0);` or `digitalRead(2);`	Connecting the sensor's output to the wrong pin.
Use a proper delay or filter to avoid false readings from environmental noise.	`delay(100);` or `if (sound > threshold)`	Reading data too fast without checking for stability.
Calibrate the sound sensor for the environment in which it's being used.	Set the threshold for loudness based on your room's noise level.	Using default values without adjusting for noise sensitivity.
Properly debounce input signals if using a digital sound sensor.	`if (millis() - lastTime > debounceDelay)`	Reading without debouncing, leading to multiple triggers.

Syntax Table

SL	Function	Syntax/Example	Description
1	Read sound from analog sensor	`soundValue = analogRead(pin);`	Reads the sound level from the sensor in analog format.
2	Read sound from digital sensor	`soundState = digitalRead(pin);`	Reads if the sound exceeds a set threshold (HIGH or LOW).
3	Set threshold for sound detection	`if (soundValue > threshold)`	Compares the sound value to a predefined threshold value.
4	Trigger event based on sound	`if (soundState == HIGH) { /* trigger event */ }`	Triggers an event when a sound above threshold is detected.

Syntax Explanation

1. Read sound from analog sensor

What is reading from an analog sound sensor?
 Analog sound sensors produce a variable voltage output based on the intensity of sound. The `analogRead()` function is used to capture this voltage level, which can then be mapped to sound intensity.
Syntax:
```
soundValue = analogRead(pin);
```

Example:
```
int soundValue = analogRead(A0);
```

Example Explanation:
 In this example, `analogRead(A0)` reads the analog value from pin A0. The result is a value between 0 and 1023, which corresponds to the intensity of sound detected by the sensor.

2. Read sound from digital sensor

What is reading from a digital sound sensor?
 Some sound sensors provide a simple digital output that indicates whether the sound exceeds a certain threshold (typically a preset value or one that you can adjust).
Syntax:
```
soundState = digitalRead(pin);
```

Example:
```
int soundState = digitalRead(2);
```

Example Explanation:
 In this example, `digitalRead(2)` checks if the sound level has exceeded the threshold. The return value is either HIGH (if the sound is detected) or LOW (if no sound is detected).

3. Set threshold for sound detection

What is setting a threshold?
When using a sensor that detects sound intensity, it's important to set a threshold to determine when a sound should trigger an event. This can be done by comparing the sensor's value to a predefined threshold value.

Syntax:
```
if (soundValue > threshold) { /* trigger event */ }
```

Example:
```
int threshold = 512;
if (soundValue > threshold) {
  Serial.println("Sound detected!");
}
```

Example Explanation:
This code checks if the soundValue exceeds the threshold. If it does, the program will print "Sound detected!" to the Serial Monitor. You can adjust the threshold depending on the sensitivity of the environment.

4. Trigger event based on sound

What is triggering an event based on sound?
When a sound sensor detects a sound that surpasses a certain level, you may want to trigger an action. This can be done by checking the sensor state and activating devices like LEDs or motors.

Syntax:
```
if (soundState == HIGH) { /* trigger event */ }
```
Example:
```
if (soundState == HIGH) {
  digitalWrite(LED_PIN, HIGH);  // Turn on LED when sound is detected
}
```
Example Explanation:
If the sound sensor's digital output is HIGH, it means the sound level has crossed the preset threshold, and the code triggers an event (in this case, turning on an LED).

Real-life Applications Project: Sound-Activated Light System

In this project, a sound sensor is used to turn an LED on when a loud noise (like a clap) is detected. This type of system can be useful in creating interactive environments, or for simple automation of lighting systems.

Required Components

Component	Description
Sound Sensor Module	Detects ambient sound levels (e.g., KY-038 or LM393).
Arduino Uno	Microcontroller to read sensor data and control outputs.
LED	A light that will be turned on by sound detection.
Resistor (220Ω)	Limits current to protect the LED.
Jumper Wires	For connecting components on the breadboard.
Breadboard	Used to organize and connect components.

Circuit Connection Table

Component	Pin Connection
Sound Sensor	VCC to 5V, GND to GND, OUT to Arduino pin 2
Arduino Uno	5V to VCC, GND to GND
LED	Anode to pin 13 through a 220Ω resistor, Cathode to GND

Project Code

```
const int soundPin = 2;  // Sound sensor connected to
pin 2
const int ledPin = 13;   // LED connected to pin 13

void setup() {
  pinMode(soundPin, INPUT);
  pinMode(ledPin, OUTPUT);
  Serial.begin(9600);
}

void loop() {
```

```
  int soundState = digitalRead(soundPin);  // Read
sound sensor value

  if (soundState == HIGH) {  // If sound is detected
    digitalWrite(ledPin, HIGH);  // Turn on LED
    Serial.println("Sound Detected! LED ON");
  } else {
    digitalWrite(ledPin, LOW);   // Turn off LED
    Serial.println("No sound. LED OFF");
  }
  delay(100);  // Small delay for stability
}
```

Expected Results

- **Serial Monitor Output**: When sound is detected, the Serial Monitor will print "Sound Detected! LED ON". Otherwise, it will print "No sound. LED OFF".
- **Physical Result**: The LED will turn on when the sound sensor detects sound (e.g., a clap) and turn off when there is no sound.

Chapter 36: Gas and Air Quality Sensors with Arduino

Gas and air quality sensors are used to detect the presence and concentration of various gases in the atmosphere, such as carbon dioxide (CO2), carbon monoxide (CO), methane (CH4), and other volatile compounds. These sensors are essential in applications such as air quality monitoring, environmental protection, and safety systems. When integrated with Arduino, they can be used for detecting gas leaks, monitoring air quality in homes or workplaces, and triggering alarms when dangerous levels of gases are detected.

Key Concepts of Gas and Air Quality Sensors

Gas sensors typically work by detecting changes in the electrical conductivity of a sensing material when it reacts with specific gases. These sensors may provide either analog or digital output that corresponds to the concentration of a specific gas. Understanding the various gas sensors and their output methods is key to successfully integrating them into your projects.

Concept	Description	Example
Gas Detection	Gas sensors detect the presence and concentration of specific gases.	Examples include detecting CO, CO2, CH4, or NO2 levels.
Sensor Output	Sensors can have analog or digital outputs, indicating gas concentration.	Analog output gives a continuous value; digital output indicates a threshold.
Sensitivity	The sensitivity of a sensor determines how well it can detect small concentrations of gas.	A sensor with higher sensitivity can detect lower gas concentrations.
Response Time	Response time refers to how quickly the sensor reacts to changes in gas concentration.	A quick response time is essential in safety-critical applications.

	Gas sensors are used in air quality monitoring, safety systems, and environmental research.	Home air quality monitoring, detecting gas leaks, and industrial safety.
Applicatio ns		

Basic Rules for Using Gas and Air Quality Sensors

Rule	Correct Example	Incorrect Example
Calibrate the sensor to the environment before use.	Calibrate the sensor by exposing it to known gas concentrations.	Using the sensor without calibration in variable environments.
Ensure the sensor is within its specified operating range.	Use the sensor within its specified gas concentration range.	Using the sensor in conditions outside its specified range.
Use proper ventilation around the sensor to ensure accurate readings.	Ensure the sensor is placed in a well-ventilated area.	Placing the sensor in an enclosed or poorly ventilated area.
Consider the sensor's power requirements.	Check the power supply voltage to ensure compatibility.	Connecting the sensor to an incompatible voltage source.

Syntax Table

SL	Function	Syntax/Example	Description
1	Read gas sensor analog value	`gasConcentration = analogRead(pin);`	Reads the gas sensor's output as an analog value.
2	Set threshold for gas detection	`if (gasConcentratio n > threshold)`	Checks if the gas concentration exceeds the set threshold.

		if	
3	Trigger event based on detection	`(gasConcentratio n > threshold) {` `/* trigger event */ }`	Triggers an event (e.g., turning on an alarm) based on gas levels.
4	Print gas concentration to serial	`Serial.println(g asConcentration) ;`	Displays the detected gas concentration on the Serial Monitor.

Syntax Explanation

1. Read gas sensor analog value

What is reading from a gas sensor?
Gas sensors output an analog voltage that is proportional to the concentration of a specific gas. The analogRead( ) function is used to measure this value.
Syntax:
`gasConcentration = analogRead(pin);`

Example:
`int gasConcentration = analogRead(A0);`

Example Explanation:
This code reads the analog value from the gas sensor connected to pin A0. The result will be a value between 0 and 1023, which corresponds to the concentration of the gas being detected.

2. Set threshold for gas detection

What is setting a threshold?
A threshold is set to define the concentration level at which you want to trigger an action. When the gas concentration exceeds this threshold, an event (e.g., turning on an alarm or light) is triggered.
Syntax:
`if (gasConcentration > threshold) {`
`    // trigger event`
`}`

Example:

```
int threshold = 400;   // Set threshold for gas
detection
if (gasConcentration > threshold) {
   Serial.println("Gas leak detected!");
}
```

Example Explanation:
This code compares the measured gas concentration with the threshold value. If the gas concentration exceeds the threshold, it will print "Gas leak detected!" to the Serial Monitor.

3. Trigger event based on detection

What is triggering an event based on gas concentration?
When the gas concentration exceeds the threshold, you may want to trigger an event, such as activating a buzzer, turning on a warning light, or sending a notification.

Syntax:

```
if (gasConcentration > threshold) {
   // trigger event (e.g., turn on alarm)
}
```

Example:

```
if (gasConcentration > threshold) {
   digitalWrite(LED_PIN, HIGH);   // Turn on LED when gas
detected
}
```

Example Explanation:
In this example, if the gas concentration exceeds the threshold, the LED connected to LED_PIN will be turned on, signaling the detection of dangerous gas levels.

4. Print gas concentration to serial

What is printing gas concentration?

This function is used to display the detected gas concentration on the Serial Monitor, allowing you to monitor the real-time gas levels.

Syntax:

```
Serial.println(gasConcentration);
```

Example:

```
Serial.println(gasConcentration);  // Print gas
concentration to Serial Monitor
```

Example Explanation:

This code sends the current gas concentration to the Serial Monitor for real-time monitoring.

Real-life Applications Project: Air Quality Monitoring System

In this project, a gas sensor is used to monitor the concentration of gases like carbon dioxide (CO_2) or carbon monoxide (CO) in the air. The system can trigger an alarm when dangerous gas levels are detected, providing a practical solution for home safety and environmental monitoring.

Required Components

Component	Description
Gas Sensor (e.g., MQ-7)	A gas sensor to detect carbon monoxide (CO).
Arduino Uno	Microcontroller to read the sensor data and control outputs.
Buzzer	Used to alert when dangerous gas levels are detected.
LED	Lights up when gas levels exceed threshold.
Resistor (220Ω)	For protecting the LED from excessive current.
Jumper Wires	For connecting the components on the breadboard.
Breadboard	For organizing the components and making connections.

Circuit Connection Table

Component	Pin Connection
Gas Sensor (MQ-7)	VCC to 5V, GND to GND, A0 to Arduino pin A0
Arduino Uno	5V to VCC, GND to GND
LED	Anode to pin 13 through a 220Ω resistor, Cathode to GND
Buzzer	One pin to Arduino pin 12, other pin to GND

Project Code

```
const int gasSensorPin = A0;  // Gas sensor connected
to A0
const int ledPin = 13;        // LED connected to pin
13
const int buzzerPin = 12;     // Buzzer connected to
pin 12
int gasConcentration = 0;     // Variable to store gas
concentration
int threshold = 400;          // Set threshold for gas
detection

void setup() {
  pinMode(ledPin, OUTPUT);
  pinMode(buzzerPin, OUTPUT);
  Serial.begin(9600);  // Initialize Serial Monitor
}

void loop() {
  gasConcentration = analogRead(gasSensorPin);  // Read
gas concentration from sensor

  // Print gas concentration to Serial Monitor
  Serial.println(gasConcentration);

  // Check if gas concentration exceeds threshold
  if (gasConcentration > threshold) {
    digitalWrite(ledPin, HIGH);  // Turn on LED
    digitalWrite(buzzerPin, HIGH);  // Activate buzzer
    Serial.println("Dangerous gas levels detected!");
```

```
  } else {
    digitalWrite(ledPin, LOW);    // Turn off LED
    digitalWrite(buzzerPin, LOW);  // Deactivate buzzer
  }

  delay(500);  // Wait for half a second before next
reading
}
```

Expected Results

- **Serial Monitor Output**: When the gas concentration exceeds the threshold, the Serial Monitor will print "Dangerous gas levels detected!" and display the gas concentration.
- **Physical Result**: The LED will turn on and the buzzer will sound when the gas concentration exceeds the threshold. If the gas level is safe, the LED and buzzer will remain off.

Chapter 37: Touch and Force Sensors with Arduino

Touch and force sensors are used to detect physical interactions with objects. Touch sensors allow the detection of human touch or proximity, while force sensors measure the physical force or pressure applied to an object. These sensors are used in a wide range of applications such as interactive projects, pressure-sensitive devices, and touch-sensitive buttons or screens. When integrated with Arduino, they enable the creation of responsive systems that can detect user input or environmental changes.

Key Concepts of Touch and Force Sensors

Touch and force sensors convert physical touch or pressure into electrical signals that can be interpreted by an Arduino. Touch sensors typically work through capacitive or resistive technology, while force sensors, such as load cells or piezoelectric sensors, detect applied pressure.

Concept	Description	Example
Capacitive Touch Sensing	Capacitive sensors detect changes in capacitance caused by a touch.	Touch-sensitive buttons on smartphones.
Resistive Touch Sensing	Resistive sensors change resistance when pressure is applied.	Pressure-sensitive touchpads or switches.
Force Sensing	Force sensors measure physical pressure or force applied to a surface.	Load cells, force-sensitive resistors (FSRs).
Output Type	Sensors can have analog or digital outputs, representing touch or force.	Analog sensors provide varying output based on touch or pressure.
Applications	Used in interactive displays, pressure monitoring, and human-machine interfaces.	Touchscreens, pressure sensors in robotics, and smart devices.

Basic Rules for Using Touch and Force Sensors

Rule	Correct Example	Incorrect Example
Calibrate sensors for accurate readings before use.	Calibrate force sensor before each measurement.	Using force sensor without calibration.
Choose the appropriate sensor type based on the required sensitivity.	Use a force-sensitive resistor (FSR) for light touch detection.	Using a pressure sensor in a low-pressure environment.
Ensure the sensor is placed in a location where force or touch can be accurately measured.	Place the sensor on a flat surface for accurate readings.	Placing the sensor in a location with high interference.
Always protect sensitive sensors from electrical overcurrent.	Use a resistor in series with a sensor to limit current.	Connecting a sensor directly without a resistor.

Syntax Table

SL	Function	Syntax/Example	Description
1	Read touch sensor value	`touchValue = digitalRead(pin);`	Reads the state of a touch sensor (HIGH for touch, LOW for no touch).
2	Read force sensor analog value	`forceValue = analogRead(pin);`	Reads the force applied using an analog value (0 to 1023).
3	Detect touch and trigger event	`if (touchValue == HIGH)`	Checks if the touch sensor has been activated (HIGH means touch detected).
4	Trigger event based on force	`if (forceValue > threshold)`	Triggers an event if the force exceeds a set threshold.

Syntax Explanation

1. Read touch sensor value

What is reading from a touch sensor?
Touch sensors are commonly digital sensors that provide either a HIGH or
LOW signal when touched or not touched, respectively. The
digitalRead() function is used to read this value.
Syntax:
```
touchValue = digitalRead(pin);
```

Example:
```
int touchValue = digitalRead(7);
```

Example Explanation:
In this code, digitalRead(7) checks if the touch sensor connected to
pin 7 has been touched. If the sensor is touched, it will return a HIGH
value, otherwise it returns LOW.

2. Read force sensor analog value

What is reading from a force sensor?
Force sensors typically output an analog value that changes based on the
amount of pressure or force applied. The analogRead() function is used
to read this continuous value.
Syntax:
```
forceValue = analogRead(pin);
```

Example:
```
int forceValue = analogRead(A0);
```

Example Explanation:
This code reads the force value from a force-sensitive resistor connected
to analog pin A0. The value will range from 0 to 1023, where higher values
represent more pressure being applied.

3. Detect touch and trigger event

What is triggering an event based on touch detection?
When the touch sensor is activated (touched), you may want to trigger an event, such as turning on an LED, activating a motor, or printing a message to the Serial Monitor.

Syntax:
```
if (touchValue == HIGH) {
    // Trigger event
}
```
Example:
```
if (touchValue == HIGH) {
    Serial.println("Sensor touched!");
}
```
Example Explanation:
This code checks if the touch sensor has been activated (i.e., if the touch value is HIGH). If so, it will print "Sensor touched!" to the Serial Monitor.

4. Trigger event based on force detection

What is triggering an event based on force detection?
You can set a threshold value for the force sensor, and if the applied force exceeds this threshold, an event (e.g., turning on an LED or activating a buzzer) is triggered.

Syntax:
```
if (forceValue > threshold) {
    // Trigger event
}
```
Example:
```
int threshold = 500;
if (forceValue > threshold) {
    digitalWrite(13, HIGH);   // Turn on LED if force
exceeds threshold
}
```
Example Explanation:
This code checks if the force value exceeds a set threshold. If the force is greater than 500, the LED connected to pin 13 will be turned on.

Real-life Applications Project: Interactive Touch and Force Detection System

In this project, we will use both a touch sensor and a force sensor to create an interactive system where a touch triggers one action, and a force triggers another. This can be used in smart home systems, touch-sensitive lighting, or interactive installations.

Required Components

Component	Description
Touch Sensor (e.g., TTP223)	Detects human touch (digital).
Force Sensor (e.g., FSR)	Detects applied pressure (analog).
Arduino Uno	Microcontroller to read the sensors and control outputs.
LED	Indicator light for touch or force event.
Buzzer	Sound indicator for force event.
Resistor (220Ω)	Protects LED from excessive current.
Jumper Wires	For connecting components to Arduino and breadboard.
Breadboard	For organizing and connecting components.

Circuit Connection Table

Component	Pin Connection
Touch Sensor (TTP223)	VCC to 5V, GND to GND, OUT to Arduino pin 7
Force Sensor (FSR)	One pin to 5V, the other to Arduino pin A0 (with a pull-down resistor to GND)
Arduino Uno	5V to VCC, GND to GND
LED	Anode to pin 13 through a 220Ω resistor, Cathode to GND
Buzzer	One pin to pin 12, other pin to GND

Project Code

```
const int touchPin = 7;        // Touch sensor
connected to pin 7
const int forcePin = A0;       // Force sensor
connected to pin A0
```

```cpp
const int ledPin = 13;          // LED connected to pin
13
const int buzzerPin = 12;       // Buzzer connected to
pin 12
int touchValue = 0;             // Variable to store
touch sensor state
int forceValue = 0;             // Variable to store
force sensor value
int threshold = 500;            // Force detection
threshold

void setup() {
  pinMode(touchPin, INPUT);
  pinMode(ledPin, OUTPUT);
  pinMode(buzzerPin, OUTPUT);
  Serial.begin(9600);           // Initialize Serial
Monitor
}

void loop() {
  touchValue = digitalRead(touchPin);   // Read touch
sensor
  forceValue = analogRead(forcePin);   // Read force
sensor

  if (touchValue == HIGH) {
    digitalWrite(ledPin, HIGH);  // Turn on LED if
touched
    Serial.println("Touch detected!");
  } else {
    digitalWrite(ledPin, LOW);    // Turn off LED if not
touched
  }

  if (forceValue > threshold) {
    digitalWrite(buzzerPin, HIGH);  // Turn on buzzer
if force exceeds threshold
```

```
    Serial.println("Force detected!");
  } else {
    digitalWrite(buzzerPin, LOW);    // Turn off buzzer
if force is below threshold
  }

  delay(

100);  // Small delay to avoid rapid state changes
}
```

Expected Results

When you touch the touch sensor, the LED will light up, and "Touch detected!" will be printed to the Serial Monitor. When a certain force threshold is applied to the force sensor, the buzzer will sound, and "Force detected!" will appear in the Serial Monitor. If neither event occurs, both the LED and buzzer will remain off.

Chapter 39: Controlling LEDs with Arduino

LEDs (Light Emitting Diodes) are one of the most basic and commonly used components in Arduino projects. They can be used for a wide variety of purposes, from simple indicator lights to creating complex visual displays. This chapter will cover how to control LEDs with an Arduino, including simple on/off control, fading effects, and even PWM-based dimming for advanced control.

Key Concepts of LED Control

LEDs can be controlled through digital or PWM signals from the Arduino. Digital control turns the LED fully on or off, while PWM allows for adjusting the brightness of the LED by varying the duty cycle of the signal.

Concept	Description	Example
Digital Output	Using digitalWrite() to turn an LED on (HIGH) or off (LOW).	digitalWrite(13, HIGH);

PWM (Pulse Width Modulation)	Varying the brightness of the LED using analogWrite() to control the duty cycle.	analogWrite(9, 128); (50% brightness)
Fading LED	Gradually changing the LED brightness over time using a loop.	Fade from dim to bright using analogWrite() in a loop.
Multiple LEDs	Controlling more than one LED using an array or multiple digital pins.	digitalWrite(LED 1, HIGH); digitalWrite(LED 2, LOW);
LED Animation	Creating visual effects by turning LEDs on and off in patterns.	"Chase" effect or blinking in a specific order.

Basic Rules for Using LEDs

Rule	Correct Example	Incorrect Example
Use a current-limiting resistor to protect the LED from overcurrent.	Use a 220Ω resistor in series with the LED.	Connect the LED directly to the pin without a resistor.
Always connect the longer leg (anode) to the positive voltage.	Anode (longer leg) to 5V, cathode (shorter leg) to ground.	Reverse the LED connection.
PWM can control LED brightness, while digitalWrite() only turns it on/off.	analogWrite(9, 128); for 50% brightness.	digitalWrite(9, HIGH); (No brightness control with digitalWrite)
LEDs are typically connected to ground (cathode) or VCC (anode).	Anode to pin 9, cathode to ground with a resistor.	LED connected to ground and pin without proper orientation.

Syntax Table

SL	Function	Syntax/Example	Description
1	Turn LED on	`digitalWrite(pin, HIGH);`	Turns the LED connected to a pin on.
2	Turn LED off	`digitalWrite(pin, LOW);`	Turns the LED connected to a pin off.
3	Control LED brightness (PWM)	`analogWrite(pin, value);`	Varies the brightness of the LED connected to a PWM-capable pin.
4	Fade LED (gradual brightness change)	`analogWrite(pin, brightness);`	Gradually changes the brightness of an LED.

Syntax Explanation

1. Turn LED on

What is turning an LED on?
Using `digitalWrite()` with the HIGH argument turns the LED fully on, sending a 5V signal to the LED.
Syntax:
`digitalWrite(pin, HIGH);`

Example:
`digitalWrite(13, HIGH);`

Example Explanation:
This code turns the LED connected to pin 13 on by sending a HIGH signal to the pin. The LED will light up fully.

2. Turn LED off

What is turning an LED off?
Using `digitalWrite()` with the LOW argument turns the LED off, sending a 0V signal to the pin.

Syntax:
```
digitalWrite(pin, LOW);
```

Example:
```
digitalWrite(13, LOW);
```

Example Explanation:
This code turns the LED connected to pin 13 off by sending a LOW signal to the pin. The LED will stop emitting light.

3. Control LED brightness (PWM)

What is controlling LED brightness using PWM?
Using analogWrite(), you can adjust the brightness of the LED by varying the duty cycle. A value between 0 (off) and 255 (full brightness) determines how bright the LED will be.

Syntax:
```
analogWrite(pin, value);
```

Example:
```
analogWrite(9, 128);   // 50% brightness
```

Example Explanation:
This code sets the brightness of the LED connected to pin 9 to 50% (a value of 128). The analogWrite() function uses Pulse Width Modulation (PWM) to vary the brightness smoothly.

4. Fade LED (gradual brightness change)

What is fading an LED?
Fading an LED is achieved by gradually changing the brightness over time. This can be done by increasing or decreasing the PWM value in a loop.

Syntax:
```
analogWrite(pin, brightness);
```

Example:
```
for (int brightness = 0; brightness <= 255;
brightness++) {
  analogWrite(9, brightness);
```

```
  delay(10);  // Wait for 10 milliseconds
}
for (int brightness = 255; brightness >= 0; brightness-
-) {
  analogWrite(9, brightness);
  delay(10);  // Wait for 10 milliseconds
}
```

Example Explanation:
This code fades the LED connected to pin 9 by gradually increasing the brightness from 0 to 255 and then decreasing it back to 0. The `delay(10)` adds a short pause between each change to make the fade effect smooth.

Real-life Applications Project: LED Fade Effect

In this project, we will create an LED fade effect that smoothly transitions from dim to bright and back to dim. This is often used for visual effects in displays, lighting systems, and even decorations.

Required Components

Component	Description
LED	The light-emitting diode to be controlled.
Resistor (220Ω)	Used to limit current and protect the LED from damage.
Arduino Uno	Microcontroller to control the LED and generate PWM signals.
Breadboard	A tool for organizing and connecting components.
Jumper Wires	Used for connecting components to the Arduino.

Circuit Connection Table

Component	Pin Connection
LED	Anode to pin 9, Cathode to ground through a 220Ω resistor
Arduino Uno	5V to VCC, GND to GND

Project Code

```
int ledPin = 9;   // LED connected to PWM-
capable pin 9
int brightness = 0;   // Initial brightness
int fadeAmount = 5;   // Amount by which to
change brightness each loop

void setup() {
  pinMode(ledPin, OUTPUT);
}

void loop() {
  analogWrite(ledPin, brightness);   // Control
LED brightness

  brightness = brightness + fadeAmount;   //
Change brightness for next loop

  // Reverse the fading direction if the
brightness is at the limits
  if (brightness <= 0 || brightness >= 255) {
    fadeAmount = -fadeAmount;   // Reverse the
fade direction
  }

  delay(30);   // Wait for 30 milliseconds to
see the fade effect
}
```

Expected Results
The LED will gradually fade in from off (0 brightness) to full

brightness (255) and then fade out back to off. This process will repeat, creating a smooth fade-in and fade-out effect.

Chapter 40: Working with Servos with Arduino

Servos are motors that can be precisely controlled to move to specific positions. Unlike DC motors, which rotate continuously, servos have a limited range of motion, typically 0° to 180°. This makes them ideal for tasks like controlling the position of robotic arms, cameras, or steering mechanisms in RC vehicles. In this chapter, we'll explore how to use servos with Arduino to control their movement.

Key Concepts of Working with Servos

Servos are controlled by sending a Pulse Width Modulation (PWM) signal to the control wire. The Arduino provides an easy-to-use library (Servo.h) to control the angle of the servo based on the PWM signal. By adjusting the pulse width, you can command the servo to move to a specific position.

Concept	Description	Example
Servo Control	Using Servo.write() to set the servo's position between 0° and 180°.	myservo.write(90); (Moves to 90° position)
Servo Motor	A small motor that moves to a specified angle.	Standard servo with a 180° range.
PWM Signal	A signal used to control the angle of the servo motor.	Control pin receives PWM signal corresponding to the angle.
Servo Library	Servo.h is a built-in Arduino library for controlling servos.	#include <Servo.h>

Basic Rules for Using Servos

Rule	Correct Example	Incorrect Example
Always use a separate power source if controlling high-power servos.	Use 5V or 6V external power supply for large servos.	Power the servo directly from the Arduino board.
Make sure the servo is properly calibrated before use.	Move servo slowly to avoid mechanical stress.	Send large angle commands without calibration.
Only use PWM pins for servo control.	Connect servo to pin 9 for PWM control.	Use pin 2 for servo control, which is a non-PWM pin.
Use Servo.attach() to initialize the servo before controlling it.	myservo.attach(9);	Call myservo.write() without attaching the servo first.

Syntax Table

SL	Function	Syntax/Example	Description
1	Attach a servo to a pin	myservo.attach(pin);	Initializes the servo and associates it with a pin.
2	Set servo angle	myservo.write(angle);	Sets the servo to a specific angle (0-180 degrees).
3	Sweep servo continuously	myservo.write(90);	Moves servo to a specific angle (90° for center position).
4	Detach servo (optional)	myservo.detach();	Stops the servo from being controlled by the Arduino.

Syntax Explanation

1. Attach a Servo to a Pin

What is attaching a servo to a pin?
Before controlling the servo, you need to attach it to a specific pin on the Arduino using the `attach()` function. This function tells the Arduino which pin is used to send PWM signals to the servo.
Syntax:
```
myservo.attach(pin);
```

Example:
```
#include <Servo.h>

Servo myservo;   // Create a Servo object

void setup() {
    myservo.attach(9);   // Attach the servo to pin 9
}
```

Example Explanation:
This code initializes the servo and attaches it to pin 9 of the Arduino. From this point, you can use the `myservo.write()` function to control the servo's position. The `attach()` function ensures that the Arduino knows which pin is controlling the servo. It's important to attach the servo before using the `write()` function to move it.

2. Set Servo Angle

What is setting the servo angle?
After attaching the servo to a pin, you can set its position by specifying an angle between 0° and 180° using the `write()` function. This tells the servo to move to that angle. The servo will turn to that angle within its range of motion.
Syntax:
```
myservo.write(angle);
```

Example:
```
myservo.write(90);   // Move the servo to the 90°
position (center)
```

Example Explanation:
 In this code, the servo moves to the 90° position, which is typically the center of its range. The write(90) command sends a PWM signal to the servo to move it to this position. The servo will stop rotating when it reaches the target angle. This is a fundamental operation that can be used to position the servo accurately.

The servo will not spin continuously, it will only rotate from its current position to the angle specified. The movement will happen in one swift motion, depending on the speed of the servo.

3. Sweep Servo Continuously

What is sweeping a servo?
 Sweeping a servo means gradually moving it through its entire range of motion, typically from 0° to 180° and back. This can be done by incrementally changing the servo's position in a loop, creating a sweeping or oscillating motion.
Syntax:
```
myservo.write(angle);
```

Example:
```
#include <Servo.h>

Servo myservo;

void setup() {
   myservo.attach(9);
}

void loop() {
   for (int pos = 0; pos <= 180; pos++) {
     myservo.write(pos);   // Sweep the servo from 0° to
180°
```

```
    delay(15);  // Wait for the servo to reach the
position
    }
  for (int pos = 180; pos >= 0; pos--) {
    myservo.write(pos);  // Sweep the servo from 180°
to 0°
    delay(15);  // Wait for the servo to reach the
position
    }
}
```

Example Explanation:
 In this example, the servo motor is moved through its full range of motion (from 0° to 180°) using a for loop. The loop starts with pos = 0 and gradually increases pos until it reaches 180. The `myservo.write(pos)` command moves the servo to each of the incremented positions. After reaching 180°, the loop reverses, decreasing pos from 180° back down to 0°.

The `delay(15)` adds a small pause between each step to give the servo time to reach each new position. Without the delay, the servo could attempt to move too quickly for us to see the motion, making it appear as if it is not moving smoothly.

4. Detach Servo (Optional)

What is detaching a servo?
 You can stop the servo from being controlled by the Arduino by using the `detach()` function. This is useful when you no longer need to control the servo and want to free up the pin for other uses. The servo motor will not receive any more commands after being detached.
Syntax:
```
myservo.detach();
```

Example:
```
myservo.detach();  // Detach the servo from the control
pin
```

Example Explanation:

In this code, the detach() function stops the servo from being controlled by the Arduino, releasing the pin so it can be used for other purposes. Once detached, the servo motor will not respond to any further write() commands until it is re-attached using the attach() function.

This is a useful feature when you have multiple servos or devices that need to share pins, or when you want to conserve power after the servo is no longer needed.

Real-life Applications Project: Servo Arm Control

In this project, we will control the position of a robotic arm using a servo motor. This is a practical example of how servos can be used in robotics, automation, and hobby projects.

Required Components

Component	Description
Servo Motor	Used to control the movement of the robotic arm.
Arduino Uno	Microcontroller that controls the servo.
Potentiometer (optional)	Used to control the servo's angle manually.
Breadboard	Used for connecting components.
Jumper Wires	Used for connecting components to the Arduino.

Circuit Connection Table

Component	Pin Connection
Servo Motor	Control pin to pin 9, VCC to 5V, GND to GND
Arduino Uno	5V to VCC, GND to GND
Potentiometer (optional)	Middle pin to A0 (analog input), side pins to 5V and GND

Project Code

```
#include <Servo.h>

Servo myservo;  // Create a Servo object
int potPin = A0;  // Pin for potentiometer
int val = 0;  // Variable to store potentiometer value

void setup() {

  myservo.attach(9);  // Attach the servo to pin 9

}

void loop() {

  val = analogRead(potPin);              // Read
potentiometer value

  val = map(val, 0, 1023, 0, 180);       // Map the
potentiometer value to 0-180

  myservo.write(val);                    // Set servo to
the mapped value

  delay(15);                             // Wait for the
servo to reach the position

}
```

Expected Results

When you rotate the potentiometer, the servo motor will rotate accordingly. The potentiometer's position will directly control the angle of the servo, from 0° (fully counterclockwise) to 180° (fully clockwise). This project demonstrates how you can use a potentiometer to control the position of a robotic arm or any other servo-driven mechanism, providing you with real-time control over the servo's motion.

Chapter 41: Using DC Motors with Arduino

DC motors are one of the most common types of motors used in Arduino projects. These motors rotate in one direction when supplied with power and can be reversed by changing the polarity. DC motors are ideal for driving wheels, fans, and other mechanical devices. In this chapter, we'll explore how to control DC motors using Arduino and some of the key considerations when working with them.

Key Concepts of Using DC Motors

DC motors work by converting electrical energy into mechanical motion. The rotation speed of a DC motor is proportional to the voltage applied, and the direction of rotation is determined by the polarity of the voltage. Using an H-Bridge, you can easily control both the speed and direction of the motor.

Concept	Description	Example
Speed Control	Use PWM to control the speed of the motor.	analogWrite(motorPin, 128); (50% speed)
Direction Control	Reverse motor direction by changing polarity using an H-Bridge.	Change the logic on IN1 and IN2 pins in the H-Bridge circuit.
H-Bridge	An electronic circuit used to control the direction of the DC motor.	Using an H-Bridge to control motor direction.
PWM	Pulse Width Modulation is used for controlling the motor's speed.	analogWrite(motorPin, 255); (Full speed)

Basic Rules for Using DC Motors

Rule	Correct Example	Incorrect Example
Always use a motor driver or an H-Bridge to control motor direction.	Use L298N H-Bridge to control motor direction.	Connect motor directly to Arduino pins.
Provide sufficient power to the motor.	Use a separate power source for the motor.	Power motor directly from the Arduino.

Use PWM to control the motor speed for smoother operation.	analogWrite(motorPin, 128);	digitalWrite(motorPin, HIGH);
Ensure the motor can handle the load.	Choose a motor with appropriate torque for your application.	Use a motor without considering load requirements.

Syntax Table

SL	Function	Syntax/Example	Description
1	Set motor speed	analogWrite(motorPin, value);	Controls the motor's speed via PWM (value 0-255).
2	Change motor direction	digitalWrite(IN1, HIGH); digitalWrite(IN2, LOW);	Controls the motor direction using an H-Bridge.
3	Initialize motor driver	motorDriver.begin();	Initializes the motor driver for use.
4	Start motor	digitalWrite(motorPin, HIGH);	Turns the motor on (without speed control).

Syntax Explanation

1. Set Motor Speed

What is setting motor speed?
Motor speed can be controlled using PWM by sending a signal with varying duty cycles. The analogWrite() function allows you to send a PWM signal to a pin, where a value between 0 and 255 determines the speed. A value of 0 turns the motor off, and 255 runs it at full speed.
Syntax:
analogWrite(motorPin, value);

Example:
```
int motorPin = 9;
analogWrite(motorPin, 128);  // Set motor speed to 50%
(128 out of 255)
```

Example Explanation:
 In this example, the analogWrite() function sends a PWM signal to pin 9, setting the motor speed to 50% (128 out of 255). The value of 128 represents a 50% duty cycle, which results in the motor running at half speed. You can adjust this value from 0 (off) to 255 (full speed) to control the motor's speed.**2. Change Motor Direction**

What is changing motor direction?

 Motor direction is controlled by reversing the polarity of the voltage supplied to the motor. This is done by controlling the input pins of an H-Bridge circuit (such as the L298N motor driver). The two inputs (IN1 and IN2) determine whether the motor rotates clockwise or counterclockwise.
Syntax:
```
digitalWrite(IN1, HIGH);
digitalWrite(IN2, LOW);
```

Example:
```
int IN1 = 4;
int IN2 = 5;
digitalWrite(IN1, HIGH);  // Rotate motor clockwise
digitalWrite(IN2, LOW);
```

Example Explanation:
 In this code, by setting IN1 to HIGH and IN2 to LOW, the motor will rotate in one direction (clockwise). To reverse the direction, you would switch the values: IN1 = LOW and IN2 = HIGH. The direction of rotation can be changed depending on the logic applied to the H-Bridge's control pins.

3. Initialize Motor Driver

What is initializing the motor driver?
Before using the motor driver, you must initialize it in the `setup()` section of the code. This can be done using the `begin()` function of the motor driver object. Initialization prepares the driver to control the motor, ensuring that signals sent from the Arduino will be correctly processed.

Syntax:
```
motorDriver.begin();
```

Example:
```
#include <MotorDriver.h>

MotorDriver motorDriver;   // Create motor driver object

void setup() {
  motorDriver.begin();   // Initialize motor driver
}
```

Example Explanation:
In this example, the motor driver object is initialized with the `begin()` function. Once initialized, you can control the motor's speed and direction using the functions provided by the motor driver library. This step is crucial for setting up the motor driver for communication with the Arduino.

4. Start Motor

What is starting the motor?
To start the motor, you can send a `HIGH` signal to the motor pin, which will activate the motor. This is often used when you want to turn the motor on without controlling its speed using PWM. However, for speed control, you should use `analogWrite()`.

Syntax:
```
digitalWrite(motorPin, HIGH);
```

Example:

```
int motorPin = 9;
digitalWrite(motorPin, HIGH);   // Start the motor
```

Example Explanation:

In this example, the motor will start running when the `motorPin` is set to HIGH. This method turns the motor on, but to control its speed, you should use `analogWrite()` instead.

Real-life Applications Project: DC Motor Powered Vehicle

In this project, we will build a simple vehicle that is powered by two DC motors. The Arduino will control the direction and speed of the motors to move the vehicle forward, backward, and turn left or right.

Required Components

Component	Description
DC Motor (x2)	Motors used to drive the wheels of the vehicle.
Arduino Uno	Microcontroller for controlling the motors.
L298N Motor Driver	Motor driver to control the direction and speed of the motors.
Power Supply (9V or 12V)	Power source for the motors.
Jumper Wires	Wires for connecting the components to the Arduino.
DC Vehicle Chassis	Chassis to hold the motors and other components.

Circuit Connection Table

Component	Pin Connection
DC Motor 1	Motor pins connected to output pins of L298N motor driver
DC Motor 2	Motor pins connected to output pins of L298N motor driver
L298N IN1, IN2	Connected to Arduino pins 8 and 9 (for motor 1 direction control)
L298N IN3, IN4	Connected to Arduino pins 10 and 11 (for motor 2 direction control)

| L298N ENA, ENB | Connected to Arduino 5V or PWM pins for speed control |
| Power Supply (9V or 12V) | VCC to the motor driver and motors, GND to common ground |

Project Code

```
int motor1Pin1 = 8;
int motor1Pin2 = 9;
int motor2Pin1 = 10;
int motor2Pin2 = 11;
int enablePinA = 5;
int enablePinB = 6;

void setup() {
  pinMode(motor1Pin1, OUTPUT);
  pinMode(motor1Pin2, OUTPUT);
  pinMode(motor2Pin1, OUTPUT);
  pinMode(motor2Pin2, OUTPUT);
  pinMode(enablePinA, OUTPUT);
  pinMode(enablePinB, OUTPUT);
}

void loop() {
  // Move forward
  digitalWrite(motor1Pin1, HIGH);
  digitalWrite(motor1Pin2, LOW);
  digitalWrite(motor2Pin1, HIGH);
  digitalWrite(motor2Pin2,

 LOW);
  analogWrite(enablePinA, 255);  // Full speed for
motor 1
  analogWrite(enablePinB, 255);  // Full speed for
motor 2
  delay(2000);  // Move forward for 2 seconds

  // Stop
```

```
    digitalWrite(motor1Pin1, LOW);
    digitalWrite(motor1Pin2, LOW);
    digitalWrite(motor2Pin1, LOW);
    digitalWrite(motor2Pin2, LOW);
    delay(1000);  // Stop for 1 second

    // Move backward
    digitalWrite(motor1Pin1, LOW);
    digitalWrite(motor1Pin2, HIGH);
    digitalWrite(motor2Pin1, LOW);
    digitalWrite(motor2Pin2, HIGH);
    analogWrite(enablePinA, 255);  // Full speed for
motor 1
    analogWrite(enablePinB, 255);  // Full speed for
motor 2
    delay(2000);  // Move backward for 2 seconds

    // Stop
    digitalWrite(motor1Pin1, LOW);
    digitalWrite(motor1Pin2, LOW);
    digitalWrite(motor2Pin1, LOW);
    digitalWrite(motor2Pin2, LOW);
    delay(1000);  // Stop for 1 second
}
```

Expected Results

The DC motor-powered vehicle should move forward,
backward, and stop in a controlled manner based on the
logic in the code. The motors will rotate at full speed for a
set duration, and the vehicle should exhibit the expected
behaviors (forward and backward motion) when the code
runs.

Chapter 42: Controlling Stepper Motors with Arduino

Stepper motors are widely used in applications that require precise control of rotational position, such as robotics, CNC machines, and camera platforms. Unlike DC motors, which rotate continuously, stepper motors rotate in discrete steps, making them ideal for precise position control. In this chapter, we will explore how to control stepper motors using Arduino, including the basics of stepper motors, libraries, and various control techniques.

Key Concepts of Controlling Stepper Motors

A stepper motor divides a full rotation into a large number of steps, giving it precise control over its position. This is achieved by energizing different coils in a specific sequence. Stepper motors can be controlled in two main ways: **full-step mode** and **half-step mode**. In full-step mode, the motor takes a step in one full rotation, while in half-step mode, the motor takes smaller steps for finer control.

Concept	Description	Example
Full-Step Mode	Each step moves the motor by one full step.	`stepper.step(1);` (moves motor 1 step forward)
Half-Step Mode	The motor takes smaller steps, allowing for finer control.	`stepper.step(1);` (smaller increments per step)
Stepper Motor Driver	An electronic component used to control the stepper motor.	Use an **ULN2003** for controlling the motor.
Stepper Motor Control	The process of controlling the motor's speed, direction, and steps.	Use the `AccelStepper` library for smoother control.

Basic Rules for Using Stepper Motors

Rule	Correct Example	Incorrect Example
Use a motor driver to control the stepper motor.	Use ULN2003 driver to control motor.	Directly connect stepper motor to Arduino pins.
Specify the number of steps per revolution for proper control.	Set steps per revolution to 200 for a 1.8-degree motor.	Set incorrect steps, resulting in inaccurate positioning.
Use the Stepper library for basic control or AccelStepper for advanced control.	Stepper stepper(200, 8, 9, 10, 11);	Without a control library, controlling stepper becomes complex.
Adjust motor speed using setSpeed() function for smooth operation.	stepper.setSpeed(200);	Not setting the speed may result in jerky motor movement.

Syntax Table

SL	Function	Syntax/Example	Description
1	Initialize Stepper Motor	Stepper stepper(steps, pin1, pin2, pin3, pin4);	Initializes a stepper motor with the specified number of steps and pins.
2	Set Motor Speed	stepper.setSpeed(speed);	Sets the speed of the motor (in RPM).
3	Move Motor by a Specific Number of Steps	stepper.step(steps);	Moves the stepper motor by the specified number of steps.
4	Move Motor to Specific Position	stepper.step(steps);	Moves motor to a defined position in a given number of steps.

Syntax Explanation

1. Initialize Stepper Motor

What is initializing a stepper motor?
To use a stepper motor with Arduino, the first step is to initialize it using the `Stepper` library. This involves defining the motor's number of steps per revolution and specifying the pins used for controlling the motor.
Syntax:
```
Stepper stepper(steps, pin1, pin2, pin3, pin4);
```

Example:
```
#include <Stepper.h>

const int steps = 200;  // Number of steps per
revolution (typically 200 for 1.8° stepper motor)
Stepper stepper(steps, 8, 9, 10, 11);  // Pins
connected to the motor driver
```

Example Explanation:
In this example, we create a stepper motor object, specifying that the motor has 200 steps per revolution (1.8° per step) and that the motor is connected to pins 8, 9, 10, and 11. These pins control the stepper motor's coils.

2. Set Motor Speed

What is setting the motor speed?
The speed of the stepper motor is specified in revolutions per minute (RPM). By adjusting the speed, you can control how fast the motor moves. The `setSpeed()` function is used to set this speed.
Syntax:
```
stepper.setSpeed(speed);
```

Example:
```
stepper.setSpeed(60);  // Set motor speed to 60 RPM
```

Example Explanation:
Here, the motor speed is set to 60 RPM using
`stepper.setSpeed(60);`. This will make the motor rotate at a moderate speed. You can increase or decrease the speed based on the needs of your project.

3. Move Motor by a Specific Number of Steps

What is moving the motor by a specific number of steps?
The `step()` function is used to move the stepper motor by a specified number of steps. Each step corresponds to a specific angular movement of the motor. Positive values rotate the motor in one direction, while negative values rotate it in the opposite direction.
Syntax:
```
stepper.step(steps);
```

Example:
```
stepper.step(100);   // Move the motor forward by 100
steps
```

Example Explanation:
In this example, the motor will move forward by 100 steps. The number of steps corresponds to the amount of rotation. If the motor has 200 steps per revolution, 100 steps would rotate it by half a revolution.

4. Move Motor to Specific Position

What is moving the motor to a specific position?
By repeatedly using `step()` or `step()` with a defined number of steps, you can move the motor to a specific position. Combining these movements allows for precise control of the motor's position in applications like robotic arms or CNC machines.
Syntax:
```
stepper.step(steps);
```
Example:
```
stepper.step(50);   // Move the motor forward by 50
steps
```

Example Explanation:

This command moves the motor forward by 50 steps. You can use this approach to move the motor to a desired location by providing the appropriate number of steps.

Real-life Applications Project: Stepper Motor-Controlled 3D Printer

In this project, we will use stepper motors to build a basic 3D printer-like movement system. The stepper motors will control the X, Y, and Z axes to position the print bed or a nozzle.

Required Components

Component	Description
4-Stepper Motors	Motors used for controlling movement along the X, Y, and Z axes.
Arduino Uno	Microcontroller for controlling the motors.
ULN2003 Stepper Motor Driver	Driver used to control the stepper motors.
Power Supply (12V)	Provides power for the stepper motors.
Jumper Wires	For making the necessary connections.

Circuit Connection Table

Component	Pin Connection
Stepper Motor 1 (X-axis)	Connect motor to ULN2003 driver (pins IN1, IN2, IN3, IN4).
Stepper Motor 2 (Y-axis)	Connect motor to ULN2003 driver (pins IN5, IN6, IN7, IN8).
Stepper Motor 3 (Z-axis)	Connect motor to ULN2003 driver (pins IN9, IN10, IN11, IN12).
ULN2003 ENA, ENB	Connect to 5V or Arduino pin for speed control.
Power Supply (12V)	Connect to motor driver and motors.

Project Code

```c
#include <Stepper.h>
const int steps = 200;   // Steps per revolution for the
stepper motor
Stepper stepperX(steps, 8, 9, 10, 11);   // Motor 1 (X-
axis)
Stepper stepperY(steps, 12, 13, A0, A1);   // Motor 2
(Y-axis)
Stepper stepperZ(steps, A2, A3, A4, A5);   // Motor 3
(Z-axis)
void setup() {
  stepperX.setSpeed(60);   // Set speed for motor 1
  stepperY.setSpeed(60);   // Set speed for motor 2
  stepperZ.setSpeed(60);   // Set speed for motor 3
}
void loop() {
  stepperX.step(100);   // Move motor 1 (X-axis) 100
steps forward
  stepperY.step(
100);   // Move motor 2 (Y-axis) 100 steps forward
  stepperZ.step(100);   // Move motor 3 (Z-axis) 100
steps forward
  delay(1000);   // Wait for 1 second
  stepperX.step(-100);   // Move motor 1 (X-axis) 100
steps backward
  stepperY.step(-100);   // Move motor 2 (Y-axis) 100
steps backward
  stepperZ.step(-100);   // Move motor 3 (Z-axis) 100
steps backward
  delay(1000);   // Wait for 1 second
}
```

Expected Results

Upon running the code, the three stepper motors will move
sequentially along the X, Y, and Z axes. Each motor will rotate
forward by 100 steps, pause for 1 second, and then move backward
by 100 steps. The motors will move in unison, mimicking a simple
3D printer-like mechanism.

Chapter 43: Using Relays with Arduino

Relays are electrically operated switches used to control a high-power device with a low-power control signal, such as turning on a lamp or controlling the power to an appliance using an Arduino. In this chapter, we will explore how to use relays with Arduino, including the basics of how relays work, how to connect them, and examples of controlling high-power devices like motors, lights, or other electrical appliances.

Key Concepts of Using Relays

A relay works as an electrical switch that allows you to control a higher voltage circuit with a lower voltage signal. Arduino can be used to control the relay with its digital outputs, which in turn controls the power supply to connected high-power devices.

Concept	Description	Example
Relay Coil	The part of the relay that is energized to activate the switch.	5V is used to energize the relay coil.
Relay Switch	The switch inside the relay that opens or closes to control current.	NO (Normally Open) contacts close when energized.
NO and NC Contacts	**NO (Normally Open)** allows current when energized, **NC** works when not energized.	You can use NO for turning a device on and NC for turning it off.
Relay Driver	Used to interface a low-power microcontroller with a high-power relay.	Use a transistor or driver IC for controlling the relay.

Basic Rules for Using Relays

Rule	Correct Example	Incorrect Example
Use a transistor to drive the relay coil if needed.	`Use a transistor (e.g., 2N2222) to drive the relay.`	`Directly connect relay to Arduino pin without a transistor.`

Make sure to use a diode across the relay coil to protect the circuit from back EMF.	Use a diode (e.g., 1N4007) across the relay coil.	Do not use a diode, which may cause damage due to back EMF.
Ensure the relay's voltage and current ratings are appropriate for the device you are controlling.	Choose a relay with the appropriate voltage and current ratings.	Using a low-rated relay can cause overheating or failure.
Use the digitalWrite() function to control the relay.	digitalWrite(relayPin, HIGH);	analogWrite(relayPin, 255); (This is for PWM signals, not relays.)

Syntax Table

SL	Function	Syntax/Example	Description
1	Set relay pin as OUTPUT	pinMode(relayPin, OUTPUT);	Initializes the relay control pin as an output.
2	Turn on relay (close switch)	digitalWrite (relayPin, HIGH);	Energizes the relay, closing the switch to allow current.
3	Turn off relay (open switch)	digitalWrite (relayPin, LOW);	De-energizes the relay, opening the switch to stop current.
4	Control relay with delay	delay(1000);	Pauses the program, allowing the relay to stay on/off for a set time.

Syntax Explanation
1. Set Relay Pin as OUTPUT
What is setting the relay pin as an output?
 Before controlling the relay, you need to set the pin connected to the relay as an output pin using the pinMode() function. This allows the Arduino to send a HIGH or LOW signal to control the relay.
Syntax:
pinMode(relayPin, OUTPUT);

Example:
```
const int relayPin = 7;  // Pin to control the relay
pinMode(relayPin, OUTPUT);  // Set relayPin as output
```

Example Explanation:
 In this example, we declare `relayPin` as pin 7 and use `pinMode()` to set it as an output. This is essential because we need to control the relay by sending HIGH and LOW signals to the relay pin.

2. Turn on Relay (Close Switch)

What does turning on the relay do?
 When you send a HIGH signal to the relay pin, it energizes the relay coil, closing the internal switch and allowing current to flow to the connected device.

Syntax:
```
digitalWrite(relayPin, HIGH);
```

Example:
```
digitalWrite(relayPin, HIGH);  // Turn on relay, close
the switch
```

Example Explanation:
 In this example, we use `digitalWrite(relayPin, HIGH)` to energize the relay. This closes the switch, allowing power to flow to the connected device, such as a motor or lamp.

3. Turn off Relay (Open Switch)

What does turning off the relay do?
 Sending a LOW signal to the relay pin de-energizes the relay coil, causing the internal switch to open and stop the current from flowing to the device.

Syntax:
```
digitalWrite(relayPin, LOW);
```

Example:
```
digitalWrite(relayPin, LOW);  // Turn off relay, open
the switch
```

Example Explanation:
Here, we use `digitalWrite(relayPin, LOW)` to turn off the relay, which opens the switch and disconnects the power to the connected device.

4. Control Relay with Delay

What does using a delay do?
The `delay()` function allows you to keep the relay in its current state (on or off) for a specified period of time. This is useful if you want the relay to stay on for a specific amount of time before turning it off or vice versa.

Syntax:
```
delay(milliseconds);
```

Example:
```
digitalWrite(relayPin, HIGH);  // Turn on relay
delay(2000);  // Wait for 2 seconds
digitalWrite(relayPin, LOW);  // Turn off relay
```

Example Explanation:
In this example, the relay is turned on for 2 seconds (`delay(2000)`) and then turned off. This simple delay ensures the relay stays on for a fixed period before turning off.

Real-life Applications Project: Home Automation System

In this project, we will use a relay to control a lamp from an Arduino, demonstrating how to turn on/off household appliances remotely.

Required Components

Component	Description
Relay Module	Used to control a high-power appliance like a lamp or fan.
Arduino Uno	Microcontroller used for controlling the relay.
Lamp or Fan	The appliance to be controlled via the relay.
Diode (1N4007)	Used to protect the circuit from back EMF generated by the relay coil.
Jumper Wires	For connecting components together.
Power Source (AC or DC)	Power supply for the relay-controlled appliance.

Circuit Connection Table

Component	Pin Connection
Relay Module	VCC to 5V, GND to GND, IN pin to Arduino digital pin (e.g., Pin 7)
Lamp or Fan	Connect to Normally Open (NO) and Common (COM) terminals of the relay.
Diode (1N4007)	Connect across relay coil (anode to GND, cathode to VCC).
Arduino Uno	Connect digital pin (e.g., Pin 7) to relay IN pin.

Project Code

```
const int relayPin = 7;  // Relay control pin

void setup() {
  pinMode(relayPin, OUTPUT);  // Set relayPin as output
}

void loop() {
  digitalWrite(relayPin, HIGH);  // Turn on relay (lamp
or fan)
  delay(2000);  // Keep the appliance on for 2 seconds
  digitalWrite(relayPin, LOW);  // Turn off relay
  delay(2000);  // Wait for 2 seconds before the next
cycle
}
```

Expected Results

When the code is uploaded to the Arduino, the relay will energize and de-energize every 2 seconds, turning the connected lamp or fan on and off in a repeating cycle. The appliance will stay on for 2 seconds, then off for 2 seconds, demonstrating basic relay control.

Chapter 44: LCD Displays with Arduino

LCD (Liquid Crystal Display) screens are commonly used in Arduino projects to display text, numbers, or even graphics. This chapter will guide you through using LCD displays with Arduino, including how to connect them, how to send data to them, and examples of practical applications.

Key Concepts of LCD Displays

LCD displays are widely used because they can show text and numeric data without requiring an external monitor or computer. They are often used in projects like digital clocks, thermometers, or information displays.

Concept	Description	Example
Pins	The number of pins on the LCD display that need to be connected to the Arduino.	Most common LCDs use 16 pins, including power, ground, and data pins.
Backlight	Provides illumination to the LCD screen for better visibility.	Can be controlled through a pin, turning it on or off.
Commands	Instructions to control the display, such as clearing the screen or moving the cursor.	lcd.clear(), lcd.setCursor(0, 0)
Data	The actual text or data to be displayed.	lcd.print("Hello World");

Basic Rules for Using LCDs

Rule	Correct Example	Incorrect Example
Use the correct library for LCD communication.	#include <LiquidCrystal.h>	#include <LCD.h> (incorrect library)
Ensure the correct wiring between the Arduino and LCD.	Connect pin 12, 11, 5, 4, 3, 2 for a 16x2 LCD display.	Connect random pins, which might cause the display to malfunction.

Initialize the LCD properly before using it.	lcd.begin(16, 2);	lcd.begin(); (missing parameters)
Use lcd.print() to send text to the display.	lcd.print("Hello World");	lcd.print(123); (this is valid, but it's good practice to be explicit)

Syntax Table

SL	Function	Syntax/Example	Description
1	Initialize the LCD display	lcd.begin(16, 2);	Initializes the LCD with specified column and row dimensions.
2	Set cursor position	lcd.setCursor(0, 0);	Sets the cursor to a specified column and row on the display.
3	Print text to the display	lcd.print("Text");	Prints text or data to the display.
4	Clear the display	lcd.clear();	Clears the screen, making it ready for new text.
5	Turn on/off backlight	lcd.noBacklight() ; / lcd.backlight();	Controls the backlight of the LCD display.

Syntax Explanation
1. Initialize the LCD display
What does initializing the LCD do?
Before you can use the LCD, you must initialize it with the number of columns and rows it has. For example, a common 16x2 LCD has 16 columns and 2 rows.

Syntax:
```
lcd.begin(16, 2);
```
Example:
```
#include <LiquidCrystal.h>
LiquidCrystal lcd(12, 11, 5, 4, 3, 2);
void setup() {
  lcd.begin(16, 2);  // Initialize a 16x2 LCD
}
```

Example Explanation:
Here, `lcd.begin(16, 2)` initializes the LCD with 16 columns and 2 rows. This step must be done in the `setup()` function to ensure the display is ready for use.

2. Set cursor position

What does setting the cursor position do?
You can move the cursor to any position on the screen using the `setCursor()` function. The first parameter specifies the column (horizontal position), and the second parameter specifies the row (vertical position).
Syntax:
```
lcd.setCursor(column, row);
```

Example:
```
lcd.setCursor(0, 0);   // Move cursor to the first
column, first row
lcd.print("Hello World");
```

Example Explanation:
In this example, `lcd.setCursor(0, 0)` moves the cursor to the first column (0) of the first row (0). Then, `lcd.print("Hello World")` displays "Hello World" starting from that position.

3. Print text to the display

What does printing text do?
To display text or numbers on the LCD, you can use the `print()` function. This function will send the string or numeric data to the LCD, starting from the current cursor position.
Syntax:
```
lcd.print("text or number");
```
Example:
```
lcd.print("Temperature: 25C");
```
Example Explanation:
This example displays the text "Temperature: 25C" on the LCD screen. The text will appear at the current cursor position.

4. Clear the display

What does clearing the display do?
If you need to clear the screen and start fresh, you can use the `clear()` function. It removes all content currently displayed on the LCD.

Syntax:
```
lcd.clear();
```

Example:
```
lcd.clear();  // Clears the display screen
```

Example Explanation:
Calling `lcd.clear()` will erase any text or numbers currently displayed on the LCD. This is useful if you want to reset the display before printing new information.

5. Turn on/off backlight

What does controlling the backlight do?
Some LCDs have a backlight that you can turn on or off to save power or to control the visibility of the display.

Syntax:
```
lcd.backlight();    // Turn on backlight
lcd.noBacklight(); // Turn off backlight
```

Example:
```
lcd.backlight();   // Turn on backlight
lcd.noBacklight(); // Turn off backlight
```

Example Explanation:
The `backlight()` function turns the LCD's backlight on, while `noBacklight()` turns it off. These functions help in controlling the power consumption and visibility of the display.

Real-life Applications Project: Digital Thermometer Display

In this project, we will use an LCD display to show the temperature measured by a temperature sensor (e.g., LM35 or DHT11). The LCD will show the temperature in Celsius and Fahrenheit.

Required Components

Component	Description
16x2 LCD Display	Used to display temperature readings.
LM35 Temperature Sensor	Sensor that outputs an analog voltage corresponding to temperature.
Arduino Uno	Microcontroller for reading sensor data and controlling the LCD.
10k Ohm Potentiometer	Used for adjusting contrast of the LCD.
Jumper Wires	For connecting components.

Circuit Connection Table

Component	Pin Connection
16x2 LCD Display	VCC to 5V, GND to GND, SDA to A4, SCL to A5 (for I2C LCD)
LM35 Temperature Sensor	VCC to 5V, GND to GND, Analog Pin A0 to Output Pin of LM35
Arduino Uno	Connect I2C pins or digital pins (based on LCD type)

Project Code

```
#include <LiquidCrystal_I2C.h>  // Include LCD library
for I2C
LiquidCrystal_I2C lcd(0x27, 16, 2);  // Initialize LCD,
16 columns, 2 rows

const int tempPin = A0;  // LM35 sensor connected to
analog pin A0

void setup() {
  lcd.begin(16, 2);  // Initialize the LCD
  lcd.backlight();    // Turn on the LCD backlight
```

```
  lcd.setCursor(0, 0);  // Set cursor to first row,
first column
  lcd.print("Temperature:");
}

void loop() {
  int tempReading = analogRead(tempPin);  // Read
analog value from LM35
  float voltage = tempReading * 5.0 / 1024.0;  //
Convert to voltage
  float temperatureC = voltage * 100;  // Convert
voltage to Celsius
  float temperatureF = (temperatureC * 9.0 / 5.0) + 32;
// Convert to Fahrenheit

  lcd.setCursor(0, 1);  // Set cursor to second row
  lcd.print("C: ");
  lcd.print(temperatureC);
  lcd.print(" F: ");
  lcd.print(temperatureF);

  delay(1000);  // Wait for 1 second before updating
}
```

Expected Results

After uploading the code to the Arduino, the LCD will display the current temperature in both Celsius and Fahrenheit. The display will update every second with the new temperature reading.

Chapter 45: OLED and TFT Displays with Arduino

OLED (Organic Light Emitting Diode) and TFT (Thin-Film Transistor) displays are becoming increasingly popular in Arduino projects for their ability to display high-quality text, images, and graphics. This chapter will guide you on how to use both OLED and TFT displays with Arduino, including wiring, programming, and real-life applications.

Key Concepts of OLED and TFT Displays

OLED and TFT displays are capable of showing detailed information with great clarity. While OLEDs are known for their vibrant colors and high contrast, TFT displays are popular for their ability to display full-color graphics and higher resolution.

Concept	Description	Example
OLED	Organic LED screens that offer high contrast, brightness, and color.	Typically use I2C or SPI communication with Arduino.
TFT	Color displays that are capable of showing full-color graphics.	Generally use SPI communication with Arduino.
Resolutio n	Refers to the number of pixels on the display.	Common resolutions are 128x64 for OLED and 320x240 for TFT.
Commun ication Protocol	OLED often uses I2C or SPI, while TFT uses SPI for faster data transfer.	I2C is simpler to wire, while SPI offers faster data transfer.

Basic Rules for Using OLED and TFT Displays

Rule	Correct Example	Incorrect Example
Choose the correct display library for the display type.	#include <Adafruit_SSD1 306.h> (for OLED)	#include <Adafruit_TFT.h> (for OLED display)
Use the correct wiring for I2C or SPI.	SDA to A4, SCL to A5 for I2C OLED	Connecting I2C pins to wrong pins or improper power supply.

Initialize the display in the setup() function.	display.begin(SSD1306_I2C_AD DRESS, OLED_RESET);	Forgetting to initialize display (display.begin())
Use display.print() to send text or graphics to the display.	display.print("Hello World!");	display.write("He llo World!");

Syntax Table

SL	Function	Syntax/Example	Description
1	Initialize OLED or TFT	display.begin(SSD1306_I2C_AD DRESS, OLED_RESET);	Initializes the OLED or TFT display, specifying address and reset pin.
2	Set cursor position	display.setCur sor(x, y);	Sets the position on the screen where text will begin.
3	Print text to the display	display.print("Hello World!");	Prints the specified text at the current cursor position.
4	Draw shapes (TFT)	tft.fillRect(x , y, width, height, color);	Draws shapes like rectangles or circles on the TFT screen.
5	Clear the display	display.clearD isplay();	Clears the display before printing new information.

Syntax Explanation

1. Initialize OLED or TFT display

What does initializing the display do?
Before any data can be shown on the screen, you need to initialize the display using the appropriate library and communication protocol (I2C or SPI).
Syntax:
```
display.begin(SSD1306_I2C_ADDRESS, OLED_RESET);
```

Example:

```
#include <Wire.h>
#include <Adafruit_SSD1306.h>
Adafruit_SSD1306 display(128, 64, &Wire, -1);

void setup() {
  display.begin(SSD1306_I2C_ADDRESS, OLED_RESET);  //
Initializes the OLED
  display.display();  // Updates the display
}
```

Example Explanation:
In this example, `display.begin()` initializes the OLED screen with a specific I2C address and reset pin. Once initialized, `display.display()` ensures the display is updated and ready to show content.

2. Set cursor position

What does setting the cursor position do?
Setting the cursor position determines where text will appear on the screen. The coordinates (x, y) correspond to the horizontal (x) and vertical (y) positions on the display.

Syntax:
```
display.setCursor(x, y);
```

Example:
```
display.setCursor(0, 0);  // Set the cursor to the top-
left corner
display.print("Hello, Arduino!");
```

Example Explanation:
Here, the cursor is placed at position (0, 0), which is the top-left corner of the screen. The text "Hello, Arduino!" is then printed at this position.

3. Print text to the display

What does printing text to the display do?
To display text, you use the `print()` function. This function can be used to display strings, numbers, or other data types.
Syntax:
```
display.print("text or data");
```

Example:
```
display.print("Temperature: 25C");
```

Example Explanation:
This will print the text "Temperature: 25C" at the current cursor position. The display will automatically update once the text is printed.

4. Draw shapes (TFT specific)

What does drawing shapes do?
With TFT displays, you can draw basic shapes like rectangles, circles, and lines. These are useful for creating graphical user interfaces or visualizations.
Syntax:
```
tft.fillRect(x, y, width, height, color);
```

Example:
```
tft.fillRect(10, 10, 50, 30, ILI9341_RED);  // Draw a
red rectangle
```

Example Explanation:
This example draws a filled red rectangle with the top-left corner at (`10, 10`), a width of 50 pixels, and a height of 30 pixels. The color is defined by the `ILI9341_RED` constant.

5. Clear the display

What does clearing the display do?
To refresh the screen and remove previous content, you use the
clearDisplay() function.
Syntax:
```
display.clearDisplay();
```

Example:
```
display.clearDisplay();  // Clears the screen
```

Example Explanation:
This clears any text or graphics on the display, making it ready for
new content to be shown.

Real-life Applications Project: Graphical Data Display
In this project, we will use a TFT display to show real-time data,
such as a sensor reading, graphically. The display will show both
numerical values and graphs to visualize data.

Required Components

Component	Description
TFT Display	A color screen used to display graphical data.
Arduino Uno	Microcontroller to read data and control the TFT display.
Analog Sensor (e.g., Potentiometer)	Sensor for testing the display with real-time data.
Jumper Wires	For making the necessary connections.

Circuit Connection Table

Component	Pin Connection
TFT Display	VCC to 5V, GND to GND, CS to pin 10, RESET to pin 9, DC to pin 8, SCK to pin 13, MOSI to pin 11
Analog Sensor	VCC to 5V, GND to GND, Output to analog pin A0
Arduino Uno	Connect necessary pins to the corresponding TFT pins

Project Code

```
#include <Adafruit_GFX.h>
#include <Adafruit_ILI9341.h>
#define TFT_CS     10
#define TFT_RST    9
#define TFT_DC     8
Adafruit_ILI9341 tft = Adafruit_ILI9341(TFT_CS,
TFT_RST, TFT_DC);
const int sensorPin = A0;
void setup() {
  tft.begin();
  tft.setRotation(3);   // Adjust screen rotation if
necessary
  tft.fillScreen(ILI9341_BLACK);   // Set background
color to black
  tft.setTextColor(ILI9341_WHITE);   // Set text color
to white
  tft.setTextSize(1);   // Set text size
}
void loop() {
  int sensorValue = analogRead(sensorPin);   // Read
sensor data
  float voltage = sensorValue * (5.0 / 1023.0);   //
Convert to voltage
  tft.setCursor(10, 10);
  tft.print("Sensor Value: ");
  tft.println(sensorValue);
  tft.setCursor(10, 30);
  tft.print("Voltage: ");
  tft.print(voltage);
  delay(500);
}
```

Expected Results

After uploading the code to the Arduino, the TFT screen will display
the real-time sensor value and its corresponding voltage. The
display will be updated every 500 milliseconds with the latest data.

Chapter 46: Buzzer and Speaker Output with Arduino

Buzzers and speakers are common components used in Arduino projects to provide audio feedback. They can be used to indicate different states, generate sounds or melodies, or create alarms. This chapter will cover how to use buzzers and speakers with Arduino, including wiring, programming, and real-life applications.

Key Concepts of Buzzer and Speaker Output

Buzzers and speakers are both used to generate sound, but they operate differently. A buzzer typically produces a constant or pulsed tone, while a speaker can generate more complex sound patterns, including music and other audio effects.

Concept	Description	Example
Buzzer	A simple component that produces a sound when powered.	Typically used for alarms, notifications, or beeps.
Speaker	A component capable of producing more complex sounds, including tones and music.	Often used for playing melodies, music, or sound effects.
Frequency	The pitch of the sound produced, controlled by the duration of the ON/OFF cycles.	Higher frequencies = higher-pitched sounds.
Pulse Width Modulation (PWM)	Used to control the intensity or volume of the sound produced by a buzzer or speaker.	Control the volume by adjusting the duty cycle in PWM.

Basic Rules for Using Buzzers and Speakers

Rule	Correct Example	Incorrect Example
Use `tone()` function to generate sound from a speaker.	`tone(8, 1000);`	`tone(8);` (missing frequency)

Use noTone() to stop sound from a buzzer or speaker.	noTone(8);	Forgetting to stop the tone when it's no longer needed.
Set PWM value for controlling the volume of the sound.	analogWrite(9, 128);	Using digitalWrite() for volume control, which is incorrect.
Use the correct pin for generating a tone.	tone(8, 500);	tone(13, 500); (pin 13 might not work with tone() on some boards)

Syntax Table

SL	Function	Syntax/Example	Description
1	Generate tone	tone(pin, frequency);	Generates a tone at the specified frequency on the given pin.
2	Stop tone	noTone(pin);	Stops the tone on the specified pin.
3	Control sound intensity	analogWrite(pin, value);	Controls the intensity of the sound with PWM on specified pin.
4	Play melody (sequence of tones)	tone(pin, melody[n]); delay(duration[n]);	Plays a sequence of notes or melody with delays.

Syntax Explanation

1. Generate tone

What does generating a tone do?
The tone() function generates a square wave of the specified frequency on a pin. This can create sounds at different pitches. The frequency is given in Hertz (Hz), and the sound will continue until you stop it using noTone().

Syntax:
tone(pin, frequency);

Example:
tone(8, 1000); // Generate a 1000 Hz tone on pin 8

Example Explanation:
This will generate a 1000 Hz tone on pin 8. The tone will continue indefinitely until the `noTone()` function is called.

2. Stop tone

What does stopping a tone do?
The `noTone()` function stops the tone being played on the specified pin.
Syntax:
```
noTone(pin);
```

Example:
```
noTone(8);   // Stops the tone on pin 8
```

Example Explanation:
This stops any tone currently being played on pin 8. If you want to stop a tone after it has played for a while, you would call `noTone()` within the `loop()` or after a specified delay.

3. Control sound intensity

What does controlling sound intensity do?
Using `analogWrite()` with PWM allows you to control the volume of the sound produced by a buzzer or speaker. The value you provide (0 to 255) controls the intensity, with 0 being silent and 255 being full volume.
Syntax:
```
analogWrite(pin, value);
```

Example:
```
analogWrite(9, 128);   // Set 50% intensity on pin 9
```

Example Explanation:
This example adjusts the sound intensity. A value of 128 results in 50% intensity, while 255 would result in the maximum volume.

4. Play melody (sequence of tones)

What does playing a melody do?
You can create a melody by generating multiple tones at different frequencies with delays in between. This allows you to play a song or sound sequence on a buzzer or speaker.

Syntax:
```
tone(pin, melody[n]);
delay(duration[n]);
```

Example:
```
int melody[] = {262, 294, 330, 349, 392, 440, 494};
int duration[] = {500, 500, 500, 500, 500, 500, 500};

for (int i = 0; i < 7; i++) {
  tone(8, melody[i]);
  delay(duration[i]);
  noTone(8);
}
```

Example Explanation:
This example plays a melody using an array of frequencies (melody[]) and their corresponding durations (duration[]). The tone() function generates each note, and delay() controls the timing between each note.

Real-life Applications Project: Melody Player

In this project, we will use a speaker to play a melody on the Arduino. The melody will be stored in an array and played by cycling through it in a loop.

Required Components

Component	Description
Buzzer or Speaker	To output sound or melody.
Arduino Uno	Microcontroller for controlling the buzzer or speaker.
Jumper Wires	For making necessary connections.

Circuit Connection Table

Component	Pin Connection
Buzzer or Speaker	Positive lead to pin 8, Negative lead to GND
Arduino Uno	Pin 8 connected to the positive lead of the buzzer/speaker

Project Code

```
int melody[] = {262, 294, 330, 349, 392, 440, 494};
int duration[] = {500, 500, 500, 500, 500, 500, 500};

void setup() {
  pinMode(8, OUTPUT);   // Set pin 8 as output
}

void loop() {
  for (int i = 0; i < 7; i++) {
    tone(8, melody[i]);   // Play the current note
    delay(duration[i]);   // Wait for the duration of
the note
    noTone(8);            // Stop the tone
    delay(50);            // Wait a bit before the next
note
  }
  delay(1000);   // Wait before repeating the melody
}
```

Expected Results

After uploading the code to the Arduino, the speaker will play a melody in sequence, starting with a 262 Hz note and moving up the scale. Each note will play for 500 milliseconds, with a brief pause between notes.

Chapter 47: Using RGB LEDs with Arduino

RGB LEDs are popular components in Arduino projects, providing the ability to display a wide range of colors by mixing red, green, and blue light. By adjusting the brightness of each individual color, you can create custom colors and dynamic light patterns. In this chapter, we'll explore how to use RGB LEDs with Arduino, including wiring, programming, and real-life applications.

Key Concepts of RGB LEDs

An RGB LED combines three LEDs (red, green, and blue) into one unit. Each LED can be controlled independently to generate different colors by varying the intensity of each light source.

Concept	Description	Example
RGB LED	An LED that combines red, green, and blue lights in one package.	Can produce any color by mixing RGB components.
PWM	Pulse Width Modulation controls the brightness of each color.	Adjusting PWM values determines color intensity.
Common Anode	The common leg is connected to the positive supply.	Typically used with positive voltage control.
Common Cathode	The common leg is connected to ground.	Typically used with negative voltage control.

Basic Rules for Using RGB LEDs

Rule	Correct Example	Incorrect Example
Use PWM for controlling color intensity.	`analogWrite(9, 255);`	`digitalWrite(9, 255);` (doesn't provide smooth control)

Ensure correct wiring.	Connect red, green, and blue pins to PWM pins.	Incorrect pin assignments causing color malfunction.
Adjust brightness with PWM.	analogWrite(9, 128);	Using digitalWrite() for brightness control.

Syntax Table

SL	Function	Syntax/Example	Description
1	Set PWM value for color	analogWrite(pin, value);	Controls the brightness of the LED on the specified pin.
2	Change color using PWM	analogWrite(redPin, value); analogWrite(greenPin, value); analogWrite(bluePin, value);	Adjusts RGB components to create a color.
3	Turn off RGB LED	analogWrite(redPin, 0); analogWrite(greenPin, 0); analogWrite(bluePin, 0);	Turns off all LEDs by setting PWM to 0.
4	Create a color pattern	analogWrite(redPin, 255); analogWrite(greenPin, 0); analogWrite(bluePin, 255);	Creates purple by adjusting red and blue.

Syntax Explanation

1. Set PWM Value for Color

What does setting a PWM value do?
The `analogWrite()` function adjusts the intensity of each color channel (red, green, and blue) on the RGB LED. PWM allows you to set a value between 0 (off) and 255 (full brightness) for each color.
Syntax:
```
analogWrite(pin, value);
```
Example:
```
analogWrite(9, 255);  // Full brightness on pin 9
```

Example Explanation:
This sets the brightness of pin 9 (where the RGB LED is connected) to its maximum value, making the color fully bright.

2. Change Color Using PWM

What does changing the color using PWM do?
By adjusting the individual PWM values for red, green, and blue, you can create a wide range of colors. For example, setting the red channel to full brightness (255), green to zero (0), and blue to half brightness (128) will create a yellow color.
Syntax:
```
analogWrite(redPin, value);
analogWrite(greenPin, value);
analogWrite(bluePin, value);
```

Example:
```
analogWrite(9, 255);   // Red at full brightness
analogWrite(10, 0);    // Green off
analogWrite(11, 128);  // Blue at half brightness
```

Example Explanation:
This creates a mix of red and blue light, which results in purple. You can adjust these values to experiment with different colors.

3. Turn Off RGB LED

What does turning off the RGB LED do?
By setting the PWM values to zero for each color channel, the RGB
LED turns off, effectively producing no light.
Syntax:
```
analogWrite(redPin, 0);
analogWrite(greenPin, 0);
analogWrite(bluePin, 0);
```

Example:
```
analogWrite(9, 0);  // Turn off red
analogWrite(10, 0); // Turn off green
analogWrite(11, 0); // Turn off blue
```

Example Explanation:

This completely turns off the RGB LED by setting the intensity of all
color components to zero.

4. Create a Color Pattern

What does creating a color pattern do?
Using analogWrite(), you can create dynamic patterns by altering
the color values over time, such as a fading effect or a moving light
pattern.
Syntax:
```
analogWrite(redPin, value);
analogWrite(greenPin, value);
analogWrite(bluePin, value);
```

Example:
```
analogWrite(9, 255); // Red at full brightness
analogWrite(10, 0);  // Green off
analogWrite(11, 255); // Blue at full brightness
```
Example Explanation:
This code produces a purple light by setting the red and blue
channels to full brightness and turning off the green.

Real-life Applications Project: RGB LED Mood Light

In this project, we will use an RGB LED to create a mood light that changes colors based on the time of day, cycling through red, green, and blue.

Required Components

Component	Description
RGB LED	Used to display colors.
Arduino Uno	Microcontroller for controlling the RGB LED.
Jumper Wires	For making necessary connections.

Circuit Connection Table

Component	Pin Connection
RGB LED	Red -> Pin 9, Green -> Pin 10, Blue -> Pin 11, Common pin to GND
Arduino Uno	Pin 9, Pin 10, Pin 11 connected to the RGB LED pins

Project Code

```
void setup() {
  pinMode(9, OUTPUT);  // Red pin
  pinMode(10, OUTPUT); // Green pin
  pinMode(11, OUTPUT); // Blue pin
}

void loop() {
  // Red color
  analogWrite(9, 255);  // Red at full brightness
  analogWrite(10, 0);   // Green off
  analogWrite(11, 0);   // Blue off
  delay(1000);          // Wait for 1 second
```

```
// Green color
analogWrite(9, 0);     // Red off
analogWrite(10, 255); // Green at full brightness
analogWrite(11, 0);    // Blue off
delay(1000);           // Wait for 1 second

// Blue color
analogWrite(9, 0);     // Red off
analogWrite(10, 0);    // Green off
analogWrite(11, 255); // Blue at full brightness
delay(1000);           // Wait for 1 second
}
```

Expected Results

After uploading the code, the RGB LED will cycle through red, green, and blue colors every second. This creates a dynamic mood light that continuously changes colors.

Chapter 48: Bluetooth with Arduino

Bluetooth modules are commonly used in Arduino projects for wireless communication. By connecting a Bluetooth module like the HC-05 or HC-06 to an Arduino, you can send and receive data wirelessly, making it perfect for remote control projects, home automation, and data transfer applications. In this chapter, we'll cover how to use Bluetooth with Arduino, including wiring, programming, and real-life applications.

Key Concepts of Bluetooth with Arduino

Bluetooth allows for wireless data transmission between devices. The most common Bluetooth modules for Arduino are the HC-05 (for master/slave communication) and HC-06 (for slave communication). These modules are used to establish a wireless connection between the Arduino and Bluetooth-enabled devices like smartphones or computers.

Concept	Description	Example
Bluetooth Module	A module that enables wireless communication over Bluetooth.	HC-05, HC-06 are common Bluetooth modules used with Arduino.
Serial Communication	Used to send and receive data between the Arduino and Bluetooth.	Data is sent over pins TX (Transmit) and RX (Receive).
Master/Slave	Bluetooth modules can work in master (controller) or slave (receiver) mode.	HC-05 can work in both modes, while HC-06 is typically a slave.

Basic Rules for Using Bluetooth with Arduino

Rule	Correct Example	Incorrect Example
Pair your Bluetooth module with the	Use `Serial.begin(9600);` for communication.	Forgetting to initialize serial communication.

Arduino.		
Use correct pins for TX/RX communication.	Connect TX to RX and RX to TX between the Arduino and Bluetooth module.	Reversing TX and RX connections.
Control Bluetooth connection using AT commands.	Send AT commands to configure module settings.	Forgetting to switch the Bluetooth module to AT mode.

Syntax Table

SL	Function	Syntax/Example	Description
1	Start Serial Communication	`Serial.begin(9600);`	Initializes the serial communication at 9600 baud rate.
2	Send Data Over Bluetooth	`Serial.print("Hello, Bluetooth!");`	Sends data over the Bluetooth connection to the paired device.
3	Receive Data from Bluetooth	`String data = Serial.readString();`	Receives data sent over Bluetooth.
4	Switch Bluetooth to AT mode	Send AT command through Serial Monitor.	Allows configuration of Bluetooth module.

Syntax Explanation

1. Start Serial Communication

What does starting serial communication do?
The `Serial.begin()` function sets up communication between the Arduino and Bluetooth module, or any serial device, at a specific baud rate. This is required for sending and receiving data.
Syntax:
```
Serial.begin(baudRate);
```
Example:
```
Serial.begin(9600);  // Start serial communication at
9600 baud
```

Example Explanation:
This code sets up the serial communication at a baud rate of 9600, which is standard for most Bluetooth modules, ensuring that data can be sent and received correctly.

2. Send Data Over Bluetooth

What does sending data over Bluetooth do?
The `Serial.print()` or `Serial.println()` function sends data over the serial connection to the paired Bluetooth device. You can send text, numbers, or even formatted data.
Syntax:
```
Serial.print(data);
```
Example:
```
Serial.print("Hello, Bluetooth!");
```

Example Explanation:
This code sends the string "Hello, Bluetooth!" over the Bluetooth connection to the paired device, which can be received by a smartphone or computer.

3. Receive Data from Bluetooth

What does receiving data from Bluetooth do?
The `Serial.readString()` function allows you to receive data sent from a paired Bluetooth device, such as a command from a smartphone or computer.
Syntax:
```
String data = Serial.readString();
```
Example:
```
String data = Serial.readString();
```

Example Explanation:
This code reads the incoming data from Bluetooth and stores it in the data variable, where it can be processed further, such as by controlling an LED or motor.

4. Switch Bluetooth to AT Mode

What does switching to AT mode do?
Sending the AT command to the Bluetooth module switches it to AT command mode, allowing you to change the module's settings like name, baud rate, or password.
Syntax:
```
Serial.println("AT");
```
Example:
```
Serial.println("AT");  // Send AT command to the
Bluetooth module
```

Example Explanation:
This sends the "AT" command to the Bluetooth module, which will respond with its settings and allow you to change configuration parameters.

Real-life Applications Project: Bluetooth Controlled LED

In this project, we will use Bluetooth to control an LED connected to an Arduino. A smartphone app will send commands over Bluetooth to turn the LED on and off.

Required Components

Component	Description
Bluetooth Module	HC-05 or HC-06 for wireless communication.
Arduino Uno	Microcontroller to control the Bluetooth module and LED.
LED	To display the output (on/off) when controlled via Bluetooth.
Jumper Wires	For making necessary connections.

Circuit Connection Table

Component	Pin Connection
Bluetooth Module	TX -> Pin 10, RX -> Pin 11 (make sure to cross TX/RX)
Arduino Uno	Pin 13 -> LED (anode), GND -> LED (cathode)

Project Code

```
const int ledPin = 13;  // LED connected to pin 13

void setup() {
  pinMode(ledPin, OUTPUT);  // Set LED pin as output
  Serial.begin(9600);        // Start serial
communication with Bluetooth module
}

void loop() {
  if (Serial.available()) {
    char command = Serial.read();  // Read the incoming
data

    if (command == '1') {
      digitalWrite(ledPin, HIGH);  // Turn LED on
```

```
  } else if (command == '0') {
    digitalWrite(ledPin, LOW);    // Turn LED off
  }
 }
}
```

Expected Results

After uploading the code, you can pair your smartphone with the
Bluetooth module (HC-05 or HC-06). Using a Bluetooth terminal
app, send '1' to turn the LED on and '0' to turn it off. The LED will
respond based on the commands sent over Bluetooth.

Chapter 49: Wi-Fi and ESP8266 Modules with Arduino

Wi-Fi and the ESP8266 module have revolutionized IoT (Internet of Things) projects by providing easy wireless communication with the internet. By integrating Wi-Fi with an Arduino, you can create projects that send and receive data over the internet, control devices remotely, and interact with web services. In this chapter, we'll explore how to use the ESP8266 module with Arduino, including wiring, programming, and real-life applications.

Key Concepts of Wi-Fi and ESP8266 Modules with Arduino

The ESP8266 is a Wi-Fi module that allows your Arduino to connect to a wireless network and communicate with other devices via the internet. It can be used to send data to a web server, control devices over the internet, or create smart home systems.

Concept	Description	Example
ESP8266 Module	A low-cost Wi-Fi module that can be connected to Arduino for wireless communication.	ESP8266 connects Arduino to Wi-Fi networks.
Wi-Fi Communication	Allows Arduino to connect to a local Wi-Fi network and communicate over the internet.	Data sent from Arduino to a cloud server or web service.
HTTP Requests	Used to send and receive data from web servers.	Sending data from Arduino to a remote server via HTTP.
AT Commands	Commands used to configure and communicate with the ESP8266.	Use AT commands to connect ESP8266 to Wi-Fi networks.

Basic Rules for Using Wi-Fi and ESP8266 with Arduino

Rule	Correct Example	Incorrect Example
Use `Serial.begin()` to communicate with the ESP8266.	`Serial.begin(115200);`	Forgetting to initialize serial communication with the ESP8266.
Ensure correct wiring for TX/RX.	Connect TX (ESP8266) to RX (Arduino) and RX (ESP8266) to TX (Arduino).	Reversing TX and RX connections between Arduino and ESP8266.
Use `WiFi.begin()` to connect to Wi-Fi.	`WiFi.begin("SSID", "password");`	Forgetting to enter the correct network credentials.

Syntax Table

SL	Function	Syntax/Example	Description
1	Start Serial Communication	`Serial.begin(115200);`	Initializes communication between Arduino and ESP8266.
2	Connect to Wi-Fi	`WiFi.begin("SSID", "password");`	Connects ESP8266 to a Wi-Fi network.
3	Check Wi-Fi Status	`WiFi.status() == WL_CONNECTED;`	Checks if the ESP8266 is connected to the Wi-Fi network.
4	Send HTTP GET Request	`http.begin("http://example.com"); http.GET();`	Sends an HTTP GET request to a web server.

Syntax Explanation

1. Start Serial Communication

What does starting serial communication do?
The `Serial.begin()` function initializes serial communication with a specified baud rate. This is important to enable communication between Arduino and ESP8266 for sending and receiving data.
Syntax:
`Serial.begin(baudRate);`
Example:
`Serial.begin(115200);  // Start serial communication at 115200 baud`

Example Explanation:
This code sets up serial communication between the Arduino and ESP8266 at a baud rate of 115200, which is standard for the ESP8266 module.

2. Connect to Wi-Fi

What does connecting to Wi-Fi do?
The `WiFi.begin()` function connects the ESP8266 module to a Wi-Fi network by specifying the network's SSID (name) and password.
Syntax:
`WiFi.begin(SSID, password);`
Example:
`WiFi.begin("YourNetworkSSID", "YourNetworkPassword");`
Example Explanation:
This code connects the ESP8266 module to a Wi-Fi network using the provided SSID and password. It's essential to have the correct credentials to establish a successful connection.

3. Check Wi-Fi Status

What does checking Wi-Fi status do?
The `WiFi.status()` function is used to check if the ESP8266 has successfully connected to a Wi-Fi network. It returns the status of the connection, such as `WL_CONNECTED` for a successful connection.

Syntax:
```
WiFi.status();
```
Example:
```
if (WiFi.status() == WL_CONNECTED) {
  Serial.println("Connected to WiFi!");
}
```

Example Explanation:
This code checks the Wi-Fi connection status. If the ESP8266 is connected to the network, it prints "Connected to WiFi!" to the Serial Monitor.

4. Send HTTP GET Request

What does sending an HTTP GET request do?
The http.begin() function initializes an HTTP client to communicate with a web server. The http.GET() function sends a GET request to a specified URL, allowing data retrieval.
Syntax:
```
http.begin("url"); http.GET();
```
Example:
```
http.begin("http://example.com");
int httpResponseCode = http.GET();
```

Example Explanation:
This code sends an HTTP GET request to the specified URL (http://example.com). The server's response can be processed using the httpResponseCode.

Real-life Applications Project: Wi-Fi Controlled LED

In this project, we will use the ESP8266 to control an LED over the internet. By sending an HTTP request from a smartphone or computer to the Arduino, the LED will turn on or off based on the command.

Required Components

Component	Description
ESP8266 Module	Wi-Fi module for internet connectivity.
Arduino Uno	Microcontroller to control the ESP8266 and LED.
LED	To visually indicate the output (on/off) status.
Jumper Wires	For making necessary connections.

Circuit Connection Table

Component	Pin Connection
ESP8266 Module	TX -> Pin 10, RX -> Pin 11 (crossed TX/RX).
Arduino Uno	Pin 13 -> LED (anode), GND -> LED (cathode)

Project Code

```
#include <ESP8266WiFi.h>

const char* ssid = "YourNetworkSSID";      // Wi-Fi
network name
const char* password = "YourNetworkPassword"; // Wi-Fi
network password

const int ledPin = 13;   // LED connected to pin 13

WiFiServer server(80);   // Set up a web server on port
80

void setup() {
  pinMode(ledPin, OUTPUT);  // Set LED pin as output
  Serial.begin(115200);     // Start serial
communication

  WiFi.begin(ssid, password);  // Connect to Wi-Fi
```

```
network
  while (WiFi.status() != WL_CONNECTED) {
    delay(1000);  // Wait for the Wi-Fi connection to
be established
    Serial.println("Connecting to WiFi...");
  }
  Serial.println("Connected to WiFi!");
  server.begin();  // Start the server
}
void loop() {
  WiFiClient client = server.available();  // Listen
for incoming client connections
  if (client) {
    String request = "";
    while (client.available()) {
      request += char(client.read());  // Read the
incoming request
    }
    if (request.indexOf("/ON") != -1) {
      digitalWrite(ledPin, HIGH);  // Turn LED on
    } else if (request.indexOf("/OFF") != -1) {
      digitalWrite(ledPin, LOW);   // Turn LED off
    }
    client.print("HTTP/1.1 200 OK\n\n");  // Send HTTP
response
    client.print("LED control: <a href='/ON'>ON</a> |
<a href='/OFF'>OFF</a>");
    delay(10);
  }
}
```

Expected Results

After uploading the code, the ESP8266 will connect to the Wi-Fi
network and start a web server. Using a web browser, you can
control the LED by navigating to the following URLs:

- http://[ESP8266 **IP address]/ON** – Turns the LED on.
- http://[ESP8266 **IP address]/OFF** – Turns the LED off.

Chapter 50: LoRa Communication with Arduino

LoRa (Long Range) communication is a popular wireless technology for long-range, low-power communication in IoT (Internet of Things) projects. It is ideal for applications where devices need to communicate over large distances without relying on cellular or Wi-Fi networks. The combination of Arduino and LoRa modules like the SX1278 or SX1276 enables you to create wireless networks that can span miles, making it perfect for remote sensors, data transmission, and smart agriculture projects. In this chapter, we'll explore how to use LoRa with Arduino, including wiring, programming, and real-life applications.

Key Concepts of LoRa Communication with Arduino

LoRa is a wireless communication technology that uses radio frequencies to transmit data over long distances. The LoRa module communicates with Arduino to send and receive data at ranges from several kilometers to tens of kilometers, depending on the environment and module used. LoRa is ideal for IoT applications, as it operates on low power and can cover large distances.

Concept	Description	Example
LoRa Module	A module that enables long-range communication using LoRa technology.	SX1278, SX1276 are common LoRa modules used with Arduino.
Frequency Bands	LoRa operates on different frequency bands based on region (e.g., 868 MHz, 915 MHz).	Choose the correct frequency for your region.
Spread Spectrum	LoRa uses spread spectrum modulation, which spreads the signal over a wide frequency range for better range and interference immunity.	Allows long-range communication with minimal interference.
Low Power	LoRa modules use very little power, which is ideal for battery-powered devices.	LoRa is often used in remote sensors, weather stations, and

		agriculture.

Basic Rules for Using LoRa with Arduino

Rule	Correct Example	Incorrect Example
Use `LoRa.begin()` to initialize the LoRa module.	`LoRa.begin(915E6);`	Forgetting to initialize LoRa with the correct frequency.
Ensure proper wiring for SPI communication.	Connect the LoRa module to the correct SPI pins (MOSI, MISO, SCK, and NSS).	Incorrect wiring of SPI pins between Arduino and LoRa module.
Use `LoRa.beginPacket()` and `LoRa.endPacket()` to send data.	`LoRa.beginPacket();` `LoRa.print("Message");` `LoRa.endPacket();`	Forgetting to call `endPacket()` to finalize sending data.

Syntax Table

SL	Function	Syntax/Example	Description
1	Initialize LoRa Module	`LoRa.begin(frequency);`	Initializes the LoRa module with the specified frequency.
2	Start LoRa Packet	`LoRa.beginPacket();`	Starts the transmission of a new LoRa packet.
3	Send Data Over LoRa	`LoRa.print("data");`	Sends data in the current packet over LoRa.
4	End LoRa Packet	`LoRa.endPacket();`	Finalizes the packet transmission.
5	Receive LoRa Data	`LoRa.parsePacket();`	Reads incoming data from a LoRa packet.

Syntax Explanation

1. Initialize LoRa Module

What does initializing the LoRa module do?
The `LoRa.begin()` function sets the frequency and initializes the LoRa module. It's essential to specify the correct frequency according to the regional regulations (e.g., 915 MHz for North America, 868 MHz for Europe).
Syntax:
```
LoRa.begin(frequency);
```
Example:
```
LoRa.begin(915E6);  // Initialize LoRa at 915 MHz
```

Example Explanation:
This code initializes the LoRa module at a frequency of 915 MHz, suitable for regions like North America. Make sure to select the correct frequency depending on your location.

2. Start LoRa Packet

What does starting a LoRa packet do?
The `LoRa.beginPacket()` function starts the process of sending data over LoRa. You can send any type of data inside the packet, such as text, numbers, or sensor readings.
Syntax:
```
LoRa.beginPacket();
```
Example:
```
LoRa.beginPacket();  // Start sending a packet
```

Example Explanation:
This code starts the process of transmitting a LoRa packet. After calling `beginPacket()`, you can send data by using functions like `LoRa.print()` or `LoRa.write()`.

3. Send Data Over LoRa

What does sending data over LoRa do?
The `LoRa.print()` or `LoRa.write()` function sends data to the
LoRa module. This data is added to the current packet, which will be
transmitted when `endPacket()` is called.
Syntax:
`LoRa.print(data);`
Example:
`LoRa.print("Hello from Arduino!");`

Example Explanation:
This code sends the string "Hello from Arduino!" inside the current
LoRa packet. You can send any data, such as sensor readings or
control signals.

4. End LoRa Packet

What does ending a LoRa packet do?
The `LoRa.endPacket()` function completes the packet
transmission. It sends the packet over LoRa and clears the buffer,
making it ready for the next transmission.
Syntax:
`LoRa.endPacket();`
Example:
`LoRa.endPacket();  // Send the packet`
Example Explanation:
This code sends the current packet over LoRa and finishes the
transmission. Without calling `endPacket()`, the data would not be
sent.

5. Receive LoRa Data

What does receiving LoRa data do?
The `LoRa.parsePacket()` function reads incoming LoRa data. After
this function is called, you can read the received data using
`LoRa.read()` or `LoRa.readString()`.
Syntax:
`LoRa.parsePacket();`

Example:

```
int packetSize = LoRa.parsePacket();  // Read incoming
data packet
if (packetSize) {
  String received = LoRa.readString();  // Read the
received data
  Serial.println(received);  // Print received data to
Serial Monitor
}
```

Example Explanation:

This code checks if there is a packet available. If a packet is received, it reads the data and prints it to the Serial Monitor.

Real-life Applications Project: LoRa-based Weather Station

In this project, we will use two Arduino boards with LoRa modules to create a weather station. One Arduino will collect weather data (e.g., temperature, humidity) and send it via LoRa to the second Arduino, which will display the data on an LCD screen.

Required Components

Component	Description
2 x LoRa Modules	Used for long-range communication between two Arduino boards.
2 x Arduino Uno	One will send data and the other will receive and display it.
DHT11 Sensor	For measuring temperature and humidity.
LCD Display	To display the received weather data.
Jumper Wires	For making necessary connections.

Circuit Connection Table

Component	Pin Connection
LoRa Module (Transmitter)	Connect LoRa module's SPI pins (MOSI, MISO, SCK, NSS) to Arduino Uno.
LoRa Module (Receiver)	Connect LoRa module's SPI pins to the second Arduino Uno.
DHT11 Sensor	VCC -> 5V, GND -> GND, DATA -> Pin 2
LCD Display	Use I2C pins (SDA, SCL) to connect to Arduino Uno.

Project Code (Transmitter - Sending Weather Data)

```cpp
#include <LoRa.h>
#include <DHT.h>

#define DHTPIN 2
#define DHTTYPE DHT11

DHT dht(DHTPIN, DHTTYPE);

void setup() {
  Serial.begin(115200);
  LoRa.begin(915E6);  // Initialize LoRa at 915 MHz
  dht.begin();  // Initialize DHT sensor
}

void loop() {
  float temp = dht.readTemperature();
  float humidity = dht.readHumidity();

  LoRa.beginPacket();  // Start sending packet
  LoRa.print("Temperature: ");
  LoRa.print(temp);
  LoRa.print("C, Humidity: ");
  LoRa.print(humidity);
  LoRa.println("%");
  LoRa.endPacket();  // Send packet

  delay(10000);  // Wait for 10 seconds before sending
next data
}
```

Project Code (Receiver - Displaying Data)

```cpp
#include <LoRa.h>
#include <Wire.h>
#include <LiquidCrystal_I2C.h>
LiquidCrystal_I2C lcd(0x27, 16, 2);  // I2C address
  for LCD
```

```
void setup() {
  Serial.begin(115200);
  LoRa.begin(915E6);   // Initialize LoRa at 915 MHz
  lcd.begin(16, 2);    // Initialize LCD
}

void loop() {
  int packetSize = LoRa.parsePacket();
  if (packetSize) {
    String received = LoRa.readString();
    lcd.clear();
    lcd.print(received);   // Display received data on
LCD
  }
}
```

Expected Results

Once the transmitter Arduino reads the temperature and humidity, it will send the data via LoRa to the receiver Arduino, which will then display it on the LCD screen. Every 10 seconds, the transmitter will send a new reading.

Chapter 51: Using GSM Modules with Arduino

GSM (Global System for Mobile Communications) modules allow Arduino to communicate over cellular networks, enabling it to send text messages (SMS), make phone calls, and access the internet through a mobile network. The GSM module is perfect for remote communication where Wi-Fi is not available, such as in remote sensing, security systems, or IoT applications. This chapter will cover how to use a GSM module with Arduino, including wiring, programming, and real-life applications.

Key Concepts of GSM Modules with Arduino

A GSM module is a device that uses cellular networks to send and receive data. It typically interfaces with Arduino through serial communication. The most commonly used GSM modules with Arduino are the **SIM900** and **SIM800**. These modules allow you to send SMS messages, make voice calls, and even connect to the internet via GPRS (General Packet Radio Service).

Concept	Description	Example
GSM Module	A module that connects to cellular networks for communication.	SIM900, SIM800, or SIM5320 GSM modules used with Arduino.
SIM Card	A small chip that connects to the GSM module to access mobile networks.	Insert the SIM card to enable communication through GSM.
Serial Communica tion	GSM modules communicate with Arduino using UART (serial communication).	Use SoftwareSerial to interface with the GSM module on different pins.
AT Commands	Text-based commands used to control the GSM module.	AT, AT+CMGF=1 (set SMS mode), ATD (dial number).

Basic Rules for Using GSM Modules with Arduino

Rule	Correct Example	Incorrect Example
Use SoftwareSerial for communication with the GSM module.	SoftwareSerial gsmSerial(7, 8);	Using the hardware serial port (Serial) for the GSM module.
Use gsm.begin() to initialize communication with the GSM module.	gsm.begin(9600);	Forgetting to initialize the GSM module with gsm.begin().
Send commands to the GSM module using gsm.print() or gsm.println().	gsm.println("AT+CMGF=1");	Forgetting to send AT commands properly.

Syntax Table

SL	Function	Syntax/Example	Description
1	Initialize GSM Module	gsm.begin(baudRate);	Initializes the GSM module at the specified baud rate.
2	Send AT Command to GSM Module	gsm.println("AT+CMGF=1");	Sends an AT command to the GSM module.
3	Send SMS Message	gsm.println("AT+CMGS=\"phoneNumber\"");	Sends an SMS message to the specified phone number.
4	Make a Phone Call	gsm.println("ATDphoneNumber;");	Dials the specified phone number.
5	Receive SMS Message	gsm.println("AT+CMGL=\"REC UNREAD\"");	Reads unread SMS messages from the GSM module.

Syntax Explanation

1. Initialize GSM Module

What does initializing the GSM module do?
The `gsm.begin()` function sets up serial communication between Arduino and the GSM module. It ensures the GSM module is ready to receive and send commands.
Syntax:
`gsm.begin(baudRate);`
Example:
`gsm.begin(9600);  // Initialize GSM module at 9600 baud rate`

Example Explanation:
This code initializes the GSM module for communication at 9600 baud. Make sure the baud rate matches the GSM module's default setting, usually 9600 or 115200.

2. Send AT Command to GSM Module

What does sending an AT command do?
AT commands are used to communicate with the GSM module. These commands control the module's functions, such as sending SMS or making calls. The `gsm.println()` function sends the AT command to the GSM module.
Syntax:
`gsm.println("AT command");`
Example:
`gsm.println("AT+CMGF=1");  // Set GSM module to SMS mode`

Example Explanation:
This code sends the AT command `AT+CMGF=1` to set the GSM module to SMS text mode. Without this, the GSM module would not understand text messages.

3. Send SMS Message

What does sending an SMS message do?
To send an SMS, you must first send the AT+CMGS command with the recipient's phone number. After this, you type the message and end it with a Ctrl+Z character (ASCII 26). This command sends an SMS to the specified phone number.

Syntax:
```
gsm.println("AT+CMGS=\"phoneNumber\"");
```
Example:
```
gsm.println("AT+CMGS=\"+1234567890\"");   // Set the
recipient's phone number
gsm.println("Hello from Arduino!");       // The message
text
gsm.write(26);                            // Ctrl+Z to
send
```

Example Explanation:
This code sends an SMS with the text "Hello from Arduino!" to the phone number +1234567890. The `gsm.write(26)` sends the Ctrl+Z character to indicate the end of the message.

4. Make a Phone Call

What does making a phone call do?
The ATD command is used to dial a phone number. The number should be followed by a semicolon (;) to indicate it's a voice call.

Syntax:
```
gsm.println("ATDphoneNumber;");
```
Example:
```
gsm.println("ATD+1234567890;");   // Dial the specified
phone number
```

Example Explanation:

This code dials the phone number +1234567890. The semicolon (;) indicates that the call is a voice call, not a data call.

5. Receive SMS Message

What does receiving an SMS message do?
The AT+CMGL command reads SMS messages stored in the GSM module's memory. You can specify message types like "REC UNREAD" for unread messages.

Syntax:
```
gsm.println("AT+CMGL=\"REC UNREAD\"");
```
Example:
```
gsm.println("AT+CMGL=\"REC UNREAD\"");  // Read unread messages
```

Example Explanation:
This code asks the GSM module to return unread messages. You can further process the messages by reading them using the gsm.read() or similar functions.

Real-life Applications Project: SMS-based Security System

In this project, we will create a simple security system that sends an SMS alert when a motion sensor is triggered. When the motion sensor detects movement, the Arduino sends an SMS message to a predefined phone number.

Required Components

Component	Description
GSM Module	Sends and receives SMS messages.
Arduino Uno	Microcontroller for controlling the GSM module.
PIR Motion Sensor	Detects movement.
Jumper Wires	For making necessary connections.

Circuit Connection Table

Component	Pin Connection
GSM Module	Connect GSM's TX to Arduino's RX (Pin 7) and GSM's RX to Arduino's TX (Pin 8).
PIR Motion Sensor	VCC -> 5V, GND -> GND, OUT -> Pin 2

Project Code

```
#include <SoftwareSerial.h>
SoftwareSerial gsm(7, 8);  // RX, TX for GSM module
int motionPin = 2;         // PIR motion sensor input
pin
String phoneNumber = "+1234567890";  // Phone number to
send SMS
void setup() {
  Serial.begin(9600);  // Start Serial Monitor
  gsm.begin(9600);     // Start GSM communication
  pinMode(motionPin, INPUT);  // Set PIR sensor as
input
  gsm.println("AT+CMGF=1");  // Set SMS mode
  delay(1000);
}
void loop() {
  int motionState = digitalRead(motionPin);
  if (motionState == HIGH) {  // If motion is detected
    gsm.println("AT+CMGS=\"" + phoneNumber + "\"");  //
Send SMS
    delay(1000);
    gsm.println("Motion detected!");  // SMS content
    gsm.write(26);  // Ctrl+Z to send message
    delay(1000);
  }
}
```

Expected Results

When the motion sensor detects movement, the Arduino will send an SMS alert with the message "Motion detected!" to the specified phone number. This project can be expanded to trigger an alarm, activate a camera, or even send additional data.

Chapter 52: Gesture Recognition with Arduino

Gesture recognition technology enables devices to interpret human gestures as input. With Arduino, you can create simple systems that recognize various hand movements or gestures using sensors. This chapter will cover how to use sensors such as the **APDS-9960** or **GY-521 (Accelerometer and Gyroscope)** for gesture recognition with Arduino, including wiring, programming, and real-life applications.

Key Concepts of Gesture Recognition with Arduino

Gesture recognition involves detecting specific movements or orientations of the hand or body and using those movements as input for a system. Arduino can interface with sensors like accelerometers, gyroscopes, and infrared sensors to detect these gestures.

Concept	Description	Example
Accelerometer	A sensor that detects movement or changes in orientation.	GY-521 module, which has both an accelerometer and gyroscope.
Infrared Sensors	Sensors that detect hand movements through infrared light.	APDS-9960, a gesture sensor that detects proximity and gestures.
Gyroscope	A sensor that measures rotation and angular velocity.	GY-521 module, for detecting rotational gestures.
Sensor Calibration	The process of adjusting sensors to accurately detect gestures.	Calibrating the accelerometer for detecting specific movements.

Basic Rules for Gesture Recognition with Arduino

Rule	Correct Example	Incorrect Example
Use `Wire.begin()` to initialize I2C communication with sensors.	`Wire.begin();`	Forgetting to initialize I2C communication.

Use `sensor.begin()` to initialize the sensor.	`sensor .begin ();`	Forgetting to call `sensor.begin()` before using the sensor.
Implement proper sensor calibration.	`sensor .calib rate() ;`	Ignoring the need for calibration before gesture detection.

Syntax Table

SL	Function	Syntax/Example	Description
1	Initialize I2C Communicatio n	`Wire.begin();`	Initializes I2C communication with the sensor.
2	Initialize Gesture Sensor	`sensor.begin();`	Initializes the gesture sensor.
3	Read Gesture Data	`sensor.readGestu re();`	Reads data from the gesture sensor.
4	Detect Gesture	`if (gesture == GESTURE_UP) { ... }`	Detect specific gestures like UP, DOWN, LEFT, RIGHT.
5	Control Output Based on Gesture	`if (gesture == GESTURE_RIGHT) { digitalWrite(LED , HIGH); }`	Perform actions based on detected gestures.

Syntax Explanation

1. Initialize I2C Communication

What does initializing I2C communication do?

The `Wire.begin()` function initializes the I2C communication protocol, which is required for communication with many sensors like the APDS-9960 or GY-521.

Syntax:

`Wire.begin();`

Example:

`Wire.begin();  // Initialize I2C communication`

Example Explanation:

This line of code initializes the I2C bus, allowing Arduino to communicate with I2C devices (like gesture sensors).

2. Initialize Gesture Sensor

What does initializing the gesture sensor do?
Each sensor has its own initialization function, which sets up communication between Arduino and the sensor, ensuring it is ready to detect gestures.
Syntax:
```
sensor.begin();
```
Example:
```
sensor.begin();  // Initialize the gesture sensor
```

Example Explanation:
This line of code initializes the sensor (e.g., APDS-9960). After this, the sensor will be ready to start detecting gestures.

3. Read Gesture Data

What does reading gesture data do?
The `sensor.readGesture()` function reads the data from the gesture sensor. It returns a gesture, such as UP, DOWN, LEFT, or RIGHT, which can be used to trigger specific actions.
Syntax:
```
sensor.readGesture();
```
Example:
```
gesture = sensor.readGesture();  // Read the detected
gesture
```

Example Explanation:
This code reads the gesture from the sensor. The gesture could be one of several values, like `GESTURE_UP`, `GESTURE_DOWN`, etc.

4. Detect Gesture

What does detecting a gesture do?
This function checks the gesture value returned by the sensor and triggers specific actions based on it. For example, if the detected gesture is "UP," you can turn on an LED.
Syntax:
```
if (gesture == GESTURE_UP) { ... }
```

Example:
```
if (gesture == GESTURE_RIGHT) {
  digitalWrite(LED_PIN, HIGH);  // Turn on LED for a
right gesture
}
```

Example Explanation:
This code checks if the detected gesture is "RIGHT." If it is, the program turns on an LED connected to LED_PIN.

5. Control Output Based on Gesture

What does controlling output based on gesture do?
You can use the gestures detected to control various outputs such as turning on an LED, sending data to a display, or controlling motors.

Syntax:
```
if (gesture == GESTURE_RIGHT) { digitalWrite(LED,
HIGH); }
```

Example:
```
if (gesture == GESTURE_LEFT) {
  digitalWrite(LED_PIN, LOW);  // Turn off LED for a
left gesture
}
```

Example Explanation:
This code turns off an LED when the "LEFT" gesture is detected.

Real-life Applications Project: Gesture-Controlled LED

In this project, we will create a simple system where an LED is controlled by hand gestures using the APDS-9960 sensor. The system will turn the LED on when the "RIGHT" gesture is detected and off when the "LEFT" gesture is detected.

Required Components

Component	Description
Gesture Sensor (APDS-9960)	Detects hand gestures (e.g., UP, DOWN, LEFT, RIGHT).
Arduino Uno	Microcontroller for controlling the sensor and output.
LED	A simple LED that will be controlled by gestures.
Jumper Wires	For making necessary connections.

Circuit Connection Table

Component	Pin Connection
APDS-9960 Gesture Sensor	VCC -> 5V, GND -> GND, SDA -> A4, SCL -> A5 (for I2C communication)
LED	Anode -> Pin 13, Cathode -> GND

Project Code

```
#include <Wire.h>
#include <APDS9960.h>


APDS9960 sensor;   // Create an instance of the gesture
sensor
int LED_PIN = 13;   // LED pin

void setup() {
  Serial.begin(9600);
  Wire.begin();
  sensor.begin();   // Initialize the sensor
  sensor.enableProximitySensor();   // Enable the
proximity sensor
  pinMode(LED_PIN, OUTPUT);   // Set LED pin as output
}


void loop() {
  int gesture = sensor.readGesture();   // Read the
gesture

  if (gesture == GESTURE_RIGHT) {
    digitalWrite(LED_PIN, HIGH);   // Turn on LED for
```

```
right gesture
  }
  else if (gesture == GESTURE_LEFT) {
    digitalWrite(LED_PIN, LOW);   // Turn off LED for
left gesture
  }
  delay(100);  // Small delay for smooth operation
}
```

Expected Results

Once the code is uploaded to the Arduino, the LED will respond to gestures:

- When you move your hand to the right of the sensor, the LED will turn on.
- When you move your hand to the left, the LED will turn off.

Chapter 53: Speech Recognition with Arduino

Speech recognition allows you to convert spoken words into commands that can control devices. With Arduino, you can integrate speech recognition to create interactive systems that respond to voice commands. This chapter will explore how to set up speech recognition with Arduino using different modules and technologies, enabling hands-free control of devices.

Key Concepts of Speech Recognition with Arduino

Speech recognition systems capture audio signals and convert them into text or actions. Arduino doesn't have the processing power to handle complex speech recognition natively, so external modules like the **Elechouse Voice Recognition Module** or **Arduino-compatible speech-to-text APIs** are used. These modules process audio and send the recognized command to Arduino, which then triggers actions accordingly.

Concept	Description	Example
Voice Recognition Module	A module designed to recognize a set of predefined voice commands.	Used to create a speech-controlled system with Arduino.
Speech-to-Text	Converting spoken words into text for further processing.	Speech is converted into text and mapped to specific actions.
Audio Processing	Filtering and processing the audio signals from microphones.	To capture clear voice commands and reduce background noise.
Command Mapping	Associating recognized speech with specific actions on Arduino.	Mapping voice commands like "turn on light" to trigger an LED.

Basic Rules for Using Speech Recognition with Arduino

Rule	Correct Example	Incorrect Example
Use an external module for speech recognition.	`VoiceRecognition Module.begin();`	Attempting to process speech without a dedicated module.
Train the speech recognition module with predefined commands.	`VoiceRecognition Module.loadComma nds(commandsArra y);`	Forgetting to train the module with commands before use.
Ensure clear audio input for recognition.	Use a microphone with noise cancellation for clearer input.	Using low-quality microphones without noise reduction.

Syntax Table

SL	Function	Syntax/Example	Description
1	Initialize the Voice Recognition Module	`VoiceRecognitio nModule.begin() ;`	Initializes the voice recognition module for use.
2	Load predefined commands	`VoiceRecognitio nModule.loadCom mands(commandsA rray);`	Loads a set of recognized voice commands into the module.
3	Listen for a voice command	`int command = VoiceRecognitio nModule.listen( );`	Listens for a recognized voice command and returns a result.
4	Map commands to actions	`if (command == COMMAND_ON) { digitalWrite(LE D_PIN, HIGH); }`	Maps the recognized command to a specific action on Arduino.

Syntax Explanation

1. Initialize the Voice Recognition Module

What does initializing the voice recognition module do?
The `VoiceRecognitionModule.begin()` function initializes the module, setting up necessary configurations and preparing it to listen for commands. This function should be called in the `setup()` section of the code.

Syntax:
`VoiceRecognitionModule.begin();`

Example:
`VoiceRecognitionModule.begin();  // Initializes the voice recognition module`

Example Explanation:
This example initializes the voice recognition module, ensuring that it is ready to process voice commands once the system is powered on.

2. Load Predefined Commands

What does loading predefined commands do?
The `VoiceRecognitionModule.loadCommands()` function loads a predefined set of commands into the module. These commands are what the module will recognize and respond to.

Syntax:
`VoiceRecognitionModule.loadCommands(commandsArray);`

Example:
`VoiceRecognitionModule.loadCommands(commandsArray);  // Loads predefined commands`

Example Explanation:
This function loads the voice commands stored in the `commandsArray`. Each command in the array corresponds to a specific action that the system will execute when recognized.

3. Listen for a Voice Command

What does listening for a voice command do?
The `VoiceRecognitionModule.listen()` function listens for a recognized command. When a command is spoken and recognized, it returns the corresponding command ID.
Syntax:
```
int command = VoiceRecognitionModule.listen();
```
Example:
```
int command = VoiceRecognitionModule.listen();  //
Listen for a recognized command
```

Example Explanation:
In this example, the system listens for a command. Once a command is detected, it returns the command ID, which is then used to trigger a specific action, such as turning on a light or activating a motor.

4. Map Commands to Actions

What does mapping commands to actions do?
Once a command is recognized, you can map it to specific actions in your Arduino program. For example, you can turn on an LED or activate a motor when certain voice commands are heard.
Syntax:
```
if (command == COMMAND_ON) { digitalWrite(LED_PIN,
HIGH); }
```
Example:
```
if (command == COMMAND_ON) {
  digitalWrite(LED_PIN, HIGH);  // Turn on LED when
"ON" command is recognized
}
```

Example Explanation:
This code checks if the command ID matches the "ON" command. If it does, it executes the action within the curly braces—in this case, turning on an LED connected to pin 13.

Real-life Applications Project: Voice-Controlled Light

In this project, we will use a voice recognition module to control an LED using voice commands like "on" and "off." The system will listen for these commands and toggle the LED accordingly.

Required Components

Component	Description
Elechouse Voice Recognition Module	Recognizes voice commands and sends them to Arduino.
Arduino Uno	Microcontroller to process voice commands and control the LED.
LED	Indicator light controlled by voice commands.
Jumper Wires	For connecting the components.

Circuit Connection Table

Component	Pin Connection
Voice Recognition Module	Connect to Arduino via RX/TX pins for communication
LED	Anode (long leg) to pin 13, Cathode (short leg) to GND

Project Code

```
#include <VoiceRecognition.h>

VoiceRecognitionModule voiceRecognitionModule;
int ledPin = 13;   // LED connected to pin 13
int command = -1;

void setup() {
  Serial.begin(9600);
  voiceRecognitionModule.begin();  // Initialize voice
recognition module
  voiceRecognitionModule.loadCommands(commandsArray);
// Load predefined commands
  pinMode(ledPin, OUTPUT);   // Set LED pin as output
}

void loop() {
```

```
  command = voiceRecognitionModule.listen();   // Listen
for a voice command

  if (command == COMMAND_ON) {
    digitalWrite(ledPin, HIGH);   // Turn on LED if "on"
command is detected
    Serial.println("LED ON");
  }
  else if (command == COMMAND_OFF) {
    digitalWrite(ledPin, LOW);   // Turn off LED if
"off" command is detected
    Serial.println("LED OFF");
  }
}
```

Expected Results

Once the code is uploaded and the system is powered on, you can
issue voice commands such as "on" and "off" to control the LED.
When "on" is spoken, the LED will turn on; when "off" is spoken, the
LED will turn off.

Chapter 54: Image Processing with Arduino

Image processing involves manipulating and analyzing visual data (images or video) to extract useful information or enhance certain features. While Arduino has limited computational power for complex image processing tasks, it can still perform basic image manipulation with the help of external components like cameras and image processing libraries. In this chapter, we will explore how to set up image processing systems with Arduino using cameras, external processing units, and basic image processing techniques.

Key Concepts of Image Processing with Arduino

Arduino can be paired with external modules like the **OV7670 Camera Module** or **TCS3200 Color Sensor** to capture images and process them. Image processing in Arduino typically involves tasks like object detection, color recognition, and edge detection. While Arduino doesn't have the computing power for sophisticated image processing, it can interact with these sensors and pass data to a more powerful system (like a PC or Raspberry Pi) for heavy processing.

Concept	Description	Example
OV7670 Camera Module	A low-cost camera module used with Arduino to capture images.	Used for basic image capture and simple processing tasks.
TCS3200 Color Sensor	A sensor used to detect colors in the surrounding environment.	Used for basic color detection and processing.
External Processing	Offloading heavy image processing tasks to more powerful systems.	Sending captured data from Arduino to a PC or Raspberry Pi.
Edge Detection	A technique used to find boundaries within an image.	Identifying edges of objects in an image for object detection.

Basic Rules for Using Image Processing with Arduino

Rule	Correct Example	Incorrect Example
Use compatible camera modules with Arduino.	camera.begin();	Trying to use unsupported cameras without proper libraries.
Send image data to an external processor.	sendDataToPi(imageData);	Trying to process complex images directly on Arduino.
Use image processing algorithms efficiently.	applyEdgeDetection(imageData);	Trying to apply complex algorithms without proper optimization.

Syntax Table

SL	Function	Syntax/Example	Description
1	Initialize camera module	camera.begin();	Initializes the camera module for capturing images.
2	Capture image	camera.capture(imageData);	Captures an image from the camera module and stores it in memory.
3	Process image (send to external processor)	sendDataToPC(imageData);	Sends the captured image data to an external processor for analysis.
4	Apply edge detection	applyEdgeDetection(imageData);	Applies edge detection to the image data to find object boundaries.

Syntax Explanation

1. Initialize Camera Module

What does initializing the camera module do?
The camera.begin() function initializes the OV7670 camera module, preparing it for capturing images. This function sets up the necessary configurations, such as resolution and output format, before capturing an image.

Syntax:
```
camera.begin();
```
Example:
```
camera.begin();  // Initialize the OV7670 camera module
```

Example Explanation:
This initializes the camera module, allowing it to start capturing images once the system is powered on.

2. Capture Image

What does capturing an image do?
The `camera.capture(imageData)` function captures an image and stores it in memory. This allows the captured image to be processed further, either on Arduino or by sending it to an external processor for more complex analysis.

Syntax:
```
camera.capture(imageData);
```
Example:
```
camera.capture(imageData);  // Capture image and store
it in imageData
```

Example Explanation:
This function captures an image and stores the image data in the `imageData` variable, which can then be processed or sent to an external processor.

3. Process Image (Send to External Processor)

What does sending image data to an external processor do?
The `sendDataToPC(imageData)` function sends the captured image data to an external processing unit (like a PC or Raspberry Pi). Since Arduino cannot handle complex image processing, offloading the task allows for better performance and analysis.

Syntax:
```
sendDataToPC(imageData);
```
Example:
```
sendDataToPC(imageData);  // Send captured image data
to PC for processing
```

Example Explanation:
This sends the captured image data to a connected PC or Raspberry Pi, where more advanced image processing algorithms can be applied.

4. Apply Edge Detection

What does applying edge detection do?
The applyEdgeDetection(imageData) function is a simple image processing algorithm that detects the edges of objects within the image. It is commonly used in object detection and analysis.
Syntax:
```
applyEdgeDetection(imageData);
```
Example:
```
applyEdgeDetection(imageData);  // Apply edge detection
to the captured image
```

Example Explanation:
This function analyzes the captured image and identifies the boundaries of objects within the image. It helps highlight objects for further analysis or recognition.

Real-life Applications Project: Simple Color Detection System

In this project, we will use the **TCS3200 Color Sensor** to detect and process the color of an object placed in front of the sensor. The Arduino will capture the color and respond by turning on an LED of the corresponding color.
Required Components

Component	Description
TCS3200 Color Sensor	Detects the color of objects based on reflected light.
Arduino Uno	Controls the color sensor and processes the data.
RGB LED	Displays the detected color by lighting up the corresponding LED.
Jumper Wires	For making necessary connections.

Circuit Connection Table

Component	Pin Connection
TCS3200 Color Sensor	S0 to pin 2, S1 to pin 3, S2 to pin 4, S3 to pin 5, OUT to pin 6
RGB LED	Connect red, green, and blue pins to Arduino PWM pins (e.g., pins 9, 10, 11)

Project Code

```
#include <TCS3200.h>

TCS3200 colorSensor;  // Create TCS3200 color sensor
object
int redPin = 9;
int greenPin = 10;
int bluePin = 11;

void setup() {
  Serial.begin(9600);
  colorSensor.begin();  // Initialize color sensor
  pinMode(redPin, OUTPUT);  // Set LED pins as output
  pinMode(greenPin, OUTPUT);
  pinMode(bluePin, OUTPUT);
}

void loop() {
  int color = colorSensor.getColor();  // Get color
value from sensor

  if (color == RED) {
    digitalWrite(redPin, HIGH);  // Turn on red LED
    digitalWrite(greenPin, LOW);
    digitalWrite(bluePin, LOW);
    Serial.println("Red Detected");
  }
  else if (color == GREEN) {
    digitalWrite(redPin, LOW);
    digitalWrite(greenPin, HIGH);  // Turn on green LED
    digitalWrite(bluePin, LOW);
```

```
    Serial.println("Green Detected");
  }
  else if (color == BLUE) {
    digitalWrite(redPin, LOW);
    digitalWrite(greenPin, LOW);
    digitalWrite(bluePin, HIGH);   // Turn on blue LED
    Serial.println("Blue Detected");
  }
}
```

Expected Results

When an object of a particular color (e.g., red, green, or blue) is placed in front of the TCS3200 sensor, the corresponding color LED will light up, and the color name will be printed on the Serial Monitor.

Chapter 55: Arduino in Robotics

Robotics is an interdisciplinary field that integrates mechanical engineering, electrical engineering, and computer science to create machines capable of carrying out tasks autonomously or semi-autonomously. Arduino is widely used in robotics due to its versatility, ease of use, and large community support. In this chapter, we will explore how Arduino can be used in robotics for building robots, controlling motors, sensors, and actuators, and implementing basic robot behaviors.

Key Concepts of Arduino in Robotics

Arduino is a popular platform for robotics because it allows easy integration of sensors, motors, and other components necessary for robot design. Here are the essential concepts for using Arduino in robotics:

Concept	Description	Example
Microcontroller	The brain of the robot that executes the program logic.	Arduino Uno, Arduino Mega, etc.
Sensors	Devices that gather data from the environment, such as distance, touch, and temperature.	Ultrasonic sensor, accelerometer, gyroscope, IR sensor.
Actuators	Devices that perform physical actions, such as motors or servos.	DC motor, stepper motor, servo motor.
Motor Drivers	Circuitry that controls the power supplied to motors.	L298N, L293D motor driver.
Communication	Methods used by the robot to communicate with other devices or controllers.	Bluetooth, Wi-Fi, RF modules, serial communication.

Basic Rules for Using Arduino in Robotics

Rule	Correct Example	Incorrect Example
Use the correct power supply for motors.	`motorDriver.s etPower(255);`	Using a 5V pin to power high-power motors (could damage the board).
Ensure proper wiring for sensors and actuators.	`ultrasonicSen sor.ping();`	Incorrectly wiring the sensor, causing incorrect readings.
Use motor drivers to control motors.	`motorDriver.f orward();`	Directly controlling a motor without a driver.
Write a modular program with separate control functions.	`void moveForward() { motorDriver.f orward(); }`	Writing all code in the `loop()` function without structure.

Syntax Table

SL	Function	Syntax/Example	Description
1	Initialize motor driver	`motorDriver.beg in();`	Initializes the motor driver for controlling motors.
2	Control motor direction	`motorDriver.for ward();`	Moves the motor forward.
3	Read sensor value	`sensorValue = ultrasonicSenso r.read();`	Reads the value from the sensor (e.g., distance from an object).
4	Send control signal to actuator	`servo.write(90) ;`	Sends a signal to an actuator (e.g., setting a servo position).
5	Communicate with external device	`Serial.print("D ata sent");`	Sends data to an external device via serial communication.

Syntax Explanation

1. Initialize Motor Driver

What does initializing the motor driver do?
The `motorDriver.begin()` function sets up the motor driver for use, enabling it to control the motors connected to it. This step is essential for establishing communication between Arduino and the motor driver.
Syntax:
```
motorDriver.begin();
```
Example:
```
motorDriver.begin();   // Initialize the motor driver
```

Example Explanation:
This function prepares the motor driver for controlling the motors connected to it. It must be called before attempting to move or stop the motors.

2. Control Motor Direction

What does controlling the motor direction do?
The `motorDriver.forward()` function sends a signal to the motor driver to move the motor in the forward direction. Similarly, other functions like `backward()`, `left()`, and `right()` control the motor in respective directions.
Syntax:
```
motorDriver.forward();
```
Example:
```
motorDriver.forward();   // Move the motor forward
```

Example Explanation:
This command moves the motor forward. In robotics, controlling the direction of the motor is essential for moving the robot or positioning it.

3. Read Sensor Value

What does reading a sensor value do?
The `sensor.read()` function retrieves data from a sensor, such as distance from an object (for ultrasonic sensors), or tilt data (for accelerometers). This data is essential for making decisions about the robot's behavior.
Syntax:
```
sensorValue = ultrasonicSensor.read();
```
Example:
```
sensorValue = ultrasonicSensor.read();  // Get the
distance reading from the ultrasonic sensor
```

Example Explanation:

This function reads the distance from the ultrasonic sensor, which could be used for obstacle avoidance or path planning in a robot.

4. Send Control Signal to Actuator

What does sending a signal to an actuator do?
The `servo.write(90);` function sends a control signal to the servo motor, telling it to move to the specified position (in this case, 90 degrees).
Syntax:
```
servo.write(degrees);
```
Example:
```
servo.write(90);  // Move servo to 90 degrees
```
Example Explanation:
This function controls the position of a servo motor. This can be used to move parts of the robot, like a robotic arm or camera.

5. Communicate with External Device

What does communicating with an external device do?
The `Serial.print()` function sends data from the Arduino to an external device (e.g., a PC or Raspberry Pi) via serial communication. This is useful for debugging or controlling the robot remotely.

Syntax:

```
Serial.print(data);
```

Example:

```
Serial.print("Robot is moving forward");  // Send
message to serial monitor
```

Example Explanation:

This sends a message to the serial monitor, allowing users to track the robot's actions or debug the code.

Real-life Applications Project: Autonomous Obstacle Avoidance Robot

In this project, we will build a simple autonomous robot that uses an ultrasonic sensor for obstacle detection and motors for movement. The robot will move forward until it detects an obstacle, at which point it will turn around and continue moving.

Required Components

Component	Description
DC Motors	Provide movement for the robot.
L298N Motor Driver	Controls the motors based on Arduino signals.
Ultrasonic Sensor	Detects obstacles in front of the robot.
Arduino Uno	Controls the robot's behavior and processes sensor data.
Jumper Wires	For making necessary connections.
Chassis (robot frame)	The physical structure to mount the components.

Circuit Connection Table

Component	Pin Connection
Ultrasonic Sensor	VCC to 5V, GND to GND, Trigger to pin 9, Echo to pin 10
DC Motors	Motor A connected to pins 3 and 4 (via L298N), Motor B to pins 5 and 6
L298N Motor Driver	IN1, IN2 to pins 3 and 4, IN3, IN4 to pins 5 and 6

Project Code

```
#define trigPin 9
#define echoPin 10
#define motorPin1 3
#define motorPin2 4
#define motorPin3 5
#define motorPin4 6

void setup() {
  pinMode(trigPin, OUTPUT);
  pinMode(echoPin, INPUT);
  pinMode(motorPin1, OUTPUT);
  pinMode(motorPin2, OUTPUT);
  pinMode(motorPin3, OUTPUT);
  pinMode(motorPin4, OUTPUT);
  Serial.begin(9600);
}

void loop() {
  long duration, distance;

  digitalWrite(trigPin, LOW);
  delayMicroseconds(2);
  digitalWrite(trigPin, HIGH);
  delayMicroseconds(10);
  digitalWrite(trigPin, LOW);

  duration = pulseIn(echoPin, HIGH);
  distance = (duration / 2) / 29.1;

  if (distance < 15) {
    stopMovement();
    delay(1000);
    turnAround();
    delay(1000);
  } else {
```

```
      moveForward();
   }
}

void moveForward() {
  digitalWrite(motorPin1, HIGH);
  digitalWrite(motorPin2, LOW);
  digitalWrite(motorPin3, HIGH);
  digitalWrite(motorPin4, LOW);
}

void stopMovement() {
  digitalWrite(motorPin1, LOW);
  digitalWrite(motorPin2, LOW);
  digitalWrite(motorPin3, LOW);
  digitalWrite(motorPin4, LOW);
}

void turnAround() {
  digitalWrite(motorPin1, LOW);
  digitalWrite(motorPin2, HIGH);
  digitalWrite(motorPin3, LOW);
  digitalWrite(motorPin4, HIGH);
}
```

Expected Results

After uploading the code to the Arduino, the robot will move forward until it detects an obstacle within 15 cm. Once an obstacle is detected, the

robot will stop, turn around, and continue moving in the opposite direction.

Chapter 56: Smart Wearables with Arduino

Smart wearables are electronic devices that are worn on the body, often as accessories or clothing, and can interact with the user or their environment. Examples include smartwatches, fitness trackers, health-monitoring devices, and more. Arduino is a powerful tool for building such wearable devices due to its compact size, ease of programming, and compatibility with a variety of sensors and components. In this chapter, we'll explore how Arduino can be used to create smart wearables, their key components, and some real-life application examples.

Key Concepts of Smart Wearables with Arduino

Wearable technology involves embedding sensors, actuators, and communication systems into objects that can be worn on the body. Arduino offers a broad range of components that can be used for smart wearables, from simple motion sensors to advanced communication modules.

Concept	Description	Example
Sensors	Devices that collect data from the user's environment or body.	Heart rate sensor, accelerometer, temperature sensor.
Actuators	Devices that output information or cause physical movement.	Vibration motor, LED, display.
Microcontroller	The brain of the wearable device that processes sensor data.	Arduino Nano, Arduino Pro Mini, Arduino MKR series.
Communication	Methods to transmit data to other devices, such as a smartphone.	Bluetooth, Wi-Fi, Zigbee.
Power Supply	Powering the wearable device efficiently, especially with small batteries.	Lithium-ion battery, solar panel.

Basic Rules for Using Arduino in Smart Wearables

Rule	Correct Example	Incorrect Example
Use low-power components for extended battery life.	Use a sleep mode to reduce power consumption when inactive.	Using high-power components like an LCD screen without managing power.
Ensure the sensors are calibrated for accuracy.	Ensure heart rate sensor is calibrated before use.	Using uncalibrated sensors for critical measurements.
Use small and lightweight components for comfort.	Arduino Nano for compact size.	Using a bulky Arduino board that makes the wearable uncomfortable.
Ensure safe wireless communication.	Use Bluetooth Low Energy (BLE) for minimal energy consumption.	Using regular Bluetooth that consumes too much battery.

Syntax Table

SL	Function	Syntax/Example	Description
1	Read sensor data	`sensorValue = sensor.read();`	Reads the data from the sensor, such as heart rate or movement.
2	Send data via Bluetooth	`bluetooth.send(data);`	Sends data from the wearable to a mobile device.
3	Control LED or motor	`digitalWrite(ledPin, HIGH);`	Turns an LED on or controls a motor to output information.
4	Display data on screen	`lcd.print("Heart Rate: " + String(heartRate));`	Displays information like heart rate on an LCD or OLED display.

5	Put Arduino to sleep to save power	`LowPower.sleep(SLEEP_8S);`	Puts the Arduino into a sleep mode to conserve battery power.

Syntax Explanation

1. Read Sensor Data

What does reading sensor data do?
The `sensor.read()` function collects data from the sensor (e.g., accelerometer or heart rate monitor) and stores it for processing. This data can then be used to trigger actions or display on a screen.
Syntax:
```
sensorValue = sensor.read();
```
Example:
```
sensorValue = heartRateSensor.read();  // Get the
current heart rate
```

Example Explanation:
In this example, the heart rate sensor reads the current heart rate, which is then stored in the `sensorValue` variable for further processing or display.

2. Send Data via Bluetooth

What does sending data via Bluetooth do?
The `bluetooth.send()` function transmits the data collected by the wearable to an external device, such as a smartphone, tablet, or computer. Bluetooth communication allows the wearable to interface with apps for real-time monitoring or analysis.
Syntax:
```
bluetooth.send(data);
```
Example:
```
bluetooth.send(heartRateValue);  // Send heart rate
data to the mobile app
```
Example Explanation:
This sends the `heartRateValue` data over Bluetooth to a paired mobile device, enabling the user to view the data in real-time through an app.

3. Control LED or Motor

What does controlling an LED or motor do?
The `digitalWrite()` function controls the state of an actuator, such as an LED or vibration motor. It can be used to provide feedback to the user, such as indicating whether a goal has been achieved or an alert has been triggered.
Syntax:
```
digitalWrite(pin, state);
```
Example:
```
digitalWrite(ledPin, HIGH);   // Turn on the LED
```

Example Explanation:
This example turns on the LED connected to `ledPin`, which could be used to notify the user about specific conditions (e.g., exceeding a certain heart rate threshold).

4. Display Data on Screen

What does displaying data on a screen do?
The `lcd.print()` function sends data to an LCD or OLED display. This allows the wearable device to show real-time information like heart rate, step count, or notifications.
Syntax:
```
lcd.print(data);
```
Example:
```
lcd.print("Heart Rate: ");
lcd.print(heartRate);   // Display current heart rate on screen
```

Example Explanation:
This code displays the string "Heart Rate:" followed by the actual value of heartRate on an LCD screen, giving the user instant feedback about their condition.

5. Put Arduino to Sleep to Save Power

What does putting Arduino to sleep do?
The `LowPower.sleep()` function puts the Arduino board into a low-power mode to conserve battery life. This is especially important in wearable devices, where battery efficiency is critical.

Syntax:
```
LowPower.sleep(duration);
```
Example:
```
LowPower.sleep(SLEEP_8S);   // Put the Arduino to sleep
for 8 seconds
```

Example Explanation:
The Arduino is put into a low-power sleep mode for 8 seconds to save energy. During this time, the board stops executing code, conserving battery power when the device isn't actively performing tasks.

Real-life Applications Project: Smart Fitness Tracker
In this project, we will create a simple wearable fitness tracker that monitors the user's heart rate and displays it on an LCD. The device will also send the data via Bluetooth to a mobile app for real-time monitoring.

Required Components

Component	Description
Heart Rate Sensor	Measures the user's heart rate.
LCD or OLED Display	Displays real-time data (e.g., heart rate).
Arduino Nano	The microcontroller for controlling the wearable.
Bluetooth Module (HC-05)	Sends data from the Arduino to the mobile app.
Vibration Motor	Provides feedback to the user when certain thresholds are reached.
Lithium Battery	Powers the wearable device.

Circuit Connection Table

Component	Pin Connection
Heart Rate Sensor	VCC to 5V, GND to GND, Data to A0
LCD or OLED Display	SDA to A4, SCL to A5, VCC to 5V, GND to GND
Bluetooth Module (HC-05)	TX to pin 2, RX to pin 3
Vibration Motor	Connected to pin 6 (with a transistor for higher current)

Project Code

```
#include <Wire.h>
#include <LiquidCrystal_I2C.h>
#include <LowPower.h>

LiquidCrystal_I2C lcd(0x27, 16, 2);

#define heartRatePin A0
#define vibrationPin 6
#define bluetoothSerial Serial

void setup() {
  lcd.begin(16, 2);
  lcd.print("Smart Tracker");
  delay(1000);
  pinMode(heartRatePin, INPUT);
  pinMode(vibrationPin, OUTPUT);
  bluetoothSerial.begin(9600);
}

void loop() {
  int heartRate = analogRead(heartRatePin);
  int heartRateValue = map(heartRate, 0, 1023, 40,
180);  // Map value to heart rate range

  lcd.clear();
  lcd.print("Heart Rate: ");
  lcd.print(heartRateValue);
```

```
  bluetoothSerial.print("Heart Rate: ");
  bluetoothSerial.println(heartRateValue);


  if (heartRateValue > 120) {
    digitalWrite(vibrationPin, HIGH);   // Turn on
vibration motor
  } else {
    digitalWrite(vibrationPin, LOW);    // Turn off
vibration motor
  }


  LowPower.sleep(SLEEP_8S);   // Save power by sleeping
}
```

Expected Results

Once the code is uploaded to the Arduino, the wearable will start measuring the user's heart rate using the sensor. The heart rate will be displayed on the LCD screen, and if the value exceeds 120 beats per minute, the vibration motor will activate. The heart rate data will also be sent via Bluetooth to a paired mobile device, where it can be viewed in real-time. The wearable will conserve battery by going into sleep mode when inactive.

Chapter 57: Home Security Systems with Arduino

Home security systems are designed to detect intruders, monitor the safety of your home, and alert you in case of emergencies. Arduino, with its simplicity and flexibility, is an excellent platform to build custom home security systems. In this chapter, we will explore how to create a basic home security system using Arduino, sensors, and communication modules, including motion detection, alarm systems, and real-time notifications.

Key Concepts of Home Security Systems with Arduino

A home security system typically involves sensors that monitor the environment, actuators that alert or react to detected threats, and communication devices to notify users. Arduino can integrate a variety of sensors, from motion detectors to door/window sensors, and can trigger alarms or send notifications.

Concept	Description	Example
Motion Detection	Detects physical movement in a given area.	PIR (Passive Infrared) sensor.
Door/Window Sensors	Monitors whether doors or windows are opened or closed.	Magnetic reed switches.
Alarm Systems	Alerts users when an intruder is detected.	Buzzer, speaker, or siren.
Communication	Sends real-time notifications to users.	SMS, Wi-Fi, or Bluetooth to send alerts to a smartphone.
Power Supply	Ensures the system remains operational, especially in emergencies.	Battery backup or solar power.

Basic Rules for Using Arduino in Home Security

Rule	Correct Example	Incorrect Example
Ensure sensors are positioned correctly.	`Place PIR sensor in a corner where movement is most likely.`	Placing sensors in areas where movement detection will be blocked.
Use external power sources for continuous operation.	`Use a battery pack or solar panel for uninterrupted power.`	Relying on the Arduino's built-in power, which can deplete quickly.
Use communication modules for real-time alerts.	`Use Wi-Fi module (ESP8266) to send notifications.`	Using just a local buzzer without alerting the user remotely.
Integrate a fail-safe mechanism.	`Include a backup power source to keep the system running.`	No backup power during power outages.

Syntax Table

SL	Function	Syntax/Example	Description
1	Read sensor data	`sensorValue = sensor.read();`	Reads data from the sensor (e.g., motion detection).
2	Trigger alarm system	`digitalWrite(alarmPin, HIGH);`	Activates the alarm when a threat is detected.
3	Send notifications via SMS	`sms.sendMessage(phoneNumber, message);`	Sends an SMS alert to the user.
4	Send alerts via Wi-Fi	`WiFi.sendAlert(message);`	Sends a real-time alert over Wi-Fi to a mobile device.
5	Activate backup power	`switchPower(backupPowerPin, ON);`	Activates a backup power source if the main power fails.

Syntax Explanation

1. Read Sensor Data

What does reading sensor data do?
The `sensor.read()` function reads the data from a sensor, such as a motion detector (PIR sensor) or a magnetic reed switch. The data is typically used to determine whether an event (such as movement or door/window opening) has occurred.

Syntax:
```
sensorValue = sensor.read();
```
Example:
```
sensorValue = PIRSensor.read();   // Read value from PIR
sensor
```

Example Explanation:
In this example, the PIR sensor detects movement. The sensor value will be stored in `sensorValue`, which is then used to trigger further actions like sounding an alarm or sending a notification.

2. Trigger Alarm System

What does triggering an alarm system do?
The `digitalWrite()` function can be used to activate an alarm (e.g., a buzzer, speaker, or siren) when a sensor detects an intruder or unwanted event.

Syntax:
```
digitalWrite(pin, HIGH);
```
Example:
```
digitalWrite(alarmPin, HIGH);   // Trigger the alarm
```

Example Explanation:
This example sends a HIGH signal to the alarm pin, which could activate a buzzer or siren to alert the homeowner of a potential threat.

3. Send Notifications via SMS

What does sending notifications via SMS do?
The `sms.sendMessage()` function uses a GSM module to send an SMS to a phone number whenever a certain event occurs (e.g., motion detected or door opened).
Syntax:
`sms.sendMessage(phoneNumber, message);`
Example:
`sms.sendMessage("+1234567890", "Alert: Motion detected at the front door.");`

Example Explanation:
In this example, an SMS is sent to the specified phone number when motion is detected at the front door. The message provides a real-time alert to the homeowner.

4. Send Alerts via Wi-Fi

What does sending alerts via Wi-Fi do?

Using a Wi-Fi module (like ESP8266), you can send alerts through the internet. This is useful for remote monitoring via a smartphone or a web interface.

Syntax:

`WiFi.sendAlert(message);`

Example:

`WiFi.sendAlert("Motion detected! Check your security system.");`

Example Explanation:

This example sends an alert over Wi-Fi, which could trigger an app notification or email, informing the user of a detected motion.

5. Activate Backup Power

What does activating backup power do?
The `switchPower()` function turns on the backup power when the main power supply fails. This ensures the system stays operational in case of a power outage.

Syntax:
```
switchPower(pin, state);
```

Example:
```
switchPower(backupPowerPin, ON);  // Activate backup power
```

Example Explanation:
This code example turns on the backup power when needed. This ensures that the security system will continue to function even when the main power supply is lost.

Real-life Applications Project: DIY Home Security System
In this project, we will build a basic home security system that uses motion sensors to detect intruders, an alarm to alert the user, and an SMS notification system to send real-time alerts.

Required Components

Component	Description
PIR Motion Sensor	Detects movement in the monitored area.
GSM Module (SIM800L)	Sends SMS notifications.
Buzzer	Provides an audible alarm when motion is detected.
Arduino Uno	The microcontroller used to control the system.
Power Supply	Provides power to the entire system.

Circuit Connection Table

Component	Pin Connection
PIR Motion Sensor	VCC to 5V, GND to GND, OUT to pin 7
GSM Module	TX to pin 10, RX to pin 11, VCC to 5V, GND to GND
Buzzer	Positive lead to pin 9, negative lead to GND
Arduino Uno	As the controller, all components connect to the appropriate pins.

Project Code

```cpp
#include <SoftwareSerial.h>

#define PIRPin 7
#define buzzerPin 9
SoftwareSerial gsmSerial(10, 11);  // RX, TX

void setup() {
  pinMode(PIRPin, INPUT);
  pinMode(buzzerPin, OUTPUT);
  gsmSerial.begin(9600);  // Initialize GSM module
communication
  Serial.begin(9600);     // For debugging
}

void loop() {
  int motionDetected = digitalRead(PIRPin);

  if (motionDetected == HIGH) {
    digitalWrite(buzzerPin, HIGH);  // Turn on the
alarm
    sendSMS("Alert: Motion detected in your home!");
// Send SMS
    delay(10000);  // Keep alarm on for 10 seconds
    digitalWrite(buzzerPin, LOW);   // Turn off the
alarm
  }
}

void sendSMS(String message) {
  gsmSerial.println("AT+CMGF=1");  // Set SMS mode
  delay(1000);
  gsmSerial.println("AT+CMGS=\"+1234567890\"");  //
Recipient phone number
  delay(1000);
  gsmSerial.println(message);  // Send the message
```

```
  delay(1000);
  gsmSerial.write(26);   // Send Ctrl+Z to send the
message
  delay(1000);
}
```

Expected Results

Once the code is uploaded to the Arduino, the system will monitor the area for any movement using the PIR sensor. When motion is detected, the buzzer will sound as an alarm, and an SMS alert will be sent to the designated phone number. The system will continue to monitor the area, ready to react to further movement.

Chapter 58: Weather Monitoring System with Arduino

Weather monitoring systems are designed to collect and analyze environmental data, such as temperature, humidity, atmospheric pressure, and light levels. These systems are essential for various applications, including agriculture, home automation, and research. In this chapter, we will explore how to create a weather monitoring system using Arduino, sensors, and communication modules to collect and display real-time weather data.

Key Concepts of Weather Monitoring Systems with Arduino

A weather monitoring system typically includes various sensors to collect environmental data, a microcontroller (Arduino) to process the data, and a display or communication module to present the results. By integrating multiple sensors, Arduino can monitor weather conditions like temperature, humidity, air pressure, and more.

Concept	Description	Example
Temperature Measurement	Measures the current temperature of the environment.	DHT11 or DHT22 sensor for temperature readings.
Humidity Measurement	Measures the amount of moisture in the air.	DHT11, DHT22, or AM2302 sensor for humidity readings.
Atmospheric Pressure	Measures the pressure exerted by the atmosphere.	BMP180 or BME280 sensor for barometric pressure.
Light Intensity	Measures the amount of light falling on the sensor.	LDR (Light Dependent Resistor) for measuring light intensity.
Data Display	Displays the collected data to the user.	LCD display, OLED screen, or Serial Monitor.
Communication	Sends the weather data to a remote device for analysis or monitoring.	Wi-Fi (ESP8266) or GSM module for real-time weather reporting.

Basic Rules for Using Weather Monitoring Systems

Rule	Correct Example	Incorrect Example
Choose appropriate sensors for data collection.	Use DHT22 for accurate temperature and humidity readings.	Using an inaccurate sensor for the required data.
Ensure correct wiring of sensors.	Connect the DHT22 sensor correctly to the Arduino for accurate readings.	Incorrect wiring may lead to false readings or sensor malfunctions.
Use accurate libraries for data processing.	Use the DHT library for working with DHT sensors.	Using incorrect libraries that are incompatible with the sensor.
Consider power consumption.	Use a low-power mode if using the system for prolonged periods.	Keeping the Arduino running constantly without consideration of power consumption.
Calibrate sensors as needed.	Calibrate the pressure sensor for better accuracy.	Ignoring the calibration process can lead to inaccurate data.

Syntax Table

SL	Function	Syntax/Example	Description
1	Read temperature from sensor	`temperature = dht.readTemperature();`	Reads the temperature data from a DHT sensor.
2	Read humidity from sensor	`humidity = dht.readHumidity();`	Reads the humidity data from a DHT sensor.
3	Read atmospheric pressure	`pressure = bmp.readPressure();`	Reads the atmospheric pressure from a BMP sensor.

4	Display data on LCD	`lcd.print("Temp erature: " + String(temperat ure));`	Displays data on an LCD screen.
5	Send data via Wi-Fi	`wifiClient.send Data("weatherDa ta", data);`	Sends the collected data to a remote server via Wi-Fi.

Syntax Explanation

1. Read Temperature from Sensor

What does reading temperature data do?
The dht.readTemperature() function reads the current temperature from the DHT sensor, which can be displayed on a screen or sent via communication modules for further analysis.
Syntax:
temperature = dht.readTemperature();
Example:
float temperature = dht.readTemperature();   // Read temperature from DHT sensor
Example Explanation:
This example reads the temperature from a DHT sensor and stores it in the temperature variable, which can be displayed or transmitted for further processing.

2. Read Humidity from Sensor

What does reading humidity data do?
The dht.readHumidity() function reads the humidity level in the environment from the DHT sensor.
Syntax:
humidity = dht.readHumidity();
Example:
float humidity = dht.readHumidity();   // Read humidity from DHT sensor
Example Explanation:
This example reads the humidity value from the DHT sensor and stores it in the humidity variable, which can be displayed or sent to a remote device.

3. Read Atmospheric Pressure

What does reading atmospheric pressure do?
The `bmp.readPressure()` function reads the current atmospheric pressure from a BMP180 or BME280 sensor. This data is useful for weather prediction and monitoring changes in weather patterns.
Syntax:
```
pressure = bmp.readPressure();
```
Example:
```
long pressure = bmp.readPressure();   // Read
atmospheric pressure from BMP sensor
```

Example Explanation:
This code reads the atmospheric pressure from the BMP sensor and stores it in the `pressure` variable for later display or communication.

4. Display Data on LCD

What does displaying data on an LCD do?
The `lcd.print()` function is used to display the data, such as temperature and humidity, on an LCD screen for easy monitoring of the environment.
Syntax:
```
lcd.print("Temperature: " + String(temperature));
```
Example:
```
lcd.print("Temp: " + String(temperature) + "C");
lcd.setCursor(0, 1);
lcd.print("Humidity: " + String(humidity) + "%");
```

Example Explanation:
In this example, the temperature and humidity readings are displayed on an LCD screen for easy monitoring. The `lcd.print()` function prints the data to the screen.

5. Send Data via Wi-Fi

What does sending data via Wi-Fi do?
The `wifiClient.sendData()` function sends the collected weather data to a remote server, where it can be stored and analyzed. This allows you to monitor weather conditions remotely.

Syntax:
```
wifiClient.sendData("weatherData", data);
```
Example:
```
wifiClient.sendData("temperature", temperature);
wifiClient.sendData("humidity", humidity);
```

Example Explanation:
This code sends the temperature and humidity data via Wi-Fi to a remote server for real-time monitoring and storage.

Real-life Applications Project: DIY Weather Monitoring System
In this project, we will create a simple weather monitoring system that measures temperature, humidity, and atmospheric pressure, and displays the data on an LCD screen. The data will also be sent via Wi-Fi to a remote server for real-time monitoring.

Required Components

Component	Description
DHT22 Sensor	Measures temperature and humidity.
BMP180 or BME280 Sensor	Measures atmospheric pressure.
LCD Display	Displays the weather data to the user.
Arduino Uno	Microcontroller to collect and process data from sensors.
Wi-Fi Module (ESP8266)	Sends data to a remote server via Wi-Fi.
Jumper Wires	Used to connect all components together.
Breadboard	Provides a platform for building the circuit.

Circuit Connection Table

Component	Pin Connection
DHT22 Sensor	VCC to 5V, GND to GND, DATA to pin 2
BMP180/BME280 Sensor	VCC to 3.3V, GND to GND, SDA to pin A4, SCL to pin A5
LCD Display	VCC to 5V, GND to GND, SDA to A4, SCL to A5
Wi-Fi Module (ESP8266)	VCC to 3.3V, GND to GND, RX to pin 10, TX to pin 11
Arduino Uno	As the central controller for all components.

Project Code

```cpp
#include <Wire.h>
#include <Adafruit_Sensor.h>
#include <DHT.h>
#include <Adafruit_BMP085_U.h>
#include <ESP8266WiFi.h>
#include <LiquidCrystal_I2C.h>

// Define pins
#define DHTPIN 2
#define DHTTYPE DHT22

// Initialize sensors
DHT dht(DHTPIN, DHTTYPE);
Adafruit_BMP085_Unified bmp;

// Initialize display
LiquidCrystal_I2C lcd(0x27, 16, 2);

// Wi-Fi credentials
const char* ssid = "Your_SSID";
const char* password = "Your_PASSWORD";

void setup() {
  Serial.begin(9600);
  dht.begin();
  bmp.begin();
  lcd.begin(16, 2);

  // Connect to Wi-Fi
  WiFi.begin(ssid, password);
  while (WiFi.status() != WL_CONNECTED) {
    delay(1000);
    Serial.println("Connecting to WiFi...");
  }
```

```
    Serial.println("Connected to WiFi");
}


void loop()

  {
    // Read sensor data
    float temperature = dht.readTemperature();
    float humidity = dht.readHumidity();
    float pressure;
    bmp.getPressure(&pressure);

    // Display data on LCD
    lcd.setCursor(0, 0);
    lcd.print("Temp: " + String(temperature) + "C");
    lcd.setCursor(0, 1);
    lcd.print("Humidity: " + String(humidity) + "%");

    // Send data via Wi-Fi
    WiFiClient client;
    if (client.connect("your-server.com", 80)) {
      client.print("GET /update?temp=" +
String(temperature) + "&hum=" + String(humidity) +
"&pressure=" + String(pressure) + " HTTP/1.1\r\n");
      client.print("Host: your-server.com\r\n");
      client.print("Connection: close\r\n\r\n");
    }
    delay(5000); // Wait for 5 seconds before reading
again
}
```

Expected Results

After uploading the code to the Arduino, the system will measure temperature, humidity, and atmospheric pressure and display the results on an LCD screen. Additionally, it will send the data to a remote server over Wi-Fi for monitoring. You can view the weather data on a web page or use it for further analysis.

Chapter 60: Common Issues and Fixes with Arduino

Working with Arduino can be an exciting and educational experience, but like any hardware and software project, there are common issues that may arise. In this chapter, we will cover some of the most frequent problems you may encounter while working with Arduino, along with their possible causes and solutions. This will help you troubleshoot effectively and ensure your projects run smoothly.

Key Concepts of Troubleshooting Arduino

When encountering issues with your Arduino projects, it's essential to understand the root cause of the problem. Most issues can be classified into one of the following categories:

Concept	Description	Example
Power Supply Issues	Incorrect or insufficient power can lead to malfunctioning components.	Using a 5V pin to power high-power devices that need 12V.
Code Errors	Bugs in the code can cause unexpected behavior or failure.	Syntax errors, incorrect pin assignments, or missing libraries.
Hardware Connection Issues	Incorrect or loose connections can prevent components from working.	Wires not properly inserted or not connected to the correct pins.
Driver or Software Problems	Missing or outdated drivers can prevent the Arduino from communicating with your computer.	Unable to upload code or recognize the Arduino board in the IDE.
Sensor or Component Malfunctions	Faulty or damaged components may not work as expected.	A sensor not giving readings or an LED not lighting up.

Basic Rules for Troubleshooting Arduino

Rule	Correct Example	Incorrect Example
Always check your power supply.	Ensure your Arduino and components are properly powered.	Using an incorrect voltage for your components.
Double-check all connections.	Verify all wires are securely connected and match the diagram.	Loose wires or incorrectly placed connections.
Review your code for syntax errors.	Use the Arduino IDE's syntax checker to identify errors.	Skipping syntax checks or ignoring warnings.
Make sure you select the correct board and port.	Choose the correct board and port in the Arduino IDE.	Selecting the wrong board type or port.
Update drivers and software when necessary.	Ensure your Arduino IDE and drivers are up-to-date.	Ignoring software updates or using outdated versions.

Common Issues and Fixes

Issue	Cause	Fix
Arduino not recognized by the computer	Missing or outdated drivers, or incorrect USB cable.	Install or update drivers. Try using a different USB cable or port.
Unable to upload code to Arduino	Incorrect board or port selected in the Arduino IDE.	Ensure the correct board and port are selected in the IDE.
Code compiles but doesn't run on Arduino	Incorrect wiring or faulty components.	Check wiring, ensure components are properly connected.
No power to the Arduino	Power supply issues, such as incorrect voltage or a faulty power source.	Ensure you're using the correct voltage for your Arduino model and connected components.

LED not lighting up	Incorrect pin number or faulty LED.	Check the LED wiring and ensure you're using the correct pin.
Sensors not giving readings	Incorrect sensor connections or faulty sensor.	Double-check connections, and test the sensor with simple code.
Serial Monitor not displaying output	Incorrect baud rate or faulty USB connection.	Ensure the correct baud rate is set in the Serial Monitor and check the USB connection.
Servo motor not working	Power supply issues, incorrect signal pin, or faulty motor.	Check the power supply, ensure correct pin assignments, and test the motor with simple code.
Breadboard not working	Loose connections or faulty components.	Inspect the breadboard connections and test each component.

Syntax Table

SL	Issue	Cause	Solution
1	Arduino not recognized by PC	Missing or outdated drivers	Update drivers, try another USB port, or use a different cable.
2	Code not uploading	Wrong board/port selected in the IDE	Select the correct board and port in the Arduino IDE.
3	No power to Arduino	Power supply issues or incorrect voltage	Ensure proper voltage is supplied to your Arduino and components.
4	No output from Serial Monitor	Incorrect baud rate or USB issues	Set the correct baud rate and check the USB connection.
5	LED not lighting up	Incorrect pin wiring or faulty LED	Check the pin number and replace the LED if necessary.
6	Sensors not giving readings	Incorrect sensor wiring or damaged sensor	Double-check the wiring and test the sensor with sample code.

7	Servo motor not responding	Incorrect pin, power supply issue, or motor malfunction	Check wiring and power supply, and test with sample code.
8	No output from sensor	Code or hardware configuration errors	Ensure proper sensor wiring and check the code.

Example Explanations

1. Arduino Not Recognized by the Computer

What does this mean?
If your Arduino is not recognized by the computer, it could be due to missing or outdated drivers, or using a faulty USB cable. This prevents the Arduino from being detected by the IDE for uploading code.
Solution:
- Install or update the necessary drivers from the Arduino website.
- Try using a different USB cable or port on your computer.
- Ensure the Arduino is powered on.

Example:
```
Check if the board is listed in the "Tools > Port" menu
in Arduino IDE.
```

2. Unable to Upload Code to Arduino

What does this mean?
If you can compile code but can't upload it to the Arduino, the issue could be with the board or port settings in the IDE, or with the Arduino's bootloader.
Solution:
- Ensure that the correct board and port are selected in the IDE (Tools > Board and Tools > Port).
- Try resetting the Arduino before uploading the code.
- Reboot the computer or try a different USB cable.

Example:
```
Select "Arduino Uno" and the correct COM port in the
IDE.
```

3. Code Compiles but Doesn't Run

What does this mean?
Sometimes the code may compile successfully but doesn't produce the desired result. This can be caused by incorrect wiring or faulty components.

Solution:
- Double-check all component connections, especially the power and ground pins.
- Use simpler code to test individual components (like LEDs or sensors) to ensure they are functioning properly.

Example:
```
pinMode(13, OUTPUT);
digitalWrite(13, HIGH);   // Test the LED on pin 13.
```


4. No Power to the Arduino

What does this mean?
If your Arduino isn't powering on, there could be an issue with the power source or the Arduino's voltage regulator.

Solution:
- Ensure that the power supply is connected properly and providing the correct voltage.
- Use a separate power source (e.g., a 9V battery or a USB adapter) to test.

Example:
```
Make sure the Arduino is powered via USB or external
power source (e.g., 9V battery).
```

Real-life Application Project: Troubleshooting Arduino Projects
In this project, you will build a basic LED blink project and troubleshoot common issues such as code compilation errors, hardware connection problems, and power supply issues.

Required Components

Component	Description
Arduino Uno	Microcontroller board
LED	Light Emitting Diode to test the output
220Ω Resistor	To limit current to the LED
Breadboard	For building the circuit
Jumper Wires	For connecting components

Circuit Connection Table

Component	Pin Connection
LED	Anode (long leg) to pin 13, Cathode (short leg) to GND
220Ω Resistor	Between LED cathode and GND

Project Code

```
void setup() {
  pinMode(13, OUTPUT);  // Set pin 13 as output
}

void loop() {
  digitalWrite(13, HIGH);  // Turn LED ON
  delay(1000);             // Wait for 1 second
  digitalWrite(13, LOW);   // Turn LED OFF
  delay(1000);             // Wait for 1 second
}
```

Expected Results

When the code is uploaded, the LED should blink on and off every second. If the LED doesn't light up, check the wiring, the power supply, and the code.

Chapter 61: Debugging Sensor Errors

When working with sensors in Arduino projects, errors can sometimes arise due to faulty connections, incorrect code, or environmental factors. Debugging sensor issues is an essential skill to ensure your projects run smoothly. In this chapter, we will explore common sensor errors and how to debug them effectively.

Key Concepts of Debugging Sensors

Sensors often give us real-time data, but that data can be incorrect or unreliable due to several factors. Understanding how to troubleshoot sensor-related errors is crucial in ensuring accurate sensor readings and reliable project performance.

Concept	Description	Example
Sensor Calibration	Ensuring the sensor is calibrated correctly to give accurate readings.	A temperature sensor may need to be calibrated to show the right temperature.
Wiring Issues	Incorrect or loose connections can cause sensors to fail or behave erratically.	Loose wires or wrong pin connections may result in no sensor readings.
Power Supply Problems	Insufficient or unstable power supply can affect sensor performance.	A sensor requiring 5V may fail to work properly if only 3.3V is supplied.
Faulty Sensors	Physical damage or defective components can cause sensors to malfunction.	A broken temperature sensor may give a constant reading or no reading at all.
Software Errors	Coding issues such as incorrect functions or delays can cause issues in sensor output.	Using the wrong library or forgetting to initialize the sensor in code.
Environmental Factors	Environmental conditions like temperature, humidity, or interference may affect sensor readings.	A light sensor may provide incorrect values due to strong ambient light.

Basic Rules for Debugging Sensors

Rule	Correct Example	Incorrect Example
Double-check wiring connections.	Ensure all wires are connected to the correct pins as per the circuit diagram.	Incorrectly connected wires causing incorrect readings.
Use simple test code to isolate problems.	Use basic sensor code to test the sensor independently.	Running complex code before ensuring the sensor works.
Check sensor power requirements.	Verify that the sensor is receiving the required voltage.	Connecting a 5V sensor to a 3.3V pin.
Review sensor documentation.	Consult datasheets and manuals for correct sensor behavior and wiring.	Skipping datasheet reading and using sensors incorrectly.
Test with serial monitor or debugging tools.	Use the serial monitor to display sensor values for easier troubleshooting.	Not using the serial monitor to check for errors.

Common Sensor Issues and Fixes

Issue	Cause	Fix
Sensor not giving any readings	Wiring issues, incorrect sensor connection, or power supply issues.	Check all wiring and power connections. Verify the correct voltage.
Sensor giving erratic readings	Interference, unstable power supply, or environmental factors.	Use capacitors for noise filtering, ensure stable power, and shield the sensor from interference.
Incorrect	The sensor hasn't been	Calibrate the sensor using known

sensor calibratio n	calibrated properly or needs factory calibration.	standards or check the datasheet for calibration instructions.
Sensor data is inconsist ent	Environmental factors or physical damage to the sensor.	Relocate the sensor to a stable environment or replace the sensor if damaged.
Inaccurat e sensor readings	Incorrect code or sensor configuration.	Double-check the code, particularly initialization, pin setup, and sensor settings.

Syntax Table for Sensor Debugging

SL	Issue	Cause	Solution
1	No sensor data output	Wiring issue or incorrect sensor connection	Verify wiring and connections according to the sensor datasheet.
2	Inconsistent sensor readings	Power supply issues or environmental interference	Ensure stable power and minimize interference (use capacitors, shields).
3	Incorrect readings due to calibration	Uncalibrated sensor or wrong configuration in code	Calibrate the sensor or check the sensor configuration.
4	Sensor fails to initialize properly	Incorrect sensor initialization in code	Recheck the initialization code and ensure correct sensor library is used.
5	Sensor data not updating	Missing delays or improper reading intervals	Ensure code includes appropriate delays or reading intervals.

Example Explanations
1. Sensor Not Giving Any Readings
What does this mean?

If your sensor isn't providing any output data, it is often due to a connection problem, a lack of power, or incorrect sensor initialization in the code.

Solution:

- Check all wiring carefully, ensuring that the sensor is connected to the correct pins and powered correctly.
- Refer to the sensor's datasheet to verify the required voltage and pin connections.
- Use simple test code to verify if the sensor can provide basic readings.

Example:

```
#include <DHT.h>

#define DHTPIN 2   // Pin where the sensor is connected
#define DHTTYPE DHT11   // Sensor type

DHT dht(DHTPIN, DHTTYPE);

void setup() {
  Serial.begin(9600);
  dht.begin();
}

void loop() {
  float humidity = dht.readHumidity();
  float temperature = dht.readTemperature();

  if (isnan(humidity) || isnan(temperature)) {
    Serial.println("Failed to read from DHT sensor!");
  } else {
    Serial.print("Temperature: ");
    Serial.print(temperature);
    Serial.print(" °C, Humidity: ");
    Serial.print(humidity);
```

```
      Serial.println(" %");
  }
  delay(2000);   // Wait for 2 seconds
}
```

Example Explanation:
- This code checks if the sensor is reading valid data (temperature and humidity).
- If the sensor fails to provide data, it outputs an error message to the serial monitor, allowing you to identify the problem.

2. Inconsistent Sensor Readings

What does this mean?

Erratic or inconsistent sensor readings can be caused by a variety of factors, such as electrical noise, environmental interference, or unstable power supply.

Solution:
- Ensure that your power supply is stable and providing the correct voltage to the sensor.
- Use decoupling capacitors near the sensor to filter out electrical noise.
- If using analog sensors, try using a low-pass filter to smooth the readings.

Example:

```
int sensorPin = A0;   // Analog sensor connected to pin
A0
int sensorValue = 0;

void setup() {
  Serial.begin(9600);
}

void loop() {
  sensorValue = analogRead(sensorPin);
  Serial.println(sensorValue);
  delay(100);   // Add delay to allow stable readings
}
```

Example Explanation:

- The code reads the analog value from the sensor and prints it to the serial monitor.
- A short delay between readings ensures that the sensor has enough time to stabilize and provide consistent values.

3. Incorrect Sensor Calibration

What does this mean?

If a sensor is giving inaccurate readings, it may need to be calibrated. Many sensors require calibration before use to ensure they give precise measurements.

Solution:

- Refer to the sensor's datasheet for calibration procedures or factory calibration details.
- Use known reference values (e.g., a known temperature or pressure) to calibrate the sensor.
- In code, ensure that calibration factors are accounted for, such as offsets or scaling.

Example:

```
#include <DHT.h>

#define DHTPIN 2
#define DHTTYPE DHT11

DHT dht(DHTPIN, DHTTYPE);

void setup() {
  Serial.begin(9600);
  dht.begin();
}

void loop() {
  float humidity = dht.readHumidity();
  float temperature = dht.readTemperature();

  if (isnan(humidity) || isnan(temperature)) {
    Serial.println("Failed to read from DHT sensor!");
```

```
  } else {
    float calibratedTemperature = temperature + 2.0; //
Calibration offset
    Serial.print("Calibrated Temperature: ");
    Serial.print(calibratedTemperature);
    Serial.print(" °C");
  }
  delay(2000);
}
```

Example Explanation:
- If the sensor readings are consistently off, this code applies a calibration offset to correct the temperature readings.
- Always check the datasheet for the correct calibration method and apply it to the sensor readings in your code.

Real-life Application Project: Debugging a Temperature Sensor

In this project, we will work with a temperature sensor and debug common errors related to sensor calibration, wiring, and inconsistent readings.

Required Components

Component	Description
Arduino Uno	Microcontroller board
DHT11 or DHT22 Sensor	Temperature and humidity sensor
Breadboard	For building the circuit
Jumper Wires	For connecting components

Circuit Connection Table

Component	Pin Connection
DHT11 Sensor	VCC to 5V, GND to GND, Data to pin 2
Arduino Uno	Pin 2 connected to the sensor

Project Code

```
#include <DHT.h>

#define DHTPIN 2
#define DHTTYPE DHT11
```

```
DHT dht(DHTPIN, DHTTYPE);

void setup() {
  Serial.begin(9600);
  dht.begin();
}

void loop() {
  float humidity = dht.readHumidity();
  float temperature = dht.readTemperature();

  if (isnan(humidity) || isnan(temperature)) {
    Serial.println("Failed to read from DHT sensor!");
  } else {
    Serial.print("Temperature: ");
    Serial.print(temperature);
    Serial.print(" °C, Humidity: ");
    Serial.print(humidity);
    Serial.println(" %");
  }
  delay(2000);
}
```

Expected Results

After uploading the code to the Arduino, the sensor readings should appear in the serial monitor every two seconds. If there are any issues, the serial monitor will output an error message indicating that the sensor failed to provide readings.

Chapter 62: Avoiding Common Mistakes with Arduino

Arduino is an excellent platform for both beginners and experienced engineers, but it's easy to make mistakes along the way. In this chapter, we will explore some of the most common mistakes encountered by Arduino users and how to avoid them. By understanding and recognizing these issues, you can save time, reduce frustration, and build more reliable projects.

Key Concepts of Common Arduino Mistakes

When working with Arduino, beginners often encounter issues related to wiring, coding, or misunderstanding how certain components work. Being aware of these mistakes and learning how to avoid them will help you streamline your project development process.

Concept	Description	Example
Incorrect Wiring	A common issue that can result in non-functional circuits or even damaged components.	Connecting a component to the wrong pin, causing it not to work.
Misunderstanding Component Specs	Using components without properly understanding their voltage, current, or functionality.	Trying to power a 5V sensor with 3.3V.
Incorrect Library Usage	Using the wrong library or improperly including libraries in code.	Using a library not compatible with your sensor model.
Missing Code Initialization	Forgetting to initialize variables, pins, or components in the setup() function.	Not defining pinMode() for an output pin, causing unexpected behavior.
Incorrect Serial	Forgetting to call Serial.begin() or using the	Code not displaying serial output due to

Communication	wrong baud rate.	missing Serial.begin().
Using Delay in Time-sensitive Applications	Using delay() in programs requiring precise timing or multitasking.	Blocking code execution with delay() in time-sensitive projects like robotics.
Overloading I/O Pins	Trying to connect too many devices to a single pin or exceeding the current rating of an I/O pin.	Connecting too many LEDs to a single pin without using a driver.
Ignoring Proper Grounding	Failing to connect the ground of all components to the Arduino ground.	Components not working due to improper grounding connections.

Basic Rules for Avoiding Common Arduino Mistakes

Rule	Correct Example	Incorrect Example
Always double-check your wiring.	Ensure each wire is correctly connected, following the schematic.	Incorrect wiring or loose connections causing non-functionality.
Use proper libraries and initialize components.	Include the correct library and initialize variables in setup().	Forgetting to initialize components or using the wrong library.
Test small code snippets before going large.	Test small sections of your code in isolation to ensure proper behavior.	Writing large programs without testing smaller portions first.
Avoid using delay() in real-time applications.	Use millis() or timers for non-blocking delays.	Relying on delay() for controlling timing in complex projects.
Verify correct voltage and	Check the component's datasheet for voltage	Overloading components with

current requirements.	and current requirements.	too much voltage or current.
Use proper grounding.	Make sure all components share a common ground connection.	Components not sharing a ground or improper grounding.
Use external power sources when necessary.	Power high-current devices through external sources, not directly from Arduino.	Drawing too much current from the Arduino's 5V pin.

Common Mistakes and Fixes

Mistake	Cause	Fix
Wrong wiring	Components connected to the wrong pins or incorrect power supply.	Double-check all wiring according to the circuit diagram.
Component damage	Incorrect voltage or current causing component failure.	Always verify voltage and current ratings before connecting.
Incorrect pinMode setup	Failing to declare a pin as an input or output.	Always use pinMode() to initialize pins before using them in code.
Forgetting to call Serial.begin()	Serial communication not initialized in the setup function.	Add `Serial.begin(9600);` in the setup() function.
Using delay() in time-critical projects	delay() blocks execution, causing delays in other tasks.	Use millis() for non-blocking delays in real-time applications.
Overloading Arduino pins	Drawing too much current from an I/O pin or connecting too many devices.	Use transistors or external drivers for high-current devices.
Lack of external	Drawing too much current from the Arduino's 5V or	Use an external power source for high-current

power supply	3.3V pin.	components.
Not checking for available libraries	Using a library that doesn't support the sensor or component model.	Always verify the library is compatible with your hardware.

Syntax Table for Avoiding Common Mistakes

SL	Mistake	Cause	Fix
1	Missing pinMode()	Forgot to define pin modes in setup().	`pinMode(LED_PIN, OUTPUT);`
2	Not using Serial.begin()	Forgot to initialize serial communication.	`Serial.begin(9600);`
3	Incorrect voltage supply	Providing incorrect voltage to components.	Verify the voltage requirement from datasheets.
4	Incorrect library	Using the wrong library for the sensor/module.	Use the library that matches your specific component.
5	Using delay() in time-sensitive code	delay() blocks code execution for a set time.	Use `millis()` instead of delay() for non-blocking timing.
6	Overloading Arduino pins	Drawing too much current from the pins.	Use external drivers or transistors for power-heavy devices.

Example Explanations

1. Wrong Wiring

What does this mean?
If your components are not wired correctly, your project will not function as expected. Common wiring mistakes include connecting the wrong pins or not supplying the correct voltage to components.
Solution:

- Always refer to the datasheet of components to ensure you're using the correct pinout.
- Use clear diagrams, and check your circuit multiple times before powering it up.

Example:

```
const int ledPin = 13;

void setup() {
  pinMode(ledPin, OUTPUT);  // Initialize the digital
pin as an output.
}

void loop() {
  digitalWrite(ledPin, HIGH);    // Turn the LED on
  delay(1000);                   // Wait for a second
  digitalWrite(ledPin, LOW);     // Turn the LED off
  delay(1000);                   // Wait for a second
}
```

Example Explanation:
- This code blinks an LED connected to pin 13.
- Ensure the LED is connected correctly (anode to the pin, cathode to GND) for it to work.

2. Incorrect PinMode Setup

What does this mean?
If you forget to set the mode of a pin (input or output) in the setup() function, the pin may not function as expected.
Solution:
- Always define the pinMode() for each pin before using it in your code.

Example:

```
const int buttonPin = 2;  // Pin where button is
connected
const int ledPin = 13;    // Pin where LED is connected

void setup() {
```

```
  pinMode(buttonPin, INPUT);    // Set button pin as
input
  pinMode(ledPin, OUTPUT);      // Set LED pin as output
}

void loop() {
  int buttonState = digitalRead(buttonPin); // Read the
state of the button

  if (buttonState == HIGH) {
    digitalWrite(ledPin, HIGH);  // Turn LED on if
button is pressed
  } else {
    digitalWrite(ledPin, LOW);   // Turn LED off if
button is not pressed
  }
}
```

Example Explanation:
- Here, `pinMode()` is used to initialize the button as an input and the LED as an output.
- Failing to set the button pin as an input could lead to unpredictable behavior.

3. Using delay() in Time-Sensitive Applications

What does this mean?
The delay() function can block the execution of other tasks while it waits, which can be problematic in real-time systems (like robotics, or multitasking applications).
Solution:
- Use `millis()` for non-blocking delays, allowing other tasks to run concurrently.

Example:
```
unsigned long previousMillis = 0;
const long interval = 1000;   // 1 second

void setup() {
```

```
  pinMode(LED_BUILTIN, OUTPUT);
}

void loop() {
  unsigned long currentMillis = millis();

  if (currentMillis - previousMillis >= interval) {
    previousMillis = currentMillis;
    digitalWrite(LED_BUILTIN,
!digitalRead(LED_BUILTIN)); // Toggle LED
  }
}
```

Example Explanation:
- This code uses `millis()` to toggle the built-in LED without blocking other operations.
- It checks whether the specified interval has passed and only toggles the LED when it's time.

Real-life Application Project: LED Button Toggle

Project Code

```
const int buttonPin = 2;     // Pin connected
to the button
const int ledPin = 13;       // Pin connected
to the LED

void setup() {
  pinMode(buttonPin, INPUT);  // Set button as
input
  pinMode(ledPin, OUTPUT);    // Set LED as
output
}

void loop() {
```

```
    int buttonState = digitalRead(buttonPin);
// Read button state
    if (buttonState == HIGH) {
        digitalWrite(ledPin, HIGH);    // Turn on
the LED
    } else {
        digitalWrite(ledPin, LOW);     // Turn off
the LED
    }
}
```

Expected Results

After uploading the code, the LED should toggle ON or OFF based on the button's state. Ensure that the button is correctly wired, and verify the input/output configuration to avoid common mistakes.

Chapter 63: Enhancing Code Efficiency with Arduino

Arduino projects can quickly become complex, and as your code grows, performance optimization becomes essential. Writing efficient code not only improves the execution time but also minimizes memory usage, resulting in smoother and more reliable projects. In this chapter, we will explore various techniques to enhance the efficiency of your Arduino code, focusing on memory management, execution speed, and power consumption.

Key Concepts of Code Efficiency

When it comes to efficient coding with Arduino, there are several factors to consider, including minimizing delays, optimizing memory, and reducing redundant operations. Below are some of the key concepts to help enhance the performance of your code:

Concept	Description	Example	
Minimize delay() Usage	Avoid using delay() as it blocks the execution of other tasks. Use alternatives like `millis()`.	Using `millis()` for non-blocking delays in time-sensitive projects.	
Efficient Memory Usage	Arduino boards have limited memory, so it's important to use variables and data structures wisely.	Use `byte` instead of `int` when you only need small numbers.	
Avoid Floating Point Operations	Floating point calculations are slower than integer operations, so avoid them if possible.	Use integer math instead of floating-point division.	
Optimize Loops	Reducing the number of iterations or conditions in loops can significantly speed up execution.	Avoid nested loops when possible.	

Use Interrupts	Interrupts allow you to perform tasks in the background, enabling your program to respond quickly to changes.	Using interrupts for time-sensitive tasks like button presses.	
Remove Redundant Code	Eliminate unnecessary variables, functions, and conditions that don't contribute to the desired output.	Avoid using variables or functions that are not being called.	

Basic Rules for Enhancing Code Efficiency

Rule	Correct Example	Incorrect Example	
Avoid using delay() for timing	Use `millis()` for non-blocking timing.	`delay(1000); blocks code execution for 1 second.`	
Optimize memory usage by choosing proper data types	Use byte or `int` depending on the required range.	Using `int` for values that only need 1 byte of storage.	
Use bitwise operations for faster hardware control	`` `PORTB ``	`= (1 << PB0);` to turn on LED connected to pin 8.	`digitalWrite(8, HIGH);` uses more time compared to bit manipulation.
Avoid floating-point operations in time-critical code	Use integer math instead of floating point.	`float temperature = (analogRead (A0) * 5.0) / 1024.0;`	
Minimize loops and	Optimize loops by	Using nested loops where a	

conditions	avoiding unnecessary iterations.	single loop could suffice.	
Use interrupts for real-time responsiveness	Attach an interrupt to a pin to detect button presses.	Polling a pin inside a loop to detect button presses.	

Syntax Table for Code Optimization

SL	Optimization Technique	Correct Syntax/Example	Description	
1	Minimize delay() Usage	`millis()`	Use `millis()` to track elapsed time without blocking the program.	
2	Efficient Memory Usage	`byte variableName;`	Use `byte` instead of `int` for smaller numeric ranges.	
3	Bit Manipulation	`` `PORTB ``	`= (1 << PB0);`	Bitwise operation for fast pin control.
4	Avoid Floating Point Operations	`int value = analogRead (A0);`	Avoid floating-point division in critical code paths.	
5	Optimize Loop Performance	Use `for` or `while` with break conditions instead of nested loops.	Reduces unnecessary loops and improves execution time.	

6	Use Interrupts	`attachInte rrupt(digi talPinToIn terrupt(pi n), ISR, mode);`	Handles external events immediately without continuous polling.	

Example Explanations

1. Minimize delay() Usage

What does this mean?

The `delay()` function pauses the program for the specified time, blocking the execution of other tasks. This can be problematic in real-time applications where tasks need to run simultaneously.

Solution:

Use `millis()` to track elapsed time without blocking the execution of other code.

Example:

```
unsigned long previousMillis = 0;
const long interval = 1000;   // 1 second

void setup() {
   pinMode(LED_BUILTIN, OUTPUT);
}

void loop() {
   unsigned long currentMillis = millis();

   if (currentMillis - previousMillis >=
interval) {
     previousMillis = currentMillis;
     digitalWrite(LED_BUILTIN,
!digitalRead(LED_BUILTIN));   // Toggle LED
   }
```

}
Example Explanation:
- This code toggles the LED every second without blocking other operations by using `millis()`.
- The program can perform other tasks while waiting to toggle the LED, avoiding the need for `delay()`.

2. Efficient Memory Usage

What does this mean?
Arduino boards have limited memory (SRAM and EEPROM), so it's essential to use the appropriate data types for variables.
Solution:
Use smaller data types like `byte` for variables that only need small values, and use `int` when larger ranges are needed.
Example:
```
byte sensorValue = 0;  // Use byte for small values
int sensorData = analogRead(A0);  // Use int for larger values
```

Example Explanation:
- Using `byte` for the `sensorValue` variable, which only needs values from 0 to 255, saves memory.
- Using `int` for `sensorData` is appropriate since `analogRead()` returns a value between 0 and 1023, which fits in an `int`.

3. Bit Manipulation

What does this mean?

Bitwise operations can manipulate specific bits of a byte or register, allowing for faster and more efficient control of hardware like LEDs, motors, or other components.

Solution:
Use bitwise operations to control hardware directly rather than using `digitalWrite()` for each pin, which can be slower.

Example:
```
PORTB |= (1 << PB0);   // Turn on the LED on
pin 8 (PORTB, pin 0)
PORTB &= ~(1 << PB0); // Turn off the LED
```

Example Explanation:
- This approach uses direct register manipulation to turn the LED on and off.
- Bitwise operations like `PORTB |= (1 << PB0);` are faster than `digitalWrite()`, which involves multiple function calls.

4. Avoid Floating Point Operations

What does this mean?
Floating-point calculations are slower and require more memory than integer calculations. If possible, use integer math to optimize performance.

Solution:
Avoid floating-point operations in performance-critical code, especially for simple arithmetic like sensor readings.

Example:
```
int sensorValue = analogRead(A0);
int voltage = map(sensorValue, 0, 1023, 0, 5);
// Integer math for voltage mapping
```

Example Explanation:

- This avoids converting values to floating point, thus reducing processing time and memory usage.
- The `map()` function is used to scale the sensor value directly with integers.

5. Use Interrupts for Real-Time Responsiveness

What does this mean?
Interrupts allow you to respond to events (like button presses) immediately, without constantly checking for them in a loop.

Solution:
Attach interrupts to pins to respond to changes without continuously polling them in the main loop.

Example:

```
volatile int buttonState = LOW;

void setup() {
  pinMode(2, INPUT);
  attachInterrupt(digitalPinToInterrupt(2),
buttonPressed, CHANGE);
}

void loop() {
  if (buttonState == HIGH) {
    // Do something when the button is pressed
  }
}

void buttonPressed() {
  buttonState = digitalRead(2);
```

```
}
```

Example Explanation:

- The interrupt triggers immediately when the state of the button connected to pin 2 changes.
- The `buttonPressed()` function is called when the state changes, saving processing time from continuously polling the button.

Real-life Application Project: Optimized LED Blink

In this project, we will toggle an LED at regular intervals without using `delay()` and while also keeping the memory and processing time as efficient as possible.

Project Code

```
unsigned long previousMillis = 0;
const long interval = 1000;  // 1 second

void setup() {
  pinMode(LED_BUILTIN, OUTPUT);
}

void loop() {
  unsigned long currentMillis = millis();

  if (currentMillis - previousMillis >=
interval) {
    previousMillis = currentMillis;
    digitalWrite(LED_BUILTIN,
!digitalRead(LED_BUILTIN));  // Toggle LED
  }
}
``
 `
```

Chapter 64: Calibrating Sensors

Calibrating sensors is an essential part of working with Arduino projects that involve measurements, as it ensures accurate and reliable data collection. In this chapter, we will cover the basics of sensor calibration, including why it's necessary, common techniques, and how to implement them in your Arduino projects. We will also go through the steps involved in calibrating various sensors, ensuring that your measurements are as precise as possible.

Key Concepts of Sensor Calibration

Sensor calibration is the process of adjusting the sensor's readings to match a known standard or reference. It involves compensating for any errors or inconsistencies in sensor data, which may arise due to environmental factors or sensor limitations. Calibrating sensors is crucial for achieving accurate results in applications such as temperature monitoring, distance measurement, and force detection.

Concept	Description	Example
Offset Calibration	Adjusts the sensor's baseline reading to match the expected zero point.	For a temperature sensor, this might involve setting the reading to 0°C at freezing point.
Span Calibration	Ensures that the sensor's readings scale correctly across the full measurement range.	Calibrating a humidity sensor to ensure that 100% humidity reads as the maximum value.
Linear Calibration	Adjusts the sensor output so that it responds linearly to changes in the input.	Ensuring that a light sensor's output increases linearly with light intensity.
Non-linear Calibration	Accounts for sensors whose output does not follow a simple linear relationship.	Calibrating a thermistor, which has a non-linear response to temperature.

Basic Rules for Sensor Calibration

Rule	Correct Example	Incorrect Example
Understand the sensor's characteristics	Research your sensor's datasheet and learn about its range, accuracy, and behavior.	Using a sensor without understanding its limitations and accuracy.
Perform a two-point calibration (offset & span)	Calibrate at both the minimum and maximum values to ensure accuracy.	Only calibrating at one point.
Use a known reference for calibration	Use a calibrated thermometer or multimeter to compare sensor readings.	Using uncalibrated equipment as a reference.
Apply calibration constants in your code	Adjust your sensor readings using calibration factors such as offsets or scales.	Not applying the calibration adjustments in the code.
Periodically recalibrate sensors	Calibrate sensors periodically, especially after prolonged use or changes in the environment.	Never recalibrating the sensor after the initial setup.

Syntax Table for Sensor Calibration

SL	Calibration Technique	Correct Syntax/Example	Description
1	Offset Calibration	`sensorValue = sensorValue - offset;`	Adjusts the sensor's reading to correct for the baseline error.
2	Span Calibration	`sensorValue = sensorValue * scaleFactor;`	Scales the sensor reading to match the expected range.
3	Linear Calibration	`sensorValue = slope * sensorValue +`	Adjusts the sensor's readings based on a linear equation.

		intercept;	
4	Non-linear Calibration	`sensorValue = pow(sensorValu e, exponent) * scaleFactor;`	Used when the sensor's response is non-linear.

Example Explanations

1. Offset Calibration

What does this mean?
Some sensors, like temperature sensors, may have a small offset, meaning they might show a reading slightly above or below the actual value. Offset calibration corrects for this by adjusting the sensor reading so it matches the known reference point.
Solution:
Subtract the sensor's offset from the reading.
Example:
```
int sensorValue = analogRead(A0);  // Read sensor value
float offset = 10.0;               // Known offset for
the sensor
sensorValue = sensorValue - offset;  // Apply offset
correction
```

Example Explanation:
- This example reads a value from the sensor and subtracts an offset (known from calibration) to adjust the reading.
- By applying the offset, the sensor's reading is corrected to provide accurate data.

2. Span Calibration

What does this mean?
Span calibration ensures that the sensor's output matches the expected range. For instance, if a sensor has a range of 0 to 100 units, calibration can be used to ensure that the sensor reads correctly within this range.
Solution:
Multiply the sensor's reading by a scale factor to match the expected

measurement range.

Example:

```
int sensorValue = analogRead(A0);   // Read sensor value
float scaleFactor = 0.5;            // Known scale
factor for the sensor
sensorValue = sensorValue * scaleFactor;   // Apply
scaling
```

Example Explanation:
- The sensor value is scaled using a known scale factor to map the reading to the expected measurement range.
- This ensures that the sensor's output matches the expected values within the sensor's range.

3. Linear Calibration

What does this mean?

Some sensors, like light sensors, have a linear response to changes in input. In such cases, the output value is directly proportional to the input. Linear calibration adjusts the sensor's readings using a mathematical formula.

Solution:

Use the slope and intercept from the linear equation to adjust the sensor's readings.

Example:

```
float sensorValue = analogRead(A0);   // Read sensor
value
float slope = 1.5;                    // Slope for
calibration
float intercept = 0.0;                // Intercept for
calibration
sensorValue = slope * sensorValue + intercept;   //
Apply linear calibration
```

Example Explanation:

- The sensor value is adjusted using a linear equation that takes into account the sensor's characteristics.
- This ensures that the sensor's output matches the actual input.

4. Non-linear Calibration

What does this mean?
Some sensors, like thermistors, have a non-linear response to input. In these cases, the sensor's output must be adjusted using a non-linear calibration formula, which may involve exponential or logarithmic functions.
Solution:
Use non-linear equations, such as powers or logarithms, to adjust the sensor's output.
Example:

```
float sensorValue = analogRead(A0);   // Read sensor
value
float exponent = 2.0;                 // Exponent for
non-linear calibration
float scaleFactor = 0.1;              // Scale factor
sensorValue = pow(sensorValue, exponent) * scaleFactor;
// Apply non-linear calibration
```

Example Explanation:

- The pow() function is used to apply a power function to the sensor reading to correct for non-linear behavior.
- This ensures that the sensor's output matches the expected values even with non-linear characteristics.

Real-life Application Project: Temperature Sensor Calibration

In this project, we will calibrate a temperature sensor, such as a thermistor, to ensure that it gives accurate readings based on a known reference temperature.

Project Code

```
const int sensorPin = A0;    // Pin connected
to the temperature sensor
float sensorValue = 0.0;     // Sensor reading
float temperature = 0.0;     // Calibrated
temperature value
float offset = 5.0;          // Known offset
value for calibration
float scaleFactor = 1.1;     // Scale factor
for temperature sensor

void setup() {
  Serial.begin(9600);
}

void loop() {
  sensorValue = analogRead(sensorPin);   //
Read sensor value
  sensorValue = sensorValue * scaleFactor -
offset;   // Apply calibration
  temperature = sensorValue;   // The
calibrated temperature value
  Serial.print("Temperature: ");
  Serial.println(temperature);
  delay(1000);
}
```

Expected Results

After uploading the code, the serial monitor will display the calibrated temperature reading, which is adjusted for both offset and scale. The sensor's readings will now reflect more accurate temperature data.

www.ingramcontent.com/pod-product-compliance
Lightning Source LLC
LaVergne TN
LVHW051428050326
832903LV00030BD/2973